INSTRUCTOR'S MANUAL *for* VOLUME II

CASES IN MANAGEMENT AND ORGANIZATIONAL BEHAVIOR, VOLUME II

Teri C. Tompkins
Pepperdine University

Pearson Education

Upper Saddle River, New Jersey 07458

Executive editor: David Shafer
Assistant editor: Melanie Olsen
Production editor: Wanda Rockwell
Manufacturer: Quebecor Printing Group

ISBN 0-13-035174-1

10 9 8 7 6 5 4 3 2 1

Table of Contents

PART I

INTRODUCTION

Why was this book written?

If you are like me, you value cases as a teaching tool. You may, however, be frustrated with end-of-the-chapter cases in textbooks that lack emotional tone or story line, and where the answers are blatantly obvious. Alternatively, you may have tried the more developed cases available from case catalogues, such as Harvard and IVY. These cases often require extensive preparation for you and your students, and are time consuming to teach. How can you include interesting and challenging cases in your teaching, yet still leave time for other teaching techniques, such as lectures, student presentations, and classroom exercises? The need for cases that are challenging, engaging, and not too long led to the writing of Cases in Organizational Behavior and Management and this instructor's manual.

Like me, you may have relied on teaching notes in textbook instructor's manuals that were little more than a few questions followed by a short answer. Would you prefer more detailed analysis and an idea of how much time to allow when teaching the case? Do you want teaching notes that have a consistent format, allowing you greater efficiency when preparing your courses? This instructor's manual has been designed to meet those needs; with two types of instructors in mind:
1. Busy instructors, who need a faster way to prepare for class.
2. New or inexperienced case teachers, who would benefit from explicit teaching plans and detailed answers.

In the following pages, I'll tell you a bit about the manual and why I think you'll find it supportive of your teaching. Let me begin by explaining how the book and teaching notes are organized.

Organization of the Instructor's Manual

If the instructor's manual is going to be a useful tool, it has to be more than merely twenty-one individual teaching notes. It needs integration. It must provide some logical framework that connects cases with other cases and key topics.

The Instructor's Manual is organized in four parts. In Part I, the introduction, I created a matrix table suggesting cases for key sections of several textbooks. This matrix helps when the casebook is used as a supplement with Organizational Behavior or Management texts. The teaching notes in Part II will be described in greater detail later in this introduction. In Part III, I suggest hints to use the Critical Incident Case Assignment described in the casebook. In Part IV, I indexed key topics from the teaching notes so you can quickly find an appropriate case for teaching your class. I rarely see an Instructor's Manual that has been indexed, yet I've often wished they were because they help you quickly build your teaching plan.

Components of the Teaching Notes

The cases in the casebook are rich and can be taught numerous ways. If you are an experienced case teacher, you may only glance at the teaching notes in this manual and then teach the case as you see fit. The teaching notes in this manual are for those who desire a little more support, or who find they lack sufficient time to adequately prepare their own teaching plan.

Introduction

Each teaching note begins with a list of <u>topics</u>. The topics were chosen because one or more answers to the discussion questions addressed the subject. Topics with an asterisk (*) are subjects that are covered in the teaching plan timetable, and are clearly important to the case.

An explicit <u>case overview</u> explains most of the case facts and key players. If you don't have time to read the case or need a refresher, you can become somewhat familiar with the key players' circumstances and the organization. The case overview is also useful when you are designing the course.

For instructors who organize their teaching by <u>industry</u>, the company is described including its size, if known.

<u>Case objectives</u> were written based on the answers to case questions and the primary topics. Not all objectives need to be covered when you teach the case, but they give you an overview of what to expect from the rest of the teaching note.

Each case is referenced to <u>other related cases in Volume 2</u>. You can use this feature to connect cases to each other, especially if you do cases on a week-to-week basis.

There is also a reference to <u>other related cases in Volume 1</u>. The 21 cases in Volume 1 are also organizational behavior and management cases. If you are concerned with students sharing the outcomes of the cases with students who take your course next term, you may find it convenient to switch back and forth between volumes. Alternatively, if you have a heavy emphasis on case teaching, you may want to have your students order both volumes since the combined price of <u>Cases in Organizational Behavior and Management, Volumes 1 and 2</u> is so low; and you will have an ample variety of cases in which to choose.

To find cases that are more appropriate for undergraduate, graduate, or executive students, the section on <u>intended courses and levels</u> may be useful.

Some teaching notes have a detailed <u>analysis</u> section if the case warrants it. Most analyses are imbedded in the question and answer section.

I think it is important for the instructor to know how a case was researched. The <u>research methodology</u> briefly describes how the author got the data to write the case. Every case in the casebook is real.

The <u>teaching plan</u> is the heart of the note. I designed the table because I find it a useful tool when I teach. In it, we provide a timetable to manage a 60-minute teaching session. We also provide a 25-minute timetable for instructors who want to use cases, but don't want to use them exclusively during a teaching session. The activity and expected student outcomes are described in detail. New case teachers will especially find the student outcomes column useful, as it often discusses what kind of answer you might expect from the activity.

I have always been bothered by answers to discussion questions that do not sufficiently probe the case. I usually find these in instructor manuals where cases aren't the primary concern. In the <u>discussion questions and answers</u> section, you will find detailed answers and references. Often, the answer might include a quick overview of a topic along with the specific application to the case. My hope is that you might bring organizational behavior and management topics to life by illustrating the theory with real life case examples. In some teaching notes, I provide a bullet point summary to help you quickly scan the page for the answers when you are teaching. The detailed answers in this section also make it an ideal grading reference guide when you assign the case and questions for write-up outside of class.

Please also note that each question is labeled based on Bloom's taxonomy. In days when outcome assessments are a top priority in teaching, these labels will help you evaluate your student's learning. In addition, the labels help you distinguish between undergraduate and graduate level teaching. Undergraduates teaching typically include knowledge, comprehension, application, and analysis questions. Graduate questions typically include application, analysis, synthesis, and evaluation questions.

Most cases include <u>references</u>. We tried to include a variety of organizational behavior and management textbooks to support those of you teaching from a particular text.

Finally, nearly every case has an <u>epilogue</u>. Very often students want to know what happened after they have discussed the case. Some of the epilogues are particularly poignant. I've suggested saving time to discuss the epilogue in several of the teaching plans.

A final note

There has always been a bias in case teaching toward decision focused cases. Personally, I enjoy teaching cases that require a decision. But I also think that it is appropriate to use cases to illustrate theory. In Cases in Organizational Behavior and Management, I have selected a variety of cases, some decision focused, some that illustrate theory, and some that do both. I hope you enjoy the variety.

One last point. I'm always looking for suggestions on how I can improve the case and the teaching note or suggestions for topics not currently in the books. If you have any ideas and would like to share them with me, please drop me a line. My address is 554 E. Foothill Blvd., Suite 120, San Dimas, CA 91773, USA. Or you can send me an e-mail at Teri.Tompkins@pepperdine.edu or lee@cyberg8t.com.

Acknowledgements

Thanks to Rasool Azari, Amber Borden, Lori Dick, Mittie Dick, Terri Egan, Ann Feyerherm, Dan Gilbert, Karen Hruby, Nathan Meckley, Kate Rogers, David Ruble, Jim Spee, Jonnetta Thomas-Chambers, and Tiffany Wilkerson for their support in completing this manual.

Regarding copying cases

We have tried to price Cases in Organizational Behavior and Management so that you can use only a few cases and still get value. A case and teaching note from Harvard Business School Publishing runs around $5.50 each. This means that two cases and a teaching note or three cases without teaching notes would pay for the casebook. If you decide to use this book after adoption decisions have passed at your university bookstore, I hope that you will have your students order the casebook themselves rather than making illegal copies of the cases. Universities and publishing companies take very seriously professors who disregard copyright laws. Students can order the book on-line, such as Amazon.com, and get it in a few days. Thank you for supporting intellectual property rights.

MATRIX OF CASES AND TEXTBOOKS

The tables below are sample organizational behavior and management texts where cases might supplement the sections. Instructors using other organizational behavior textbooks will find cases developed around the three levels: individual, group, and system. You should be able to readily adapt to your textbook based on the four samples given here. The management texts are organized around the four functions of management: planning, organizing, leading, and controlling. Some include management processes, global, ethics, quality, and other contemporary issues. The five samples of management texts should be illustrative if you use a different textbook than those listed. A very popular book on organizational theory and design rounds out the list of textbooks.

Sample Organizational Behavior Texts

Kreitner & Kinicki, *Organizational Behavior.*	Volume 2 Cases	Topic
Part One: The World of Organizational Behavior	Saving Private Ryan Video Case: Classic Leadership Models	Learning about OB from film
	Angry Branch Manager	Cultural Diversity
	The Volunteer	Culture, Values, and Ethics
	A Selfish Request in Japan	Managing Across Cultures

Kreitner & Kinicki, *Organizational Behavior.*	Volume 2 Cases	Topic
Part Two: Individual Behavior in Organizations	Preferential Treatment?	Attitudes and Personality
	Unprofessional Conduct	Perception
	Then There Was One	Motivation and Job Satisfaction
	Café Latte	Equity, expectancy, and Goal-Setting
	Saving Private Ryan Video Case: Classic Leadership Models	Behavioral models of leadership
Part Three: Groups and Social Processes	Cost and Schedule Team at AVIONICS	Group Dynamics
	A Selfish Request in Japan	Power, Conflict & Negotiation
	Groupware Fiasco	Group Decision Making
	Computer Services Team at AVIONICS	Teamwork and Trust
Part Four: Organizational Processes	Groupware Fiasco	Electronic Decision-Making
	Computer Services Team at AVIONICS	Self-Management
	Saving Private Ryan Video Case: Classic Leadership Models	Leadership
	Violence at the United States Postal Service	Occupational Stress
Part Five: The Evolving Organization	Insubordination or Unclear Loyalties	Structure
	Reputation in Jeopardy	Organizational Culture
	Cost and Schedule Team at AVIONICS	Organizational Learning

Robbins, *Essentials of Organizational Behavior*	Volume 2 Cases	Topic
Prologue	Violence at the United States Postal Service	Current Topic
Part Two: The Individual in the Organization	Preferential Treatment?	Attractions and Abilities
	Richard Prichard and the Federal Triad Programs	Personality and self-esteem
	Then There Was One	Basic Motivation Concepts
	The Safety Memo	Employee Involvement
	Changing Quotas	Individual Decision-Making
Part Three: Groups in the Organization	Cost and Schedule Team at AVIONICS	Group Development
	Computer Services Team at AVIONICS	Group Dynamics
	Reputation in Jeopardy	Communication
	Angry Branch Manager	Leadership and Trust
	Incident on the USS Whitney	Power & Politicking
	Negotiating Work Hours	Negotiations
Part Four: The Organization System	When Worlds Collide	Organization Structure & Work Design
	Angry Branch Manager	Performance Appraisal
	A Selfish Request in Japan	Organizational Culture
	Leading TQM in Panama	Organizational Change in a Global Context

Robbins, *Organizational Behavior.*	Volume 2 Cases	Topic
Part One: Introduction	Violence at the United States Postal Service	Current Topic
Part Two: The Individual	Unprofessional Conduct	Job Fit
	Changing Quotas	Individual Decision-Making
	Then There Was One	Job Satisfaction
	Richard Prichard and the Federal Triad Program	Expectancy Theory & Goal Setting Theory
	Leadership of TQM in Panama	Empowerment
Part Three: The Group	Temporary Employees: Car Show Turned Ugly	Group Structure
	Computer Services Team at AVIONICS; Cost and Scheduling Team at AVIONICS.	Leaderless group High-performance team
	Reputation in Jeopardy	Communication
	Saving Private Ryan Video Case: Classic Leadership Models	Leadership
	Incident Aboard the USS Whitney	Power Imbalance
	Negotiating Work Hours	Negotiation
Part Four: The Organization System	When Worlds Collide	Organization Structure & Work Design
	Angry Branch Manager	Performance Appraisal
	A Selfish Request in Japan	Global and organizational culture
Part Five: Organizational Dynamics	Computer Services Team at AVIONICS	Organizational Change and Resistance to Change

Schermerhorn, Osborn, & Hunt, *Organizational Behavior.*	Volume 2 Cases	Topic
Environment	The Volunteer	Ethics and Social Responsibility
	Leadership of TQM in Panama	High Performance Workplace
	A Selfish Request in Japan	Global Dimensions of Organizational Behavior
Managing Individuals	Unprofessional Conduct	Diversity and Individual Differences
	Angry Branch Manager	Attribution and Perception
	Richard Prichard and the Federal Triad Programs	Motivation and Rewards
	The Volunteer	Following HR Policies
	Computer Services Team at AVIONICS	Job Design
Managing Groups	Cost and Schedule Team at AVIONICS	Organizational Development
	Computer Services Team at AVIONICS	Norms and Cohesiveness
Managing Organizations	Incident on the USS Whitney	Structure and Chain of Command
	Groupware Fiasco	Technology and Organizational Design
	Reputation in Jeopardy	Organizational Culture

Schermerhorn, Osborn, & Hunt, *Organizational Behavior.*	Volume 2 Cases	Topic
Managing Processes	Saving Private Ryan Video Case: Classic Leadership Styles	Leadership Styles
	A Selfish Request in Japan	Power and authority
	The Safety Memo	Communication
	Changing Quotas	Decision-Making
	Negotiating Work Hours	Conflict and Negotiation
	Cost and Schedule Team at AVIONICS	Change, Innovation and Stress

Management Texts

Certo, *Modern Management*	Volume 2 Cases	Topic
I. Introduction to Management	Unprofessional Conduct	Management Careers
	The Volunteer	Ethics and Social Responsibility
II. Planning	Changing Quotas	Objectives
	Computer Services Team at AVIONICS	Poor Planning
	A Selfish Request in Japan	Decision-making Process
	Cost and Schedule Team at AVIONICS	Planning Tools
III. Organizing	Café Latte	Organizing People in a Small Business
	Insubordination or Unclear Loyalties?	Authority and Structure
	Unprofessional Conduct	Recruitment
	The Safety Memo	Rapid Change in an Organization
IV. Influencing: Foundations for Leading	Negotiating Work Hours	Communications & Negotiations
	Saving Private Ryan Video Case: Classic Leadership Models	Leadership Theories
	Then There Was One	Motivating Employees
	Reputation in Jeopardy	Corporate Culture
	Cost and Schedule Team at AVIONICS	Organizational Learning
V. Controlling	A Selfish Request in Japan	Controlling and Power
	Groupware Fiasco	Information Technology
VI. Topics for Special Emphasis	Leading TQM in Panama	Quality
	Angry Branch Manager	Diversity and HRM

Daft, *Management*	Volume 2 Cases	Topic
Part One: Introduction to Management	A Selfish Request in Japan	Japanese Management Practices
Part Two: The Environment of Management	Reputation in Jeopardy	Corporate Culture
	Leading TQM in Panama	Managing in a Global Environment
	The Safety Memo	Social Responsibility
	Café Latte	Small Business

Daft, *Management*	Volume 2 Cases	Topic
Part Three: Planning	Changing Quotas	Planning
	When Worlds Collide	Strategy
	The Volunteer	Creative Decision Making
Part Four: Organizing	Insubordination or Unclear Loyalties?	Vertical Structure
	When Worlds Collide	Using structural design to achieve goals
	Computer Services Team at AVIONICS	Change & Development
	Angry Branch Manager	Human Resources Management & Diversity
Part Five: Leading	Richard Prichard and the Federal Triad Program	Foundations of Behavior
	Saving Private Ryan Video Case: Classic Leadership Models	Leadership
	Then There Was One	Motivation
	The Safety Memo	Communicating
	Cost and Schedule Team at AVIONICS	High Performance Team
Part Six: Controlling	Leading TQM in Panama	Quality Control
	Groupware Fiasco	Group Decision Support Systems
	A Selfish Request in Japan	Service Management

Dessler, *Management*	Volume 2 Cases	Topic
Part 1: Introduction to Managing	Unprofessional Conduct	Managing your career
	Leading TQM in Panama	Managing in a Third World Country
	The Volunteer	Ethical Challenge at Work
Part 2: Planning	Changing Quotas	Making Better Decisions & Goal Setting
	When Worlds Collide	Planning & Strategic Planning
Part 3: Organizing	Insubordination or Unclear Loyalties?	Structure
	Cost and Schedule Team at AVIONICS	Designing to Manage Change
	Angry Branch Manager	Human Resources Management
Part 4: Leading	Saving Private Ryan Video Case: Classic Leadership Models	Leadership
	Reputation in Jeopardy	Organizational Culture
	Then There Was One	Motivating Employees
	Incident on the USS Whitney	Interpersonal Communications
	Cost and Schedule Team at AVIONICS	Group Dynamics
	Computer Services Team at AVIONICS	Leading Organizational Change
Part 5: Controlling	A Selfish Request in Japan	Human Response to Control
	Leading TQM in Panama	Controlling for Quality
	Groupware Fiasco	Managing Change with Information Technology

Robbins, *Managing Today*	Volume 2 Cases	Topic
Part One: Introduction	The Volunteer	Social Responsibility and Ethics
	Saving Private Ryan Video Case: Classic Leadership Models	What Leaders Do
Part Two: Decision and Monitoring Systems	Angry Branch Manager	Decision-Making Process
	When Worlds Collide	Environmental Scanning and Strategy
	Changing Quotas	Planning and Objectives
	Leading TQM in Panama	Controlling for Quality
Part Three: Organizing Tasks and Shaping the Organization's Culture	When Worlds Collide	Mechanistic and Organic Structures
	Negotiating Work Hours	Individual work design
	A Selfish Request in Japan	HRM laws that shape practice
	Cost and Schedule Team at AVIONICS	Successful group development
	Reputation in Jeopardy	Organizational Culture
Part Four: Leading and Empowering People	Café Latte	Attribution Theory
	Richard Prichard and the Federal Triad Program	Motivation and Rewards
	Saving Private Ryan Video Case: Classic Leadership Models	Leadership
	Computer Services Team at AVIONICS	Self-managed work teams
	Negotiating Work Hours	Negotiation skills
Part Five: Organizational Renewal	Cost and Schedule Team at AVIONICS	Team Building

Robbins & Coulter, *Management*	Volume 2 Cases	Topic
Part One: Introduction	Unprofessional Conduct	Managing your Career
	Leading TQM in Panama	Current Trends and Issues
Part Two: Defining the Manager's Terrain	The Safety Memo	Evaluating Culture
	A Selfish Request in Japan	The Legal-Political Environment
	The Volunteer	Managerial Ethics
	Angry Branch Manager	Decision-Making Process
Part Three: Planning	Changing Quotas	Objectives and Planning
	When Worlds Collide	Environmental Scanning and Strategy
Part Four: Organizing	The Volunteer	Authority & Structure
	Computer Services Team	HRM Training
	Reputation in Jeopardy	Changing Organizational Cultures
Part Five: Leading	Unprofessional Conduct	Attitudes and Personality
	Computer Services Team at AVIONICS	Unsuccessful Group Development
	Cost and Schedule Team at AVIONICS	Successful Group Development
	Then There Was One	Motivation
	Saving Private Ryan Video Case: Classic Leadership Models	Leadership
Part Six: Controlling	A Selfish Request in Japan	Adjusting Controls for National Differences
	Changing Quotas	Control by Quota

Organizational Theory and Design

Daft, *Organizational Theory and Design & Essentials of …*	Volume 2 Cases	Topic
Part Two: The Open System	When Worlds Collide	Goal; Organic & Mechanistic Structure
	Saving Private Ryan Video Case: Classic Leadership Models	Contingency Leadership
	Changing Quotas	Goals
	Richard Prichard and the Federal Triad Program	Goals
Part Three: Organization Structure and Design	Reputation in Jeopardy	Workplace culture
	A Selfish Request in Japan	Control by culture
	Then There Was One	Workplace variety
	When Worlds Collide	Differentiation and Integration
	Violence at the United States Postal Service	Organizational Size and Bureaucracy
	Insubordination or Unclear Loyalties?	Reporting Relations
	Cost & Schedule Team at AVIONICS	Matrix Structure
	Computer Services Team at AVIONICS	Matrix Structure
	Leading TQM in Panama	Contemporary Designs for Global Competition
Part Four: Organization Design Process	Leading TQM in Panama	Quality and Change
	The Volunteer	Ethical Values and Culture
	The Safety Memo	Ethical Values and Culture
	Changing Quotas	Decision Making

Cases or teaching notes that generate strong emotional impact

A Selfish Request in Japan	An American teacher at an English Language School in Japan is denied permission to miss work to take the GMAT because it is a selfish request. If he misses the test, he can't get into graduate school, but if he takes it, he is in violation of company policy, which discriminates against foreigners. What should he do?
The Safety Memo	A new safety officer at a telecommunication company points out obvious safety problems in a memo and is called on the carpet by an executive. Was the safety officer right? Or did he not gather enough data?
The Volunteer	The Director of Volunteers at a museum finds out that her boss is protecting a volunteer who is a convicted child abuser. How can she get rid of the felon, protect the children and the museum, and still keep her job?

PART II
TEACHING NOTES
FOR
VOLUME 2 CASES

A SELFISH REQUEST IN JAPAN

Topics (* = Primary topic with teaching plan)
*Hofstede's Cultural Dimensions; Organizational Culture Differences
National Culture
*Organizational Culture
*Power, Influence and Negotiation
Decision Making, Creative Problem Solving
Ethics and Legal Issues
Communication
Conflict Management
Maslow's Hierarchy of Needs
Positional Bargaining
Negotiation
Labor/Management Context
International Case Japan
Education Context

Case overview

Toby Lee worked as an English teacher in Yokohama, Japan at NOGI, the largest language school chain in Japan. Toby's work at NOGI afforded him the opportunity to secure a visa, as well as pursue a tae kwon do career. Toby's immediate plan was to attend the Drucker School of Management, in the United States, pending taking the Graduate Management Admissions Test (GMAT). Toby's problem was his employer, NOGI. Although Toby requested time off three months prior to the test date, NOGI refused to grant Toby the day off to take the GMAT. After numerous meetings with multiple levels of management, Toby failed to persuade NOGI to give him the day off.

Toby worked under a contract specifically designed for Americans. NOGI's contract did not comply with the legal guidelines of hiring American workers. Japanese law stipulated that foreign employees were allowed seven personal days per year, unless the absence endangered the operation of the business. Toby's absence would not have endangered the business, considering his request was submitted three months prior. Toby was aware of his rights, yet refrained from mentioning the law to his supervisor, planning to use the information only as a last resort. Toby discussed his predicament with Jim Crawford, Vice President of the Tokyo South General Workers, to decide how he should proceed. Upon the advice of Mr. Crawford, Toby agreed to start a teacher's union and was quickly successful at doing so.

Hisami Davies, Vice President of Human Resources, called Toby to ask him if he planned to report to work on Saturday. Toby informed Ms. Davies that he had already spoken with his manager so that she could make the appropriate accommodations for Saturday. Ms. Davies communicated her displeasure and told Toby that the regional manager, Mr. Miyake, wanted to meet with him the next day to further discuss the situation.

Toby, accompanied by Mr. Crawford, met with Mr. Miyake. Mr. Crawford outlined the illegalities within the American employee contract. Mr. Miyake responded to Mr. Crawford by referring him to NOGI's attorney. At times, Mr. Miyake attempted to persuade Toby to act in the interest of NOGI. Terry Allen, head trainer for foreign teachers, was asked to join in the conversation. Mr. Allen's demeanor mirrored Mr. Miyake's. Toby and Mr. Crawford left the meeting with confidence that NOGI was aware of its wrong doings and understood Toby's intent to take the GMAT on Saturday.

Toby's manager asked him if he would come to work to teach one class after taking the GMAT. Toby agreed, to demonstrate his ability to compromise. Although Toby was told he would not be paid for the day, he reported to work after he took the GMAT.

This teaching note was prepared by Tobias M. Lee, Ann Feyerherm, Pepperdine University, Jonnetta Thomas-Chambers and Teri C. Tompkins, University of Redlands. The case and teaching note were prepared as basis for class discussion rather than to illustrate either effective or ineffective handling of administrative situations. Suggestions for improvement of this note should be sent to Teri.Tompkins@pepperdine.edu. Credit will be given in the next revision.

A Selfish Request in Japan

Industry

One of the largest English-speaking school chains in Japan, NOGI. Education context.

Teaching objectives

1. To illustrate what it is like to be a North American working in Japan.
2. To investigate how Japanese culture and contracts are used to manage North Americans.
3. To teach the importance of culture in organizational environments.
4. To illustrate and help students diagnose the dynamics of organizational culture and power in conjunction with individual power.
5. To examine the importance of ethics and legal issues when faced with decision-making.
6. To decide what steps are appropriate when negotiating and managing a conflict.

Other related cases in Volume 1

A New Magazine in Nigeria (power). Fired! (problem solving). Heart Attack (ethics). No, Sir, Sergeant! (power). Problems at Wukmier Home Electronics Warehouse (Hofstede's cultural dimensions). Questions Matter (Maslow's hierarchy of needs). Shaking the Bird Cage (problem solving). Temporary Employees: Car Show Turned Ugly (ethics).

Other related cases in Volume 2

Leadership of TQM in Panama (Hofstede's cultural dimensions). Negotiating Work Hours (communications, negotiation). Preferential Treatment? (power).

Intended courses and levels

This course is intended for undergraduate, graduate, and executive students in human resource management, organizational behavior, and management courses. The topics include organizational culture, decision-making, ethics, Japanese law, power, influence and negotiation. This case is best positioned under global issues, culture, or power. In human resources, it works well under employee law. In management, it could also be used to illustrate control—legal and behavioral.

Analysis

All related analysis and references are embedded in the answers to the questions.

Research methodology

This case reflects the recollections of Tobias Lee, the teacher in the case. The case is a true incident that happened in Japan. The company and people have been disguised.

Teaching plan

This exercise allows participants to understand the range and dynamics of individual-to-group choices and perceptions, as well as realizing that both positive and negative aspects exist in any situation.

At the beginning of class request four volunteers. Two of these volunteers will be group facilitators, the other recorders. Give each facilitator one of the lists of phrases below:

Positive aspects of:	Negative aspects of:	Positive aspects of:	Negative aspects of:
Toby's decisions	Toby's decisions	NOGI's decisions	NOGI's decisions
Toby's culture	Toby's culture	NOGI's culture	NOGI's culture
Toby's power	Toby's power	NOGI's power	NOGI's power
Toby's influence	Toby's influence	NOGI's influence	NOGI's influence
Toby's negotiating skills	Toby's negotiating skills	NOGI's negotiating skills	NOGI's negotiating skills
Toby's ethics	Toby's ethics	NOGI's ethics	NOGI's ethics

Segregate the class into four groups. The recorders' jobs will be to record a summary of their group's responses. The facilitators' jobs will be to ensure that the groups have discussed each phrase on the list and are able to relate their responses to specific case examples as well as course theories.

Segregated group discussion time limit is approximately 15 minutes.

Bring the class together to share responses from opposite points of view. Delivery of responses are (recommended) to be done by the recorder.

Class discussion is approximately 20-25 minutes.

Topic: Dynamics of Individual-to-Group Choices and Perceptions
60-minute teaching plan

Pre-assignment: Read case A & B (15 minutes)

	Timing	Activity	Organization	Student Outcomes
I	0-15 minutes (15)	Lecturette on Hofstede	Instructor gives the 4 primary dimensions and students discuss.	Basic knowledge of cultural dimensions
II	15 - 30 minutes (15)	Application of cultural dimensions and decision-making in split groups.	Split class into 4 groups. Select a recorder and facilitator for each group. Have first group list the positive aspects of Toby's decisions, power, etc. One group list positive of NOGI; one group list negative aspects of Toby's, and the last group list negative aspects of NOGI. (see table under teaching plan.)	Penetration of knowledge and application of concepts to real situation • Hofstede's dimensions • Power sources • Decision-making in various cultures
III	30-50 minutes (20)	Four groups come together, each with flip charts or parts of the board. Go through Toby +/-, then NOGI +/-.	Full class discussion	Ability to see both perspectives, positive and negative, and to synthesize them.
IV	50 -59 minutes (9)	Summarize: Instructor asks: *What might Toby have learned to apply in new situations? What do you think NOGI management learned about dealing with Americans?*	Full class comes up with list of highlights.	Some possible answers: Toby: • Gaining credibility through power base (TSGW) • Expert knowledge of laws is complementary to Japanese power distance (Hofstede). • Don't put NOGI in a position of publicly losing face. • Allow Ms. Nakamura a way to be seen as successful.

	Timing	Activity	Organization	Student Outcomes
				NOGI: • Increase participation for American employees. • Good to use separate contracts for U.S. & Japanese.
V	59 - 60 minutes (1)	Read short epilogue		

25-minute teaching plan on dynamics of individual-to-group choices and perceptions.
Pre-assignment: Read case before class (15 minutes)
Activities. Do activities I, III, and VI in the 60 minute plan.

Topic: Japanese Culture, Hofstede, and Power
60-minute teaching plan
Pre-assignment: Read case A & B (15 minutes)

	Timing	Activity	Organization	Student Outcomes
I	0-15 minutes (15)	Lecturette on Hofstede or read case in class.	Instructor gives the 4 primary dimensions and students discuss.	Basic knowledge of cultural dimensions
II	15 - 45 minutes (30)	*Q1. According to Hofstede's Four Dimensions of Culture, citing examples from the case, explain the Japanese management's reactions and concerns to Toby's request.*	Divide the class into groups. Assign 2 questions each to the groups. Group 1	• Perceived request as disrupting because it favored individual over the system. • High power distance evident in management's decision-making process (under their conditions). • High uncertainty avoidance—strong beliefs in rules & policy. • They saw no rewards for the company. Reward should be for glory of the team, not individual.
		Q2. From a conceptual analysis of power and influence, examine NOGI's methodology in handling Toby's request. What types of power did each agent of NOGI possess?	Group 1	• Local management had no authority to authorize leave. • Head office was centralized command center. • Managers used legitimate and coercive power. Positional power respected at all levels. • When Toby didn't accept the decision, then Ms. Davis sought higher positional power through the regional manager. If Toby were Japanese, he would have felt intimidated and backed down. As an American, the strategy didn't work. (Bring up Hofstede's study, specifically the power distance differences between Japanese and American cultures.)

14

	Timing	Activity	Organization	Student Outcomes
		Q3. Examining Maslow's Need Hierarchy Model, identify NOGI's failure to account for American attitudes towards needs in their school policies. Additionally, prove how the Japanese version of Maslow's model is infused into the contract with disregard for the law.	Group 2	• American employees need to feel they can achieve a goal and contribute value to their company. • But employees with little control over their work might not feel higher level needs in their jobs. • In Japan, job security and life-long employment are stronger motivators than self-actualization. Belonging and security more important than growing needs. Maslow's hierarchy is reversed. • The manner in which NOGI attempted to embed Japanese culture into the teacher's contract was not justified by the law.
		Q5. Recommend a management strategy, at the local school level and at the corporate headquarters level, which incorporates Hofstede's four dimensions of culture to enhance employee satisfaction, minimize disruptions in the business process, and to promote a positive corporate culture.	Group 2	• Perhaps greater autonomy at local school level. • Requiring a time period where requests must be made. • Consult Americans. • Provide ways to increase American participation.
		Q6. Explain the importance of Toby's decision to recruit the help of the Tokyo South General Workers Union. Examine its role in the negotiation processes.	Group 3	• Gave Toby increased power (expert power through knowledge of Japanese law).
		Q7. Evaluate the presence of Mr. Crawford and Mr. Allen from a power and influence perspective in the meeting between Toby and Mr. Miyake. How effective were they? Did one neutralize the other?	Group 3	• Crawford leveled the playing field. • Crawford marginalized the coercive and legitimate power of Mr. Miyake. • Interestingly, Mr. Allen was likely brought in to try and neutralize Crawford's expert power. Allen argued, as a fellow American, that exceptions had to be made because NOGI was a Japanese company. • Crawford prevented Miyake from intimidating Toby.

	Timing	Activity	Organization	Student Outcomes
		Q8. Explain NOGI's reasoning for drafting two employee contracts, one for Americans and one for Japanese.	Group 4	• Two contracts for two major kinds of employees: American and Japanese. • NOGI wanted Americans to behave more like Japanese, so they used the legal contract (the Japanese conformed due to culture). • There was also an issue of trust (lack) and ethnocentrism (Japanese way is better).
		Q9. If Ms. Nakamura had been aware of the illegality in the American employee contract, would their actions have been different?	Group 4	• Even though she was highly ethical and procedural, she likely would not have stood up against NOGI even if she knew the contract was illegal. Toby was only a year-term employee and she was just beginning her career. The good of the company would likely have prevailed as a more important value than following the law.
III	40-55 minutes (15)	Discussion: *What have we learned about Japanese management systems? (If there are any foreign students ask: can you draw parallels to coming to America? What cultural norms do American's tend to expect?)*		• Discussion about Japanese management system will vary, but could be judgmental. Important for instructor to point out that every country has its own ethnocentrism. • This is a great time for foreign students to express their own observations of North American culture. North American students will be more open to seeing their ethnocentrism through a "foreigner's" observation because Toby was a foreigner.
IV	55 -60 minutes (5)	Read epilogue	Full class	

<u>25-minute teaching plan on Japanese culture, Hofstede, and Power</u>
Pre-assignment: Read case before class (15 minutes)
Activities. Do activities II (create 8 groups and answer one question in 10 minutes and III (15 minutes) in the 60-minute plan.)

Discussion questions and answers

Question 1

According to Hofstede's four dimensions of culture, citing examples from the case, explain the Japanese management's reactions and concerns to Toby's request.
<u>Application skills</u> (using information in a new context to solve a problem, answer a question, or perform a task).

Answer

Japanese business practices are a natural expansion of societal and cultural values. NOGI's collectivist attitude frowned upon Toby's (individual) challenge: the business process. NOGI's management team and employees were all bounded by a contract stipulating certain responsibilities and restrictions. Toby's exception to this contract, specifically regarding personal days, was viewed as a rebellion against the system. Regardless of his arguments, emphasizing limited availability of the test date and initiating proper written permission, NOGI management saw his request as a purely selfish one (Hall, E., 1989).

The high power distance at NOGI can be identified in management's decision-making process. The decision to not respond immediately to Toby's request, contacting him one week before his test with their decision, supports management's belief that employee relations be dictated at their pace, under their conditions.

The strong belief in rules, regulations, and policy characterizes Japanese management as high in uncertainty avoidance. The desire to minimize uncertainty and requests like Toby's protects the standardized operation at NOGI. Management was highly against Toby's request because it was perceived to potentially create chaos in the company. If one teacher was allowed to schedule his/her own personal days and independently affect the business operation, NOGI considered the impact if all teachers did it. This high degree of uncertainty motivated NOGI management to immediately reject the dangerous precedent Toby's request may have established.

Japanese and Americans both value the quantity of life and the attainment of material items. The important distinction lies in the medium and the process. NOGI believes that the team must succeed before the individual can reap the rewards. For this reason, they saw no rewards for the company by allowing Toby to take a personal day off. Furthermore, they would need to cover the classes he had contractually agreed to teach. Whereas American companies permit individuals to pursue independent endeavors that better themselves, Japanese firms frown upon an employee seeking glory in sake of the team.

Question 2
From a conceptual analysis of power and influence, examine NOGI's methodology in handling Toby's request. What types of power did each agent of NOGI possess?

<u>Comprehension skills</u> (understanding the meaning of remembered material, usually demonstrated by restating or citing examples) and <u>analysis skills</u> (breaking a concept into its parts and explaining their interrelationships, distinguishing relevant from extraneous material).

Answer

NOGI management's concept of power and its allocation in the company were demonstrated consistently throughout Toby's critical incident. Local management had no authority to authorize personal days off. Ms. Nakamura realized that Toby's request surpassed her jurisdiction and forwarded Toby's proposal to the head office. The head office existed as the centralized command center and made the final decisions.

Leaders possess 5 general types of power: *referent* (leading through admiration), *legitimate* (leading through rank in the organization), *reward* (leading through incentives), *coercive* (leading through threats of punishment), and *expert* (leading through expertise). (Hellreigel, Slocum, Woodman, 1998, pgs.305)

Due to the cultural nature of Japanese corporations, all the managers at NOGI possessed legitimate and coercive power. The degree to which a person's title outranked the other determined who had more power. For instance, as a head teacher, Ms. Yamashina had less power than the school manager Ms. Nakamura did. The managers at NOGI thoroughly understood and respected the positions of power held by their fellow employees.

When Ms. Davies, Vice President of Human Resources, informed Toby of NOGI's decision, she was representing the head office. Expecting full compliance to her demand, Toby's hesitation caused her to seek support from an even higher-ranking individual whose legitimate power was undisputed. Mr. Miyake, the regional manager, commanded not only legitimate and coercive power but referent power as well. He had worked his way up the corporate ladder at NOGI for more than 20 years and earned the respect and admiration of his fellow Japanese coworkers along the way. As a newly employed American, Toby was not influenced by his referent power but he was aware of it.

Scheduling a face-to-face interview with Mr. Miyake was NOGI's attempt to intimidate Toby so that he would change his mind.

Question 3

Examining Maslow's Needs Hierarchy Model, identify NOGI's failure to account for American attitudes towards needs in their school policies. Additionally, evaluate how the Japanese version of Maslow's model is infused into the contract that seems to disregard the law.

<u>Analysis skills</u> (breaking a concept into its parts and explaining their interrelationships, distinguishing relevant from extraneous material).

Answer

The needs hierarchy model devised by Maslow suggested that people have a complex set of exceptionally strong needs, which can be arranged in a hierarchy. Those needs begin with physiological and ascend up through security, affiliation, esteem, and self-actualization. Maslow asserts that lower level needs must be satisfied before higher level needs. The three lowest levels, deficiency needs, are necessary for an individual to be happy, physically and psychologically. The two highest levels, growth needs, are where we analyze the development of the human being. (Hellreigel, Slocum, Woodman, 1998, pgs.140)

Esteem needs are defined as feelings of personal achievement, and self-actualization needs, the highest level, are defined as feelings of self-fulfillment. American employees need to feel that they can achieve a goal and contribute value to their company. Employees who have little or no control over their work may not experience higher level needs in relation to their jobs.

NOGI's contract for American teachers was written with a Japanese mentality and did not take into consideration Maslow's model.

In Japan, job security and lifelong employment are stronger motivators than self-actualization. Belonging and security are considered more important than growing needs. The level of needs for Japanese employees may thus be reversed, as represented in Maslow's model. NOGI's contract reflected this mentality.

In addition to dictating when American teachers could schedule their personal days, the contract mandated specific dress codes (including unacceptable colors) and hairstyles. The attempt here was to present a standard appearance of professionalism and not to distinguish oneself from other teachers. However, Maslow's fourth level of needs, esteem, states that being accepted for who you are is critical to feeling that you belong to the organization. Belonging to an organization that requires one to change him/her self prevents his/her self-esteem needs from being fulfilled.

The inclusion of numerous regulations, which required American teachers to participate in non-work related activities on unscheduled workdays, was another attempt by NOGI management to ensure that American employees would behave as Japanese even if their beliefs were different.

As we have learned from Toby's case and the legal issues that arose, the manner in which NOGI attempted to imbed Japanese culture into the American teacher's contract was not justified by the law.

Question 4

Understanding where the Japanese management system falls along Hofstede's four dimensions of culture, analyze its effectiveness in a corporation that employs American employees (i.e. NOGI). Specifically, citing examples from the case, examine and identify the cultural inaccuracy of NOGI's management policies within the context of Toby's critical incident.

<u>Analysis skills</u> (breaking a concept into its parts and explaining their interrelationships, distinguishing relevant from extraneous material).

Answer

NOGI manages employees and its operations in a traditional Japanese fashion. Extremely centralized, with heavy importance placed on the corporate hierarchy, NOGI closely controls its organization in the pursuit of profits. This system poses serious problems for Japanese firms that employ Americans like Toby because it does not value individual performance or consider individual needs. NOGI failed to recognize Toby as an independent thinker and a competitor in the marketplace. In NOGI's eyes, his individual input, initially, lacked power. Unsatisfied with matching the efforts of their peers, the American employee, like Toby, seeks individual recognition and rewards for his/her work.

Often, this invites confrontation with Japanese management. The Japanese view confrontation with superiors as disrespectful because seniority is achieved through years of experience and commitment to the company.

NOGI's management system was not prepared to accommodate Toby's request because its policies were not structured to respond to challenges at a lower level. The high power distance at NOGI established many layers of ascending management to pursue before change could happen. When Toby asked his local manager for the day off to take the GMAT, his request was redirected to the head office. The head office then gave no indication of their decision to Toby or his manager until a week prior to the test date. Due to the high cultural context in which Americans are raised, Toby would have preferred an immediate response to his request. All requests and decision-making were made at the corporate level (consisting entirely of Japanese) to maintain order and minimize exceptions and uncertainty in the business process. However, this did not omit uncertainty at the local school level. For 3 months, Toby, his school manager, and co-workers waited for a decision. They were uncertain of what preparations needed to be made for the school and for Toby. Unsure of who knew what regarding the head office's decision, those 3 months built feelings of suspicion and anxiety between Toby and his coworkers. (Schermerhorn, Jr., John R., 1996, pg.42).

<u>Question 5</u>
Recommend a management strategy, at the local school level and at the corporate headquarters level, which incorporates Hofstede's four dimensions of culture to enhance employee satisfaction, minimize disruptions in the business process, and to promote a positive corporate culture.
<u>Synthesis skills</u> (putting parts together to form a new whole; solving a problem requiring creativity or originality).

<u>Answer</u>
Japanese management might consider giving greater autonomy to the local school managers at NOGI to minimize the bureaucratic process. Mandating all requests to be reviewed at the corporate level does not take into account localized knowledge of the employee, school, or circumstances which might substantiate their proposal. A move to decentralize the operations at NOGI would enhance the powers of local management and allow slight differentiation in school policies. This move towards individualism, however, must not be extreme. The head office should still review the decisions of local management and maintain standardized policies. The distinction should come when local management feels exceptions can justifiably be made.

If Ms. Nakamura had been able to decide on Toby's request, the matter would have remained local. Most likely, his request would have been approved, since his teaching record and performance were satisfactory.

Requiring a time period where requests must be made one month prior would minimize uncertainty and provide ample preparation time. The ability to utilize this much needed and scarce resource would benefit the entire corporate culture. Furthermore, the enhanced participatory role of the American employee would increase their emotional connection to the firm. Considering that NOGI is a Japanese company in Japan and the American employee is on a temporary contract, this is an extremely challenging task.

The difficulty for the local Japanese manager is balancing the more individualistic attitudes and demands of the American teachers with their Japanese counterparts. Including all teachers and staff in the establishment of local school policies would help maintain objectiveness in manager-employee relations.

Increasing participation of the American employee increases the degree of trust NOGI extends to them and makes their behavior more predictable. The behavioral intention model by Ajzen and Fishbein states that focusing on a person's specific intention to behave in certain ways makes behavior more predictable and understandable. A collaborative process between NOGI management and American teachers that seeks to define intentions before behavior is acted out would minimize uncertainty, open communication lines, and improve corporate culture. (Ajzen, I. And Fishbein, M., 1980, pg.8).

Question 6

Explain the importance of Toby's decision to recruit the help of the Tokyo South General Workers Union. Examine its role in the negotiation processes.

<u>Analysis skills</u> (breaking a concept into its parts and explaining their interrelationships, distinguishing relevant from extraneous material).

Answer

As a first year American teacher at NOGI, Toby possessed no real power over NOGI management. He did have the option to threaten to quit his job, but that provided no significant leverage against a company as large as NOGI. Instead, Toby chose to recruit the help of the Tokyo South General Workers Union (TSGW).

The TSGW provided Toby with expert power concerning the employee contract. It also helped NOGI management recognize the serious legal ramifications that would result if Toby's employment was terminated.

NOGI now had to deal with the TSGW, which gave Toby credibility and legitimized his request. Additionally, the TSGW encouraged Toby to establish a union for NOGI teachers. The power struggle was now beginning to shift as Mr. Crawford and the TSGW backed Toby's request with the highest power; that of legality. NOGI eventually withdrew its tactics.

Question 7

Evaluate the presence of Mr. Crawford and Mr. Allen from a power and influence perspective in the meeting between Toby and Mr. Miyake. How effective were they? Did one neutralize the other?

<u>Evaluation skills</u> (using a set of criteria to arrive at a reasoned judgment of the value of something).

Answer

When Toby and Mr. Crawford, the Vice President of TSGW, entered Mr. Miyake's office, the playing field leveled greatly. Mr. Crawford was also a lawyer and familiar with Japanese employment regulations, Mr. Miyake could not intimidate Toby without confronting the issues. Mr. Crawford dramatically marginalized the coercive and legitimate power of Mr. Miyake. As a high-ranking officer himself, Mr. Crawford was not intimidated by Mr. Miyake. Additionally, as a non-NOGI employee he was not threatened by the corporate power that Mr. Miyake represented because it had no relevance to his employment.

Mr. Allen was brought into the meeting as a last minute attempt to neutralize the expert power that Mr. Crawford brought with him. As a fellow American he tried to convince Toby that certain exceptions had to be made because NOGI was a Japanese company. He sympathized with Toby's situation but stressed the need to conform rather than rebel. This attempt to redirect the discussion away from the issues failed. Because Mr. Crawford possessed expert power on foreign employee contract laws, he identified the argument as pure hearsay.

At the end of the meeting NOGI refused to admit any wrongdoing or concede any reviews to their initial decision. In line with traditional Japanese negotiation tactics, Mr. Miyake hid his true emotions well as he searched for avenues to exploit or weaknesses to attack. By admitting any wrongdoing, Mr. Miyake and NOGI would lose face and weaken their corporate power, a scenario that was considered extremely shameful and embarrassing in Japanese culture. (Casse, P. and Doel, S., 1985, pg.10).

Question 8

Explain NOGI's reasoning for drafting two employee contracts, one for Americans and one for Japanese.

<u>Diagnostic question</u> (probes motives or causes).

Answer

NOGI had two contracts because they had two major kinds of employees: Japanese and Americans. NOGI wanted to exercise some degree of control over the Americans by specifying work expectations. The majority of the American employees were hired in the United States and deployed to various school locations throughout Japan. Often, the cultural differences and pressures of living in Japan exceeded the expectations of these new American teachers and contracts were broken. For this reason, NOGI devised a separate contract for American teachers that protected the company in a variety of situations. Most relevant to this case, American employees, like Toby, were controlled as much as possible due to the extremely different cultural attitudes. The different regulations between Japanese and American employees at NOGI was a continual debate at the company. Japanese employees were allowed to schedule their vacation time, while Americans could not.

Toby discovered that NOGI was obligated to provide 7 personal days per year to the American teacher, and that the law stated that those 7 days could be taken at the individual's discretion unless their absence threatened the viability of the company. Since a teacher missing a single day of work and also being covered by another teacher was hardly a threat, NOGI's contract was in violation of this employment law.

The Japanese teaching contract at NOGI was far less strict in nature and much more flexible concerning personal situations. Japanese employees requesting personal days did not need to submit their request to the head office as local Japanese managers could approve their requests. Again, this can be related to issues of trust and ethnocentrism.

Question 9

If Ms. Nakamura had been aware of the illegality in the American employee contract, would their actions have been different?

<u>Hypothetical question</u> (poses a change in the facts or issues).

Answer

Ms. Nakamura was highly ethical and procedural in her management style. Objectivity was a constant principle throughout her relations with the various employees. Despite the difficulty in developing a personal relationship with her, no one could discount her fairness.

The issue then becomes whether this fairness would outweigh her loyalty to the company. Based on NOGI's responses in the case, it can be inferred that NOGI headquarters would undoubtedly try to persuade Ms. Nakamura that this policy existed in the company's best interest.

Titles and rank are taken extremely serious and disobeying one's superior typically results in termination. The pressure to perform for the company, and not lose face, in an essential driver of employee performance.

For this reason, it is likely that Ms. Nakamura would not have stood up against NOGI and confronted their violations of employment law. In addition, Toby was a new employee with a year term. Ms. Nakamura had just begun her life-long career with the company and needed to make good impressions on senior management if she intended to escalate the corporate ladder.

References

Ajzen, I. and Fishbein, M. (1980). <u>Understanding attitudes and predicting behavior</u>. Englewood Cliffs, NJ: Prentice-Hallp.

Casse, P. and Doel, S. (1985). <u>Managing intercultural negotiations: Guidelines for trainers and negotiators</u>. Washington, D.C.: SEITAR International.10

Hall, E. (1989). <u>Understanding cultural differences</u>. Yarmouth, ME: Intercultural Press.

Hellreigel, Slocum, Woodman. (1998). <u>Organizational behavior</u>. Cincinnati, OH: South-Western College Publishing, 1998. 305

Schermerhorn, Jr., John R. (1996). <u>Management and organizational essentials</u>. New York, NY: John Wiley and Sons. 42

Epilogue

Ms. Nakamura remained manager of NOGI Tsurumi for an additional three years and was eventually permitted a school transfer (considered a type of promotion by Japanese standards). Ms. Yamashina remained the head teacher for NOGI Tsurumi for two and a half years before transferring to the head office as a trainer for children's classes. Mr. Miyake, Ms. Davies, and Mr. Allen remained in their same positions with the company. Mr. Crawford continued to fight for employee rights at the Tokyo South General Workers Union.

As a company, NOGI continues to be successful and employ thousands of American teachers. Thanks in part to the problems Toby struggled through, these teachers are now able to schedule personal days at their own convenience.

Toby left Japan for the Drucker School of Management in June 1997. He brought with him a rich experience in Japanese culture and business. The beginning of a new chapter in his life meant the closing of an old one. The doors of the Kawasaki Budokan were officially closed that year. His professional fighting career in Tokiona was very successful. He was lucky enough to win every match he fought in Japan, including one against his most challenging opponent, NOGI.

Teaching Note
ANGRY BRANCH MANAGER

Topics (* = Primary topic with teaching plan)
    *Decision Case
    *Employee Motivation (Maslow's Hierarchy of Needs, cognitive appraisal theory)
    *Cognition and Perception
    *Decision-making Process, rational
    *Racial Diversity
    *Turnover (high)
    Interpersonal Conflict
    Cultural Differences
    Interracial Differences and Conflict
    Human Resource Management
    Termination
    Banking/Financial Context

Case overview

An account executive from a high-pressure, sales-oriented mortgage lending company has called the human resource department accusing his branch manager of emotional and physical abuse. Two members of the HRM department and the area manager conduct an investigation that is inconclusive but shows:

- that the branch manager has demonstrated a pattern of complaints and high turnover,
- that the branch has increased its productivity since the branch manager took over, and
- that the branch manager had coerced other employees to change their stories during prior investigations into his conduct.

The HRM staff and the area manager must decide on a course of action.

Industry

Financial Services, Commission-Based Sales.

Teaching objectives

1. To apply motivation theories to an employee relations problem.
2. To understand how culture affects perceptions of behavior.
3. To apply a rational decision model to a difficult employee relations problem.

Other related cases in Volume 1

A Team Divided or a Team United? (termination). Heart Attack (termination). La Cabaret (racial diversity). Moon over E.R. (HRM). Problems at Wukmier Home Electronics Warehouse (HRM, racial diversity, termination). Shaking the Bird Cage (decision-making process).

Other related cases in Volume 2

The Safety Memo (decision-making process). Your Uncle Wants You! (HRM).

Intended courses and levels

This case fits with courses on human resource management and organizational behavior at the graduate and executive level. The case emphasizes the rational decision process, which fits well in management courses.

This teaching note was prepared by Joe Underwood, James C. Spee, University of Redlands, and Teri C. Tompkins, University of Redlands. The case and teaching note were prepared as the basis for class discussion rather than to illustrate either effective or ineffective handling of administrative situations. Suggestions for improvement of this note should be sent to Teri.Tompkins@pepperdine.edu. Credit will be given in the next revision.

Analysis

The analysis is included with the answers to the discussion questions.

Research methodology

This case reflects the recollections of one of the participants. The case is a true incident. The company and people have been disguised.

Teaching plan

This case takes the form of a decision-making case, leaving the reader hanging about what to do. The epilogue in this case could be used as a case B because it tells what decision was made. Students could evaluate whether the decision was a good one or not. Below are three alternative plans. Plan 2 includes a role play.

Topic: Motivation
60-minute teaching plan

Pre-assignment: Read case before class

	Timing	Activity	Organization	Student Outcomes
I	0-10 minutes (10)	Review the facts of the case.	Full group discussion	Better comprehension of the situation.
II	10-20 minutes (10)	Discuss need theories of motivation and apply to the case using discussion Question 1.	Small group discussion	Application of needs hierarchy to understand changes in employees' responses to a manager's style.
III	20-40 minutes (10)	Apply cognitive appraisal theory to the case using discussion Question 2.	Full class discussion	Students apply a second motivation theory to the situation.
IV	40-55 minutes (15)	Examine how the actions of the HRM department can help or harm the situation using discussion Question 3.	Full class discussion	Students understand implications HR role in employee relations.
V	55-60- minutes (5)	Wrap up.	Full class discussion	Reflect on learning from session.

<u>25-minute teaching plan on motivation</u>
Preassignment: Read case (15 minutes) before class.
Follow steps I (5 minutes), II, and III above.

Topic: Cultural Diversity and Perception
60-minute teaching plan

Pre-assignment: Read case before class

	Timing	Activity	Organization	Student Outcomes
I	0-10 minutes (10)	Review the facts of the case.	Full group discussion	Better comprehension of the situation
II	10-20 minutes (10)	Discuss cultural diversity issues and perception, apply to the case using discussion Question 4.	Small group discussion	Students begin to see connections between culture and management style.

	Timing	Activity	Organization	Student Outcomes
III	20-40 minutes (10)	Prepare for role play of investigation with Henry, Sal, and Joe.	Count off by threes. Group 1 will be Henrys, Group 2 will be Sals and Group 3 will be Joes.	Each group discusses how it will handle the investigation.
IV	40-55 minutes (15)	Negotiations between Joe, Henry and Sal.	Reform into groups of three, each with a Joe, a Sal and a Henry.	Students see if they can do any better than Joe at handling Henry and Sal, explore the difficulties.
V	55-60-minutes (5)	Wrap up discussion.	Full group.	Reflect on key learning points.

25-minute teaching plan on cultural diversity and perception
Preassignment: Read case (15 minutes) before class
Follow segments III and IV in the 60-minute teaching plan.

Topic: Decision-making Process
60-minute teaching plan

Pre-assignment: Read case before class

	Timing	Activity	Organization	Student Outcomes
I	0-10 minutes (10)	Review the facts of the case	Full group discussion	Better comprehension of the situation
II	10-20 minutes (10)	Discuss Decision-making Model	Full group discussion	Understand limits to use of the model due to bounded rationality an uncertainty.
III	20-55 minutes (35)	Evaluate each step of the Decision-making Model	Full group discussion	Apply the model to this situation and critique the approach used by the HRM team.
IV	55-60-minutes (5)	Wrap up discussion	Full group	Reflect on key learning points.

25-minute teaching plan on decision-making process
Preassignment: Read case (15 minutes) before class
Follow Step III above applying the Decision-Making Model to the situation at the Manhattan Beach branch of Calwest.

Discussion questions and answers

The first three questions deal with employee motivation. Questions 4 to 6 deal with cultural diversity and perception. Question 7 deals with turnover. Question 8 deals with the decision process.

Question 1
Assuming that Henry's management style stayed consistent during his management tenure, why did his employees fail to disclose any wrongdoing during the first investigation performed by Michael Griffin, the Regional Manager?
Diagnostic question (probes motives or causes)

Answer

Before Henry assumed his position, the employees were not making very much money. After he took over the management reins, Henry sat with his employees and taught them how to sell loans. Within a month, his employees were making a lot of commission – almost doubling their salaries in some cases. Not surprisingly, the employees appreciated the increase in income perhaps enough to forgive Henry of his management faults.

Abraham Maslow's Need Hierarchy is a useful tool to explain why increased income could account for the employees' failure to disclose Henry's management style during the first investigation. According to Maslow's Need Hierarchy, humans have five separate needs that they always try to satisfy. These needs are physiological, safety, love, esteem, and self-actualization. These needs are hierarchical with physiological being the lowest level need and self-actualization being the highest level need. These needs can only be satisfied on a basis of prepotency; e.g., the needs falling lower in the hierarchy must be satisfied before needs falling higher in the hierarchy can be met (Wagner & Hollenbeck, 1995).

In the case of the employees, their new increased income allowed them to satisfy their basic lower level needs. With more income, they would not have to go hungry or thirsty. Therefore, their physiological needs were satisfied. They could also afford to pay rent, so their safety needs were satisfied. Although Henry may not have satisfied their higher level needs, the lower level needs took precedence over the higher level needs. As such, they would not disclose Henry's mismanagement (or their perception of his mismanagement) to their regional manager for fear that Henry would lose his job. If this happened, they would probably start making less money and would not be able to satisfy their physiological or safety needs.

To complicate matters further, three of the employees disclosed in the second investigation that Henry had threatened them with retaliation should they admit any management wrongdoing to the regional manager. In addition, since the employee who had initiated the allegations against Henry was sent home by HR without any communication to the rest of the branch as to why she was sent home, they may have assumed that the employee had been retaliated against because she had been forthcoming. As such, they may have believed that any disclosure could lead to their own possible termination, which would once again jeopardize their physiological and safety needs.

Question 2

What happened after the first investigation to change their behavior?

Diagnostic question (probes motives or causes)

Answer

Three important events happened that swayed their behavior. First, the employee that had been put on paid leave initially returned to work. The branch employees discovered that she had been placed on a paid leave by human resources during the initial investigation. In addition, after the investigation, she was granted a transfer to another branch, which turned out to be more lucrative for her and was also closer to her house. Second, Henry fired two employees a month after the first investigation for poor production. Third, Henry became more demanding and belligerent since he believed that human resources would back his management style.

When considering Maslow's Hierarchy, it is not surprising that Sal complained to human resources or that the other employees decided to be more forthcoming during the second investigation. When they realized that not only had the employee who initiated the first complaint not been retaliated against but she had received a promising transfer, they also realized that they would not be retaliated against either. As such, they did not need to fear for their lower level needs if they disclosed. However, they did start worrying that they may not be able to satisfy their lower level needs at this particular branch when Henry terminated the two employees for their lack of performance. Although these two employees had been the worst two producers in the branch, the other employees were not performing that much better than the two terminated employees were. In fact, Henry had set production goals that were high when compared to the average Calwest branch. Instead of facing possible termination, they may have decided to disclose Henry's behavior in hopes of getting a new manager or securing a transfer for themselves.

The employees' forthcoming attitude was also due to Henry's increased belligerence. A few of the employees stated that they believed that Henry had become exceedingly aggressive to the point that they feared for their safety. The other employees were not afraid of any physical violence although they did suggest that Henry was becoming increasingly mentally abusive. Obviously, this violates their safety needs.

Whether Henry changed his behavior or not, the employees' perception that he changed his behavior for the worse could explain their willingness to disclose during the second investigation as suggested by Arnold and Lazarus's cognitive appraisal theory. According to this theory, individuals first perceive some stimulus in their environment (perception stage). They evaluate the stimulus (primary appraisal stage). If they find it satisfactory, they stop processing. If they find it dissatisfactory, they evaluate the stimulus again (secondary appraisal stage) to determine their abilities to cope with the dissatisfaction. If they believe they can cope, processing stops and they are satisfied. If they believe they can not cope with the stimulus, they become stressed and attempt to fight the stimulus or run away from it (Wagner & Hollenbeck, 1995).

During the initial investigation, the employees evaluated Henry's management style and decided that they could cope with it. Coping with an unpleasant situation is made much easier if the situation also has very pleasant consequences. In this case, Henry was making them more money than they had ever made before. As one employee stated during the second interview, "I had just made a $1200 commission check. Would you have ratted him out?" However, as they began perceiving Henry's behavior as getting more egregious, coping became more difficult especially after they felt like he was becoming mentally abusive. As suggested by cognitive appraisal theory, they had two choices: fight or run away. Sal chose to fight when he called human resources for help. The others also chose to fight when they disclosed their views of Henry's management style. Several of the employees also chose to run away by asking for immediate transfers.

Question 3

What part did the actions of human resources play in the differing responses of the employees?
<u>Cause-and-effect question</u> (asks for causal relationship between ideas, actions, or events)

Answer

Initially, the human resources department was not very involved in the first investigation process. Michael Griffin conducted the first investigation. Although he attempted to be as impartial as possible, the employees likely viewed him as one of the top corporate managers. As such, they may have found it difficult to be forthcoming with him. Since Michael decided that the preponderance of the evidence suggested that Henry's management style was sufficient, it is likely that his employees decided that the corporation would back Henry and his management style. When HR allowed the one associate who had initiated the claim against Henry to transfer to another branch, the other employees may have realized that calling HR and complaining about Henry could initiate a transfer. HR also allowed Henry to terminate two of his employees, which may have increased the level of fear within the branch. Finally, HR never followed up with the employees after the investigation to make sure that they were still comfortable with the culture within the branch. As such, the whole process affirmed that Henry could get away with almost anything without corporate or HR intervention.

During the second investigation process, however, HR took a more active role. From the start, they assured the employees that the company would not tolerate any form of retribution from anyone in the company because they contacted HR. During the actual investigation, Michael Griffin joined the two HR representatives. However, Stephanie, the HR Manager, obviously drove the process. Since they had suspended Henry while the investigation was conducted, they sent a clear message to the employees that his intervention would not be tolerated. They also assured each employee that their conversations would be as confidential as possible and assured them that Henry would not be privy to any information shared within the confines of the private office. The difference in perception between the two investigative processes, e.g., that human resources was in charge and would be fair, allowed the employees to disclose much more than they initially did. Also, Stephanie was a very skilled investigator, and she would often ask apparently innocuous questions that would be very telling by the end of the conversation. Because of this, she was able to draw more information out of the employees than they initially wanted to disclose.

Question 4
How might cultural diversity account for the behavior of the branch employees?
<u>Cause-and-effect question</u> (asks for causal relationship between ideas, actions, or events)

Answer

One of the major concerns for three of the four interviewed employees was Henry's confrontational approach to management. They suggested that Henry would be very nice and easy-going one minute then extremely heated the next minute. Whenever he spoke to them about their job performance, he would stand very close to them and raise his voice often. They found this behavior to be very intimidating and often frightening. In fact, they suggested that because he grew so angry so quickly and easily they were afraid that he might be prone to greater violent outbursts if further provoked.

Unbeknownst to the employees, Henry may not have realized how much his outbursts affected them. As Thomas Kochman (1981) suggests, different cultures have different ways of expressing themselves. According to Kochman's findings, African-Americans tend to get very passionate and confrontational when discussing matters that are important to them. For example, Henry may have assumed that raising his voice and standing close to his employees was an effective coaching or motivating tool. In fact, African-Americans have been known to find confrontation very therapeutic while other cultures find it very trying. For example, Asians' hearts begin to palpitate quickly when they are forced to confront someone else. Anglos' hearts begin to palpitate whenever they are confronted. African-Americans' hearts begin to palpitate whenever they are not allowed to confront someone else (Kochman, 1981). As such, much of the perceived anger in the branch might have been culturally specific miscommunication.

Question 5
What might have influenced Henry's statements about being a minority at Calwest?
<u>Cause-and-effect question</u> (asks for causal relationship between ideas, actions, or events)

Answer

From the beginning of Henry's employment, he had the preconception that he had to be very careful at Calwest because he was African-American. For example, he tape-recorded conversations that he had with his employees, senior management, and human resources. Typically, he tape-recorded the conversations without the knowledge or consent of the person(s) being recorded. He also told his employees that management would heavily scrutinize him because they were always looking for ways to terminate him as "they had all the other black managers." Ironically, his perception of Calwest was not warranted. Although there were only 7 African-American managers out of 178 total managers in the sales force at Calwest (over 60percent of the rest of the managerial force was some other minority status), only one of the African-American managers was currently on a performance-issued action plan. Three of the seven were top producers and were very highly regarded by top management. Michael, an African-American, was a Regional Manager, which is one of the top management positions in the whole company.

Since Calwest's history tended to be minority-friendly, why might Henry assume that his race was a detriment to his job security? According to schema theory, initial perceptions can be very powerful and are very hard to change even when faced with strong evidence that is contrary to the perception (Sternberg, 1994). If Henry had a schema, or preconception, that corporations disparage African-Americans, he would assume that Calwest would do the same. One particular type of schema, the script, is especially rigid in design. Typically, a person develops scripts when they repeatedly experience patterns in behavior. After they experience a particular series of events that are consistent, the person will assume that the series of events will continue to stay consistent. This assumption can lead to preconceptions that are incorrect. In fact, when a series of events occur that are inconsistent with a person's script, the person may disregard the events as an aberration and assume that their script is correct anyway (Sternberg, 1994; Wagner & Hollenbeck, 1998). In Henry's case, if he had previously experienced disparate treatment in other corporations that was racially motivated, he might have developed a script that incorporated racially disparate treatment. Regardless of how fairly Calwest management treated Henry, he would assume that the fair treatment was unusual and that he could expect unfair treatment at all other times.

In support of Henry's perception of potential race discrimination, it may be that Calwest does have an unfriendly atmosphere for African-Americans. Seven African-American managers of 178 managers (3.7 percent) is a smaller percentage of African-Americans than one would expect in the population, especially in Southern California. Sometimes racial privilege is not obvious to the majority population as it is to the minority.

Question 6

How might have the different cultural perceptions created an unhealthy atmosphere within the branch?
Cause-and-effect question (asks for causal relationship between ideas, actions, or events)

Answer

By themselves, the different cultural perceptions created an atmosphere that was unpleasant for Henry and his employees. When exposed to each other, their perceptions fed off of each other to the point that Henry believed that he was losing control of his staff, and his staff believed that they could no longer trust Henry. It was this interaction between the two perceptions that created an environment so hostile that the employees finally decided to discuss their problems with human resources regardless of how much money they were earning or how much they feared retaliation.

Initially, the employees were surprised when they discovered that Henry was taping every formal conversation that he had with them. Although they were not entirely comfortable with being taped, they viewed the act as one of Henry's paranoia-based quirks and decided that they could live with it. When Henry began to espouse anti-corporation platitudes, e.g., "HR is like the Gestapo and can't be trusted," they accepted his attitude as potentially plausible. This was especially true when he promised that they would never need to speak to HR or any other corporate entity since he would take care of them by judiciously handling any of their issues. Since he did treat them well initially, they also assumed that this option was plausible. When he began getting more confrontational, however, their perceptions began to change.

As his management style became more aggressive, they began viewing his behavior as more volatile and frightening, which began changing their perceptions of his other behaviors. They found his tape recordings and HR admonishments as further aggressive attempts to control their own lives. They reacted to this new perception change by withdrawing from Henry, which he viewed as a loss of control and/or insubordination. He responded by firing two of his employees. The other employees viewed this behavior as threatening. Eventually, everyone became extremely sensitive to the actions of the others, and small innocuous actions were perceived as affronts. As such, the whole branch atmosphere became intolerable, and Sal decided to call human resources.

Question 7

What inferences might you make about a 56 percent turnover rate at Calwest?
Evaluation question (using a set of criteria to arrive at a reasoned judgment of the value of something)

Answer

Fifty-six percent is high turnover for any company. One has to wonder why it is so high? We can examine several areas: (1) the context of the company; (2) the company itself and (3) the employees within the company.

We can infer that Calwest had no shortage of employees to take the place of those who left. There must have been a ready pool of applicants. Why? Either the economy was very tight (not true in the late 1990s) or the job attracted a lot of people. The latter is likely because of the promise of high pay if the employee was successful. Since sales positions don't necessarily require college education, the potential employee base was larger (high school educated people) than if it was a more technical position (requiring college or technical training).

The company practice of terminating employees within three months if the employee doesn't produce also contributed to high turnover. Management's willingness to quickly terminate an employee supports the inference that there was a ready employment base. Since Calwest offered very little training to its employees, the likelihood that an employee might not succeed was high.

Employees that are attracted to these entry-level positions may be attracted to the potentially high paying job. Once on the job, they may have found that they were not skilled at sales and may have ended their employment voluntarily or through termination. If they were successful in sales, then they might be promoted to management. An employee with skills needed for success in sales does not necessarily have the skills necessary to be successful in management. Since the company does not offer much management training, unskilled new managers may not be very successful. Therefore, we might expect a fairly high turnover rate at entry-level management positions as well.

There are hidden costs to high turnover that Calwest appeared to ignore. High turnover rate can lead to low morale because employees watch their friends leave employment. It can also cause people to ignore newcomers to the organization because they assume most of those people will leave anyway. Ignoring new employees also makes the newcomers feel less welcome, thereby, increasing the likelihood of them leaving. Since the company offered very little training, there were fewer problems often associated with turnover, that of increased training costs.

Question 8

Using the rational decision process, how would the group handle this situation?
Exploratory question (probes facts and basic knowledge)
Answer

The rational decision process can be broken down into about nine steps, as shown in the figure on the next page, (Ivancevich and Matteson, 1999, p. 515)

1. Establishing Specific Goals and Objectives and Measuring Results. The goal for the decision was to deal with Henry. Several measurable results were reported in the case: sales for the branch, commissions for the sales associates, and branch turnover. The company had pretty clear expectations for the first objective; the employees had clear expectations for the second. The HR department never determined whether 80 percent turnover was unacceptable, given the company average of 56 percent. Henry may have never been warned that his turnover was too high. The clearest objective of the decision-makers was to have this problem go away and not come back.

2. Problem Identification and Definition. They appear to have identified Henry as the problem without consideration of other systemic issues that could put other African-American managers in jeopardy if put in the same situation without training. Several problems could emerge in the discussion, including misperceptions based on cultural biases and changing needs as performance in the branch increased. To simplify the discussion, the problem could be simplified to keeping Henry or terminating him, but this would shortchange discussion of the deeper issues, including why they might avoid identification of systemic problems within the company.

3. Establishing Priorities. It is not clear from the case just what the investigating team's priorities really are. They focus on dealing with the situation quickly. They want to deal with the concerns of all employees, including Henry fairly. They want to protect the company from lawsuits from Henry if he claims discrimination or from the employees if they claim that they have been abused and the company took no action. If they put the priority on developing stronger managers and better employees, they might approach the situation differently. In this company, production is what counts, so the priority is getting people back to producing new loans as quickly as possible.

4. Consideration of Causes. The list of issues includes physical abuse, mental abuse, micromanagement, intimidation and retaliation, lack of written performance evaluations, race discrimination, and Henry's tape recordings. It is not apparent from the case how deep the assessment went into the

systemic flaws in Calwest's promotion policies and non-existent cultural diversity or management training procedures that could have contributed to the breakdown of relations between Henry and several of his subordinates.

5. <u>Development of Alternative Solutions.</u> The team has several alternatives. They can terminate Henry. They can keep him and try to work through his conflicts with the employees. They can send the entire branch to cultural diversity training and help them devise more effective ways to communicate with each other. They could demote Henry.

6. <u>Evaluation of Alternative Solutions.</u>

   ◆ *Positions that favor termination*

   - Physical abuse – although there had been assertions of physical abuse by Sal, most of the other employees did not substantiate the assertions. As a litigation-wary human resources department, however, Stephanie and Joe decided to consider the assertions of physical abuse and the potential that Henry might become physical in the future.

   - Mental abuse – these assertions were substantiated by all but one of the employees (this employee was the only other African-American in the branch). When asked for examples, the mental abuse described by the employees all centered around Henry's confrontational management style.

   - Intimidation and retaliation – three of the employees independently asserted that Henry had threatened retaliation if any of his employees ever approached Michael or human resources with an issue. They also suggested that he had coerced them to submit false written testimonies during a previous investigation.

   - Tape recordings –Henry had recorded conversations without the knowledge or consent of his subordinates and may have violated their civil rights in doing so.

   ◆ *Positions that favor no termination*

   - Lack of any formal written warnings – per Calwest policy, employees are typically counseled and then written up at least once and normally twice over a 60 day period before termination. Although Calwest is an at-will organization, they have only terminated employees without written warnings in the past when the employee had committed a major rule infraction, e.g., fraud.

   - Race discrimination – Henry had already mentioned that he believed that Calwest treated African-Americans unfairly. Although Stephanie did not believe that the organization had discriminated against Henry, Calwest was currently involved in another race discrimination case. If Henry publicly claimed racial discrimination as he had once suggested that he might do, the claim could have been very incriminating and costly for the organization in the long run.

   - Tape recordings – Michael noted that Henry had potentially recorded conversations with his area manager, who had been demoted for questionable business practices. Michael was concerned that Henry may have recorded conversations that could be potentially damaging to the company's reputation.

   - Absence of management training—No one in the company had much formal training in management. Holding Henry to a higher standard of management practices than other managers when no standards had been communicated would leave the company wide open for a discrimination lawsuit.

   - Absence of training in cultural diversity—If, as the answer to Question 6 suggests, the real issue is one of cultural perceptions, then the entire workforce may need training in cultural diversity and awareness. Holding Henry responsible for misperceptions that could have been understood through better training hints at more discrimination.

   ◆ *Positions that favor sending the entire branch to cultural diversity training and helping them devise more effective ways to communicate with each other.*

- If, as suggested in Questions 3 to 6 above, cultural differences were at the heart of the conflict, then neither terminating Henry nor keeping him will solve the problem permanently.
- The entire group contributed to the problem, although Henry was identified as the one with the problem.
- The company may have a responsibility to prevent other African-American managers from failing the way Henry has by not helping him and his employees come to a shared level of understanding both of his behavior and of their responses to it.
- *Positions that support demoting Henry*
  - Henry would have no management responsibilities at all.
  - Henry was a fantastic salesperson, so Calwest would have been able to take advantage of his sales skills.
  - If Henry felt uncomfortable being in the same branch where he used to manage, Calwest could have transferred him to any of the local branches.

7. Solution Selection. The choice will depend on the importance attached to Henry's intimidation of the other employees by forcing them to change their testimony in the previous investigation. This creates a serious ethical barrier to keeping him in the company, even if the company is responsible for not training him to be a better manager. If the reasons for Henry's lack of trust in the process can be discerned and forgiven and he is willing to accept training with the group, it is possible that termination will not be necessary.

8. Implementation. The most difficult option to implement is the training and development one because it requires people to lose selling time and forfeit commissions. The company would have to compensate them for their lost time. If they choose to terminate Henry, then they will have to give him cause and then select a successor. Ideally, the successor would receive management and cultural diversity training to prevent a recurrence of this problem.

9. Follow-Up. Michael will need to work with the new manager and the group to maintain the high level of productivity gained under Henry without duplicating the hostility he aroused.

References

Ivancevich, J.M. and Matteson, M.T. (1999). Organizational behavior and management. New York: Irwin McGraw-Hill.

Kochman, T. (1981). Black & white: Styles in conflict. Chicago: University of Chicago Press.

Sternberg, R. J. (1994). Thinking and problem solving. San Diego: Academic Press.

Wagner, J. A. & Hollenbeck, J. R. (1995). Management of organizational behavior, 2nd Edition. New Jersey: Prentice Hall.

Wagner, J. A. & Hollenbeck, J. R. (1998). Management of organizational behavior, 3rd Edition. New Jersey: Prentice Hall.

Epilogue

After conducting the investigation, Stephanie, Joe, and Michael attempted to use the rational decision-making model to decide whether or not to terminate Henry's employment. First, they framed the decision by spelling out the issues they thought were most important and deciding whether the issues were important enough to warrant termination. The group then started generating alternatives. This stage was a two-step process. First, they examined each employee's testimony and decided if there were any reasons why the employees would be less than truthful. Second, they considered possibilities other than termination but immediately decided that termination (or not termination) would be the only possible outcome should they agree with the employees. They used a historical decision model to arrive at this solution, e.g., they determined that termination was the typical result when allegations of this severity were affirmed.

They made the decision to terminate Henry. They framed this decision in terms of social responsibility (e.g., what alternative was best for the employees) and mostly economic responsibility (e.g., what alternative would cost the company less in legal fees in the long run, Wagner & Hollenbeck, 1995).

The decision was both good and bad. Henry needed to be relieved of his management responsibilities. Although a stronger area manager might have been able to guide Henry and teach him more appropriate manager skills, Henry had shown a poor lapse of judgement when he coerced his employees to falsify testimony in the previous investigation. Calwest could not afford to have an ethically challenged individual as a branch manager, whose responsibilities include regularly receiving highly confidential financial information from the company's customers.

Instead of taking the time to consider all possible alternatives, Stephanie, Joe, and Michael decided that they needed to make a quick decision (e.g., settled for the first alternative that they felt was acceptable, Wagner & Hollenbeck, 1995). As such, the decision was not necessarily a good decision. The outcome might have been the best outcome under the circumstances; however, the decision process should have included a better use of all of the components of good decision-making.

CAFÉ LATTE, LLC

Topics (* = Primary topic with Teaching Plan)
*Decision Case
*Interpersonal Conflict
*Anger Management
*Selective Perception
*Communication Barriers
*Entrepreneurship
*Family Businesses
Equity Theory
Small Business Context
Interpersonal Conflict

Case overview

This decision making case chronicles three members of the Chan family, and one family friend, examining entrepreneurial opportunities that required relatively low levels of capital to start, could be quickly profitable and could be maintained with minimal supervision. In the summer of 1997, they decided that an espresso cafe fit the profile. The opportunity to test their theory presented itself when a low rent space became available through the current landlord of the Chan family restaurant.

Each partner held equal shares and contributed equally distinct talents to the strategic planning and development of the espresso cafe. Cynthia contributed her design skills, Stuart utilized his negotiation skills, Rob used his ability to work with people and also contributed some physical labor to the project. The final partner and family friend, Jeff, was geographically removed from the endeavor and therefore only a financial contributor.

Cynthia, and her older brother Stuart, had a history of personality conflicts. Cynthia had pursued an education away from home and enjoyed her freedom from the responsibility of the family restaurant. On the other hand, Stuart attended a local college to obtain his degree and obediently fulfilled his obligations at his parent's restaurant. Frustrated by these obligations, the outwardly charming Stuart was prone to angry verbal assaults on family members in private.

One week prior to the grand opening of Cafe Latte, the contractor was substantially behind and Stuart's frustration escalated into a heated confrontation with Cynthia. Stuart told her that he felt he was the only one contributing to the project. Case A ends with Cynthia contemplating what to do.

In Part B of the case, Stuart's unacceptable behavior and his lack of appreciation offended Cynthia to the extent that she decided to take Stuart up on his threat to buy her out of the business. When faced with her imminent departure, Stuart realized his mistake, and the value of the skills that she contributed, and subsequently apologized to Cynthia.

A compromise was reached in the form of a schedule that cut down the amount of time that Stuart and Cynthia were required to work together. Rob became the manager of the operations of Café Latte while Stuart and Cynthia happily limited their daily involvement.

Industry
Hospitality, small coffee shop. Family owned, entrepreneurs.

This case was written by Kim Hui, Amber Borden and Teri C. Tompkins, University of Redlands. The case and teaching note were prepared as a basis for class discussion rather than to illustrate either effective or ineffective handling of administrative situations. Suggestions for improvement of this note should be sent to Teri.Tompkins@pepperdine.edu. Credit will be given in the next revision.

Teaching objectives

1. To illustrate equity theory and its implications in family business.
2. To evaluate differences in perceptions and communication styles.
3. To explore causes of anger and aggression.
4. To apply anger management ideas to the case.
5. To discuss challenges of family owned businesses.

Other related cases in Volume 1

A New Magazine in Nigeria (entrepreneurship). Costume Bank (entrepreneurship). Donor Services Department in Guatemala (equity theory). Handling Problems at Japan Auto (management of conflict). Questions Matter (barriers to communication).

Other related cases in Volume 2

A Selfish Request in Japan (management of conflict). Computer Services Team at AVIONICS (management of conflict). Preferential Treatment? (equity theory).

Intended course and levels

This case is intended for undergraduate and graduate students in management, organizational behavior, or entrepreneurship courses. It is especially useful in connection with discussions pertaining to the equity theory, conflict resolution techniques, selective perception, and family owned businesses.

Analysis

All related analysis and references are embedded in the answers to the questions.

Research methodology

This case reflects the recollections of one of the partners in the case and the decisions made regarding this case. The case is a true incident. However, names and the organization were disguised to promote privacy.

Teaching plan

This case can be used as an illustration of equity, communication, conflict resolution techniques and group effectiveness issues. For undergraduate students, the questions and answers will serve to guide students to the specific theories related to the case. It is decision-focused and instructors may want students to role-play the parts of Cynthia and Stuart in the case.

Topic: Conflict and Anger Management
60-minute teaching plan

Pre-assignment: None

	Timing	Activity	Organization	Student Outcomes
I	0 to 15 minutes (5)	Read the case.	Individually	Familiarity with the case facts.
II	15-25 minutes (10)	*What is your character's perception of the situation?*	Divide the class into two or four groups. Even number groups take on Cynthia's role and odd number groups take on Stuart's role.	Stuart perceives Cynthia as having the easy life, fewer responsibilities. Cynthia perceives Stuart as the bossy big brother.

	Timing	Activity	Organization	Student Outcomes
III	25-30 minutes (5)	*What is your character's goal for Cafe Latte?*	Same as II.	Stuart, Rob, and Cynthia have the same goal—to have a successful enterprise.
IV	30-45 minutes (15)	Imagine that Cynthia and Stuart talk to each other at the end of case (A). Role play Cynthia and Stuart's discussion. Before the role play, discuss in your group how you will approach the role play.	Choose one Cynthia and Stuart for first role play. Ask the first pair to role play and allow the discussion to just happen. At the end of their role play, ask the rest of the class to evaluate Stuart and Cynthia's actions. Do they have suggestions for improvement? Ask a new Cynthia and Stuart to role play the class' idea, or let the first pair redo their role play.	A variety of possible scenarios exist. Most likely is an escalation of the conflict. Another is an avoidance of the conflict. Least likely is a skillful discussion revealing problems in perceptions and a willingness to explore common ground (goals). In the second round, you may need to coach the player during the role play, to practice listening and reflecting, as well as advocating their position with a willingness to change.
V	45-50 minutes (5)	Class discussion or mini-lecture on perceptual problems and conflict resolution options.	Full-class discussion	See answer in discussion section.
VI	50-55 minutes (5)	Read Case B class		
VII	55-60 minutes (5)	*How satisfied are you with Cynthia's solution?*	Full-class discussion	See Anger Management solutions in Q & A section.

<u>25-minute plan for conflict and anger management</u>

Students read case before class.

Answer the questions: (Total 25 minutes for questions 1 through 4 below).

1. What are some perceptual problems that may explain the confrontation between Cynthia and Stuart? What were some other causes of Stuart's anger?
2. To what extent was the conflict due to a difference in communication style?
3. Suppose an anger management consultant visited Cafe Latte to help the partners deal with the issue of anger in the workplace, what might be his/her advise on anger management?
4. Summarize how conflict and anger can be managed. (5 minutes)
5. Students read Case B.

Topic: Family business and entrepreneurship
60-minute teaching plan

Pre-assignment: None

	Timing	Activity	Organization	Student Outcomes
I	0 - 15 minutes (15)	Read the case.	Individually	Familiarity with the case facts.
II	15-25 minutes	Students answer question: *What were some of the*	Small group or whole class	Anger and frustration from Stuart; 2. Feelings of inequity; 3.

	Timing	Activity	Organization	Student Outcomes
	(10)	*problems Cynthia faced?*		Communication differences; 4. Stress over new business.
III	25 -40 minutes (15)	*What are some of the challenges members of family businesses face?*	Small group or whole class	Distinction between family and economic roles often blur. Negotiation of the multiple roles can be difficult. Issues of power and control.
IV	40 - 50 minutes (10)	Read Case B. *What are some options for getting out of entrepreneurial adventures and the importance of an exit strategy?*	Small group or whole class	Cynthia's options are reasonable for getting out. Every contract should have an exit strategy that is fair to all partners.
V	50 - 55 minutes (5)	*What are your conclusions (or lessons learned) about family business?*	Full-class discussion	Various answers depending on what struck each student as important. Summarize how entrepreneurship requires the ability to oversee new projects and take risks.
VI	55-60 minutes (5)	Read epilogue.	Instructor read to class	

25-minute teaching plan for Family business and entrepreneurship
Pre-assignment: Students read case before class (15 minutes)
Do activities II (10 minutes); III (10 minutes), read Case B and epilogue (5minutes).

Discussion questions and answers

<u>Question 1</u>

Define equity theory and its implications in family business. How does this theory explain Stuart's angry confrontations with Cynthia?

<u>Application skills</u> (using information in a new context to solve a problem, answer a question, or perform a task).

<u>Answer</u>

Equity theory helps explain the process people use to decide whether they are being treated fairly in their relationships. According to this theory, people compare their own inputs and outcomes to others to see if fairness exists in a particular environment. This notion of equity is very difficult to achieve within organizations due to people's differing perceptions about inputs and outcomes (Wagner & Hollenbeck 1998, p.179-182).

When individuals perceive inequity, they consciously evaluate situational rewards and costs, and in family businesses the perceived rewards are many (Kelley and Thibaut, 1978). Some of the rewards include keeping the business in the family, togetherness, and often a greater commitment to quality (Davis, 1983). The perceived potential costs are also great; these include power struggles, favoritism, unfair workloads and compensation, and incompatibility of goals (Bork, 1986; Rosenblatt et al., 1985).

This perceived inequity tends to cause distress, and individuals may try to alleviate it by changing communication strategies or relational expectations (Canary & Stafford, 1992). Often, if the inequitable situation cannot be balanced, family members will choose to terminate the relationship or leave the business altogether (Weigel & Ballard-Reisch, 1997).

Whenever a feeling of inequity exists, an individual will likely act in one or more of the following manners to restore a sense of equity:

1. Change work inputs (reduce the amount of effort).

2. Change the outcomes (rewards) received.
3. Leave the situation.
4. Change the comparison points.
5. Psychologically distort the comparisons (rationalize that the inequity is only temporary and will be resolved in the future).
6. Take actions to change the inputs or outputs of the comparison person (e.g. get a coworker to do more work). (Schermerhorn, Jr., Hunt, Osborn, 1995, p.74).

Stuart's perception was that Cynthia and Rob were not doing their share of the work, yet they would eventually enjoy the same benefits, namely financial gains, in the end. Under the circumstances, Stuart's response to his feelings of inequity resulted in anger. Stuart felt that the only way to restore a feeling of equity was to get his partners to accept more responsibilities. Rather than discussing it with them in a professional manner, Stuart would yell at his partners to work harder. This was the way Stuart chose to release his angry feelings.

There is also a larger issue of inequity in this case that must be discussed. Stuart always thought Cynthia's life was "easier" because she had more opportunities to leave Idaho and the family business. Stuart's opinion of Cynthia had been formed well before the business venture, and it had serious effects on their working relationship.

Question 2
What are some perceptual problems that may explain the confrontation between Cynthia and Stuart? What were some other causes of Stuart's anger?
Diagnostic question (probes motives or causes) and exploratory question (probes facts and basic knowledge)

Answer
Selective perception is the tendency to single out those aspects of a situation, person, or object that are consistent with one's needs, values, or attitudes. Stuart thought Cynthia had an easy life; therefore, he attributed the lack of time she spent at the cafe over the last few days to laziness, and came to the conclusion that she was "slacking." He discounted all her other efforts and focused on this aspect which was consistent with his own belief.

Attribution theory also helps explain the complexities between Cynthia and Stuart. Attribution theory describes how people try to explain others' behaviors, by determining whether a certain behavior was internally or externally caused. Instead of looking at possible external causes of Cynthia's absence from the cafe, he attributed her lack of time spent as being lazy (internal). On the same note, Cynthia attributed Stuart's anger to a completely internal cause (his sour personality), without considering possible external explanations.

Cynthia and Stuart both underestimated the prevalence of situational factors, such as delays and long hours, and overestimated personal factors when they assessed the situation. This is a common mistake known as the fundamental attribution error.

Stuart's anger can be partially attributed to his perception of inequity. The partners of Cafe Latte and the Chan Family believed that his anger was more obscure and deeply rooted. It is reasonable to surmise that Stuart's anger stemmed from childhood, although no one can know for sure. The one thing the Chans agreed on was that his anger was usually directed at a family member. In fact, friends and acquaintances seldom saw any type of anger from Stuart. This causes one to believe that the root of the anger was familial. Stuart had also personally stated that he was mad at the family for not helping with the family business as much as he and that he was the one who was always "picking up the pieces" after the other siblings created "messes" within the business.

Another source of his anger or aggressive behavior was frustration. "Frustration always leads to some form of aggression," said John Dollard and his colleagues in studies on causes of aggression (Dollard, 1939). Frustration arises when something blocks one from attaining a goal, and it grows when the motivation to attain that goal is very strong, and when expected gratification is completely blocked (Myers, 1996).

Further studies from Leonard Berkowitz (1978,1989), revised Dollard's original theory stating that frustration did not always lead to aggression. Instead, frustration produces anger, an emotional precursor to aggression. Hence, a frustrated person is likely to lash out, releasing pent-up anger.

Both these theories relate to how Stuart may have felt during this time. He may have felt frustrated that the opening may be set back by delays in construction, or by the mere stress of beginning a business. In any event, Stuart displaced his anger (Myers, 1996) on the closest targets, Cynthia and Rob.

Question 3

Suppose an anger management consultant visited Cafe Latte to help the partners deal with the issue of anger in the workplace, what might be his/her advise on anger management?

Application skills (using information in a new context to solve a problem, answer a question, or perform a task)

Answer

According to Hendrie Weisinger, Ph.D, a psychologist and business professor at UCLA, anger is difficult to manage because people are not taught how. Dr. Weisinger states that anger in the workplace is commonplace because work is an expression of ourselves and is "the principal means of validating our self-esteem." When people feel that they have lost control and their needs are threatened, they become angry ("Be an Explosives Expert", 1995). It appears that many Americans feel this loss of control. According to a nationwide Gallup survey four out of ten workers generally felt slightly mad at work (Lee, 1998).

Dr. Albert Mehrabian, psychology professor at UCLA, believes that "anger often provides a feeling of power" and "when we are angry, we are highly aroused, displeased, and feel dominant. We feel free to strike out physically or verbally" (Raudsepp, 1994, p. 79).

Jay Schneider, a licensed clinical social worker, and Gina Simmons, a psychologist, offer some suggestions on dealing with anger:

1. Accept responsibility for his/her anger and stop blaming everyone else for his/her behavior. This will work only if Stuart recognizes his anger as a problem and wants to change.
2. Discuss the grave physiological impact on the overall health of individuals. Angry people have greater risk of cardiovascular disease. Someone would need to talk to Stuart about this. His physician or a therapist would be one possibility.
3. "Cognitive restructuring" to train one's mind to think differently and discover the real reason for the anger, which may be covering other emotions such as fear or grief. Stuart could accomplish this through reflection either on his own or with the help of another person (e.g., therapist, clergy, or skillful friend).
4. Behavioral techniques such as: taking walks, breathing exercises, or listening to music to ease tension.
5. Learn effective listening and communication skills and conflict resolution techniques (Lee, 1998, C2 p.3).

Question 4

To what extent was the conflict due to a difference in communication style?

Evaluation skills (using a set of criteria to arrive at a reasoned judgment of the value of something)

Answer

According to Cox (1994), men and women have differences in communication styles, which can be traced back to early childhood. These differences in styles often lead to behavioral differences. This can be manifested in the way men and women identify problems. According to researcher Deborah

Tannen, "Women often acknowledge problems in an effort to solicit confirmation, support, and discussion of the issues. Men often respond with a strongly worded piece of advice on how to solve the problem" (Tannen, 1990).

Since Cynthia had previous conflicts with Stuart, she knew that they had a problem communicating with one another. Usually, after any type of confrontation between Stuart and a family member, the conflicting parties would just walk away, still angry, with nothing resolved. From these past examples, Cynthia knew that she should quit arguing before either party completely lost control. Since they were children, Cynthia and Stuart had divergent communication styles, and as adults, these styles continued to be obstacles.

Question 5
What are some of the unique challenges that family enterprises face?
Evaluation skills (using a set of criteria to arrive at a reasoned judgment of the value of something)
Answer

Family businesses are unique systems because the distinction between family and economic roles often blur (Davis, 1983). For most people, the roles of "boss, employee, or laborer" (Meyers & Meyers, 1982), are left at work, and the roles of father, sibling, child, or spouse are assumed when they leave their job. In a family business, many roles are confused and sometimes compete with one another (Weigel & Ballard-Reisch, 1997). Negotiation of the multiple roles can be difficult (Ibrahim & Ellis, 1994), and "when behaviors expected of each role differed, individuals experienced stress and confusion" (Weigel & Ballard-Reisch, 1997, p. 15).

In this case, Cynthia had to react to Stuart's attempt to be the "general manager" when, in fact, he was an equal partner and a brother. Since Cynthia had a fractured relationship with Stuart already, it was difficult for her to accept orders from him. Rosenblatt, et al., (1985) found that family members alleviated this role confusion and stress by clearly defining divisions of labor or working out role expectations.

Aside from role confusion, there are also the issues of power and control that are extremely volatile in family businesses (Rosenblatt et al., 1985). In the conventional business world, power is often held within traditional boundaries of authority. When family is added, the issue of power is "negotiated in the interactions of family members;" and each family member has the power to affect and be affected within the business (Cromwell & Olson, 1975).

References

Be an explosives expert: Managing your anger on the job. (1998, December). Men's Health, 10.

Bork, (1986.) as cited in Journal of Family and Economic Issues.

Brody, G. (1981). Sibling relationship quality: Its causes and consequences. Annual Review of Psychology, 49. 1-24.

Canary & Stafford (1992) as cited in Journal of Family and Economic Issues.

Cox Jr., T. (1994). Cultural diversity in organizations: Theory, research, and practice. San Francisco, CA.: Berrett-Koehler.

Cromwell & Olson (1975) as cited in Journal of Family and Economic Issues.

Davis (1983) as cited in Weigel & Ballard-Reisch (1997). Merging family and firm: An integrated systems approach to process and change. Journal of Family and Economic Issues, 18, 7-35.

Dollard (1939) as cited in Meyers (1996). Social psychology, pp.441-442.

Ibrahim & Ellis (1994) as cited in Journal of Family and Economic Issues (1997).

Kelley and Thibaut (1978) as cited in Journal of Family and Economic Issues, p. 20.

Lee, D. (1998). Careers: Madder than ever. Los Angeles Times. Part C2, p.3.

Meyers & Meyers (1982) as cited in Journal of Family and Economic Issues, (1997) p 15.

Myers, D. (1996). Social psychology. New York: McGraw-Hill.

Raudsepp, E. (1994). Coping with anger: Workplace anger. Machine Design, 66, p. 79.

Rosenblatt, et al. (1985) as cited in Journal of Family and Economic Issues, (1997).

Schermerhorn, Jr., J, Hunt, J., Osborn, R. (1995). Basic organizational behavior. New York: John Wiley & Sons, Inc.

Tannen (1990) as cited in Cultural diversity in organizations (1994), p. 122.

Wagner III, JA, & Hollenbeck, JR (1998). Organizational behavior: Securing competitive advantage. Upper Saddle River: Prentice Hall.

Weigel, D., & Ballard-Reisch, D. (1997). Merging family and firm: An integrated systems approach to process and change. Journal of Family and Economic Issues, 18, pp.7-35.

Epilogue

Cynthia had applied to several graduate schools around the country for the fall semester. She had decided before the espresso bar even opened, that once she was accepted, she would leave the state and begin her studies in the fall of 1998.

In August, just six months after the confrontation and the grand opening, Cynthia moved to Claremont, California, and began a program in human resources design.

Rob currently works at the espresso bar full-time and seems to have a bearable relationship with Stuart. Stuart still gets angry from time to time, but seems to stay out of Rob's way for the most part. Stuart and Cynthia still do not speak to one another. Cafe Latte is doing well.

CHANGING QUOTAS

Topics (* = Primary topic with teaching plan)
- *Creative Problem Solving
- *Motivation
- *Goals and Objectives (quotas)
- *Planning (how to meet objectives)
- Decision-making Process
- Rational decision-making
- Synergy
- Expectancy Theory
- Banking Context
- Sales Context

Case overview

Susan Steele, a seasoned sales representative, knew there was a potential sale looming. Her customer, Tom Leney, senior vice president at Fidelity Federal Bank wanted to change the bank's image and considered updated ATMs as a good vehicle to initiate the change. Susan realized a deal of that size could generate $2 million in sales. This would help her exceed her quota and generate a great commission.

Susan had been working hard for a reputation as a sales representative that could produce even in the most challenging markets, Los Angeles being one of them. In Susan's first year as a representative she exceeded her quota by 127 percent in 9 months versus 12. Susan, then, had another great selling year and was able to surpass her quota by 377 percent. Susan had won numerous awards for sales over the last three years and was satisfied with her performance.

After the deal went around the company and received everyone's blessing, Susan was able to present it to the customer. After a couple of days, she phoned Tom and asked what he thought of the deal. He responded quite enthusiastically. Susan was elated, as she felt she on the right track. They discussed some other terms that Fidelity wanted and confirmed that he would take it to the CEO to get some feedback. Things were rolling in the right direction when, all of a sudden, a roadblock popped up in front of Susan.

Ron Tenuta, the vice president, began to question her current quota. He explained that she had already made her numbers for the year and that this sale would afford her to far exceed her numbers. After a heated discussion between her manager, the vice president, and Susan, it was decided that her quota would have to be raised. Susan was taken by surprise, because they usually didn't raise quotas six months into the year. They said she could wait and see if she got the order before they raised it, in which case they would raise it from $1.2 million to $3.0 million or she could let them raise it now to $2 million and, perhaps, not get the deal but have a higher quota for the rest of the year. Susan let them raise her sales quota before the deal went through. In the end, Susan got the deal and never worried about the commission.

Industry

High volume sales and manufacturing of vaults and equipment for the financial industry. In business since 1859, Diebold generates over $1 billion in sales annually.

This teaching note was prepared by Susan Steele, Jonnetta Thomas-Chambers and Teri C. Tompkins, University of Redlands. The case and teaching note were prepared as basis for class discussion rather than to illustrate either effective or ineffective handling of administrative situations. Suggestions for improvement of this note should be sent to Teri.Tompkins@pepperdine.edu. Credit will be given in the next revision.

Teaching objectives
1. To identify and practice some key ingredients of creative problem solving and decision-making.
2. To examine motivation, rewards, goals and objectives and cite its relevance to the case.

Other related cases in Volume 1

Fired! (creative problem solving). Shaking the Bird Cage (decision-making process).

Other related cases in Volume 2

A Selfish Request in Japan (creative problem solving). Angry Branch Manager (decision-making process). Richard Prichard and the Federal Triad Program (expectancy theory). The Safety Memo (decision-making process).

Intended courses and levels

This course is intended for graduate, undergraduate and executive students in human resource management, organizational behavior, and management theory courses. It can be used in other courses such as sales and marketing, or decision-making.

Analysis

All related analysis and references are embedded in the answers to the questions.

Research methodology

This case reflects the recollections of the case writer. The case is a true incident. The case is not disguised.

Teaching plan

Creative problem solving can be a fun topic for students to examine. The table below outlines one method of addressing this topic.

Motivation can also be a useful topic for this case and works well as a decision case. What caused Susan to stay motivated in spite of management's changing the rules at mid-stream? Using the case format style (everyone in class participating with instructor facilitating discussions), ask students:

- What were the concerns of Diebold management? (Some concerns were: fairness of bonuses to all employees, profit to the company, possibly the manager not getting similar rewards).
- What were Susan's concerns? (Getting management to support her out of the box proposal, landing the sale and helping her clients, internal satisfaction, fair bonus system, clarity of the bonus rules).
- If you were Susan, would you continue to work for Diebold? Why or why not? (see answer to question 2 in discussion section of TN).
- How is Susan motivated? (see similar question 4 in discussion section of TN).
- Was Susan a valuable employee for Diebold? What risks does Diebold take by changing her quota? (Possible loss of an excellent salesperson, employees not trusting management).

Topic: Creative Problem Solving & Planning Objectives
60-minute teaching plan

Pre-assignment: None

	Timing	Activity	Organization	Student Outcomes
I	0 - 15 minutes (15)	Read case.	Individually	Familiarity with case facts.

	Timing	Activity	Organization	Student Outcomes
II	15 - 25 minutes (10)	*Why did Susan seek to work with her old boss versus her current one? Why was her decision to do so successful?*	Small group or case format	To brainstorm successfully it is helpful to feel free of criticism. Susan's old boss was willing to do that, whereas her new one was not.
III	25 - 35 minutes (10)	*How did Susan capitalize from creative problem solving? What were her planning objectives?*	Small group or case format	She used brainstorming technique appropriately and was also able to build on the principles of synergy. She was able to think out of the box, which helped her get the sale.
IV	35-55 minutes (20)	Brainstorming exercise. Read the brainstorming exercise (written below this table) to students.	In small groups of 4 to 6.	Students arrive at many solutions. Among the more creative ideas students might come up with: Apply a number to each bottle, hold a raffle and have charities sell the bottles for $2 each (they get 25 percent of the sales). $1/2 million to the winner; $1/2 million to charities; $1 million to pay for bottles.
V	55-60 minutes (5)	Read epilogue to students	Whole class	Susan was successful due to her internal locus of control and her abilities. She did not let the change of quotas stop her.

Brainstorming exercise: You are the marketing director of ACME company. One of your products is a small bottle filled with water, sealed with a sponge applicator and used to seal envelopes. You boss called you this morning to tell you that there was a quality control problem and one million bottles were made without the water. The cost of removing the sponge applicator and refilling the bottles exceeds the price you can sell the applicator for (normally $1 wholesale). The boss tells you that the company was depending on the $1 million dollar revenue and without it, the company will face severe problems, you might even loss your job. The boss asks you to get together with a few other executives and brainstorm a way out of this. (Your assignment is to brainstorm what you can do with the empty sponge applicators (about 2 inches high by 3/4 inch wide by 3/8 inch deep) to recoup the $1 million dollars.

25-minute teaching plan for creative problem solving
Preassignment: Read case before coming to class (15 minutes).
Activities II, III, V in 60-minute plan above.

Discussion questions and answers
Question 1
Why did Susan seek to work with her old boss versus her current one? Why was her decision to do so successful?
Diagnostic questions (probes motives or causes) and Evaluation skills (using a set of criteria to arrive at a reasoned judgment of the value of something):

Answer
One of the prerequisites of brainstorming is the absence of criticism during the process. When Susan originally approached her current boss regarding her sales prospect, she believed he lacked enthusiasm. Susan did not perceive him as a creative thinker. Therefore, she chose to work with her old

boss because he appeared to have more of the attributes of a creative thinker. Susan was very comfortable with her old boss, because she felt that he never criticized any of her ideas and he asked constructive questions to draw out information that could help her build a better deal. In brainstorming, criticism during the process could slow or stifle the entire creative process completely.

Susan's decision to work with Carroll was a successful one because they worked well together to compose a presentation that was accepted by Fidelity. Together, their ability to brainstorm and create synergy between them allowed them to accomplish this. Susan knew how to use her resources, the primary one being Carroll.

Question 2

If you were Susan, would you continue to work for Diebold? Why or why not?
Priority questions (seeks to identify the most important issue)

Answer

If answered no: The key focus of this answer would evolve around ethics, trust, and motivation. Diebold's ethics, for some would be questionable. Is it ethical to change the rules of a sale in mid-stream? First, the question of ethics would circumvent discrimination, specifically not outlining the same rules for everyone. If all other sales representatives were prescribed quotas every 12 months, then it is discriminatory to single out one over the others. An employee that didn't plan to remain an employee at Diebold could seek legal retribution. Second, for some students, trust would be a factor. One might feel apprehensive that every time they're in the midst of negotiating a large sale that the company may seek ways to minimize the promised profit margin. In retrospect, an employee might under-achieve to avoid such perceived repercussions. Which bring us to the last point, motivation. An employee may lose their driving force to achieve if they perceive the rules are ever changing, lacking their best interest.

If answered yes: The key focus to this answer would be perseverance and self-motivation. This person would not favor Diebold's decision, but could live with it. This person has a larger concept in mind, such as working to be promoted or working to maintain status. Money is not the epicenter of their success, just one of the results. This person is self-motivated to succeed, and sometimes, obstacles are perceived as opportunities to transcend. In other words, very few circumstances or people can deter this person from their focus.

Question 3

How did Susan capitalize from creative problem solving?
Application skills (using information in a new context to solve a problem, answer a question, or perform a task)

Answer

Susan first had to define the problems that she would attempt to resolve, which were: Fidelity wanted to upgrade their relatively new ATM machines with even newer high technology machines, though they did not have enough cash to support a $2 million outlay.

Next, Susan had to find a solution to these problems. To begin, she teamed up with her former boss, Carroll Lawerence, to work to find a solution. Together they brainstormed, role played, and thought-out all options until they reached synergy. Finally, they both agreed on a plan that would be considered a good business deal.

"Brainstorming is an idea generation process that specifically encourages any and all alternatives, while withholding any criticism of those alternatives (Robbins, 1998, p.271)." Susan and Carroll used the brainstorming technique between the two of them to contribute ideas quickly. They began with a note pad and a quiet office and allowed no interruptions. First, Carroll blurted out an idea, then Susan added to it. There was no criticism or critiquing of their ideas until they were done brainstorming. After a few hours they agreed on an approach they were confident would work.

Synergy is two or more people working together in a cooperative, coordinated way so that they can accomplish more than the sum of their independent efforts. Susan felt that she could not have come up with the idea for the sale on her own. She wanted to avoid hitting roadblocks, for they can sometimes impede one from reaching a creative solution. Susan felt that Carroll's seasoned input would keep her on the right track. Their synergistic approach gave her more than what she could have produced independently.

The strength of using a creative process is the freedom it gives one to explore a myriad of possibilities that may never have been achieved without the opportunity to think, unimpaired by rules and conservative thought.

Question 4

Define Expectancy Theory. Could this define Susan's motivation to succeed before Diebold changed her quota? Why or why not?

Knowledge skills (remember previously learned material such as definitions, principles, formulas) and Analysis skills (breaking a concept into its parts and explaining their interrelationships, distinguishing relevant from extraneous material)

Answer

Expectancy theory states that individuals are predicted to be high performers when they see (1) an effort-performance relationship in which a high probability exists that their efforts will lead to high performance, (2) a performance-reward relationship in which a high probability exists that high performance will lead to favorable outcomes and (3) a rewards-potential relationship which states that these outcomes will be, on balance, attractive to them (Robbins, 1998, p.187-189).

This could define Susan's motivation before Diebold changed her sales quota. Examples can be illuminated from the case. First, people will perform more highly when they see a high probability that their efforts will lead to a high performance. Susan, a high-achiever, had been an employee for two years and worked to exceed the goals that were set for her. Second, high performers will move forward if they know that it will lead to a favorable outcome. Favorable outcomes for Susan were receiving a sizable commission, successfully meeting the needs of her customer, and making an attention-grabbing sale in her company. These, typically, can be very strong motivating factors to a salesperson's success. Finally, Susan invested her time, energy, and hard work so that the end result, or balance, would be attractive to her. The balance of a sale would have resulted in a large commission. She also had a desire to eventually become a manager in the company.

Question 5

If you were Susan's manager at Diebold, would you have opted to increase her quota in the middle of a sales negotiation? Why or why not?

Evaluation skills (using a set of criteria to arrive at a reasoned judgment of the value of something)

Answer

Diebold should not have changed Susan's quota in the midst of her sale. They were gambling with the potential of losing a $2 million deal, as well as a potentially unhappy employee, a high-achiever that could have taken her talent elsewhere. It would have been best to maintain a "win–win" situation for all parties involved, based on the current rules outlined in her sales quota. Diebold should have maintained the rules that had already been established six months prior. Had they broke even or lost money on the deal, they could have chalked it up as a learning experience and prepared not to repeat the same mistake in the future.

References

Robbins, Stephen P. (1998). Organizational behavior, 8th ed., Upper Saddle River, NJ: Prentice-Hall.

Epilogue

Susan surpassed the new quota they gave her mid year. She sold $3.7 million in 1998 and was the second highest selling sales rep in the nation out of 700 salespeople. It is interesting to note that Susan's old vice president, Ron Tenuta, had since ended his employment at Diebold. There is no connection between this and Susan's deal; however, it could be evidence that his management style might not have been a good fit for Diebold.

Susan claimed that this incident was a positive experience. Susan realized that the lesson learned from this process was that it is very important to look at the big picture, which includes all the various parties involved in the picture. She states that she looked at this incident like one looks at an obstacle course, and although there were deterrents in her way, the focus remained on the finish line.

In 1999, Susan left Diebold and now works in a new venture that just went public. She sells banking software to the same type of clients she had at Diebold.

Teaching Note
COMPUTER SERVICES TEAM AT AVIONICS

Topics (* = Primary topic with teaching plan)
> *Leaderless Group or Self-management
> *Leadership, absence of
> *Group Development, unsuccessful
> Group Dynamics
> TQM
> Management of Conflict
> Leadership of Groups
> Job Fit
> Management Skills
> Interpersonal Conflict, management of
> Organizational Change
> Restructuring
> Large Corporation (non-banking) Context

Case overview

      This case describes problems that occurred when a team was told by their manager to become a leaderless group. The case unfolds through the eyes of three main characters: 1) John Johnson (the same manager from the <u>Cost and Scheduling Team at Avionics</u> case); 2) William, the volunteer leader of the group whose management skill does not match his enthusiasm and good will; and 3) Glen, the former supervisor of the team, who John had tried to fire.

      John Johnson created the leaderless group to address three issues at once: 1) A contract directive calling for integration of the computer information systems into a service center concept; 2) Management directive to cut costs; and 3) Removing (through termination) the service manager, Glen, for poor performance. Glen immediately appeals his termination and is reinstated back on the team pending the investigation.

      To begin the process, John takes the team on a two-day retreat telling them, "No one is a leader – you are all responsible." He also taught them some basic TQM tools, such as breakthrough analysis.

      Shortly after the off-site training, team members gathered for their first meeting. It was apparent that the members didn't know what to do and some felt that their "real work was waiting." After waiting for someone to begin the meeting, William tentatively began and was soon elected leader. Realizing that he didn't have any idea how to lead, he went to the bookstore and found several book on TQM and <u>How to Make Prize Winning Teams</u>, which he thought was a real find.

      After making careful notes, William was prepared for the following week's meeting. After telling members to buy the book and telling them what they needed to do, several members state that they don't want anyone telling them what to do. The team agrees that everything should be decided by vote. Over time, members don't vote, don't participate and William feels at a loss. He goes to HR asking for training, but they tell him there is no budget for training.

      After six months of deterioration, the team votes William out and elects Glen, their former supervisor, as the team leader (he won his grievance). William is hurt.

      In the meantime, John is transferred to another assignment and a new manager is appointed. Glen, who has more leadership skills than William, begins to build trust by working on continuous process improvement. Four months later, however, the new manager pulls the plug telling them to go

48

This teaching note was prepared by Teri C. Tompkins, University of Redlands. The case and teaching note were prepared as basis for class discussion rather than to illustrate either effective or ineffective handling of administrative situations. Suggestions for improvement should be sent to Teri.Tompkins@pepperdine.edu. Credit will be given in the next revision.

back to the structure they had a year ago. Glen said, "I was just beginning to feel like we were going to make it. Management gives a lot of lip service, but there is no management commitment."

When John looked back at what happened. "They are still having problems serving their customers. I ran a bizarre experiment by cutting them loose. I took away all their support systems, and told them they were all equal people. It was a big mistake."

Industry

This case takes place in a major defense industry firm. The company is primarily a sub-contractor for companies such as TRW, Hughes Aircraft, and Boeing. The division was roughly 1,500 employees of a much larger national organization.

Teaching objectives

1. To analyze the factors that hindered group's development.
2. To evaluate management's leadership style.
3. To understand the dynamics of group cohesion and interpersonal relations.

Other related cases in Volume 1

A Team Divided or a Team United? (group dynamics). Handling Problems at Japan Auto (group development). Julie's Call: Empowerment at Taco Bell (TQM). Temporary Employees: Car Show Turned Ugly (group dynamics).

Other related cases in Volume 2

Cost and Schedule Team at AVIONICS (group development). Groupware Fiasco (absence of leadership, group dynamics, interpersonal conflict). Leadership of TQM in Panama (TQM).

Intended courses and levels

This case works well during the group level of organizational behavior courses, and during the leading function of management courses. It is especially well suited for executive and graduate students.

Analysis

All analysis is imbedded in the discussion questions and answers section.

Research methodology

Data for this case were gathered during research studying the question of how collective learning occurs. John, William, Glen, and two other members of the team were interviewed. The company and people are disguised.

Teaching plan

This case can be used as a stand alone or in comparison to The Cost and Schedule Team at AVIONICS. The teaching plan in the table below is as a stand-alone case.

The comparison case works well because the two teams had the same manager and a similar government mandate to integrate teams. Yet one team was highly successful and the other was not. Why? If used as a comparison case of group development, it might work well for the students to do the Cost and Schedule Team at AVIONICS **first**, and then to assign this case. Alternatively, you could have the students read the cases and answer some of the preliminary questions outside of class, and then do the comparison during your class session.

The following question can get things started.
After you've read the Cost and Schedule Team at AVIONICS case and the Computer Services Team at AVIONICS, compare these two teams on the following dimensions: 1) stress 2) technology

resources 3) integration 4) communication 5) conflict 6) team member interpersonal skills 7) training 8) management. What conclusions do you draw based on these comparisons?
Relational question (asks for comparisons of themes, ideas, or issues)

Answer

	Computer Team	Cost and Schedule Team
Stress	High stress to complete individual work. (e.g., 10 people who need to be hardwired breathing down my neck)	High stress to complete integrated report (e.g., weekly report due.)
Tech Resources	No apparent problems.	Not enough hardware; don't know how to use software program.
Integration	Mandated by government contract.	Mandated by government contract.
Communication	Vote on everything.	Discuss in team meetings and hallways.
Conflict	Argue about what goals should be.	Argue about performance and fairness.
Team Members' Interpersonal and Leadership Skills	Not much apparent. No one was allowed to take on the leadership role.	Several members took the lead. Members were accepted as informal leaders.
Training	Given early. No leadership training given.	None given, members taught themselves after identifying they needed training.
Management	Absent.	Supportive.

Conclusions:
- To be a successful team, the team members' stress levels can be high, but they need to be focused on group outcomes, not individual outcomes.
- Apparently, the absence of tech resources and training did not stop the successful team from working around the limitation.
- Direct communication about the task seems to be helpful.
- Supportive management appears to be helpful.
- Having people on the team with interpersonal and leadership skills helps. Acceptance by other members also makes a difference.

Topic: What makes an integrated team? Examining leadership and group development
60-minute teaching plan

Pre-assignment: none

	Timing	Activity	Organization	Student Outcomes
I	0-10 minutes (10)	Read the case.	Individually	Familiarity with case facts.
II	10 - 20 minutes (10)	*Q1. Evaluate Williams' leadership of the team. What went wrong?*	Discuss in small groups. Report conclusions back to full classroom. Instructor may want to list these on the board.	William didn't do well as the leader. Students may mention some of these reasons: • William had no experience or training as a leader. And no one (John) to develop him. • He didn't have any basis of power or authority. • Team members didn't need him to help them do their jobs. • The former leader of the team was still a member and in the middle of grievance proceedings.

	Timing	Activity	Organization	Student Outcomes
				• Team didn't really accept him. • Team may have believed that leaderless group meant that they shouldn't allow any emergent leadership.
III	20 – 25 minutes (5)	Mini lecture or reminder of the five stages of group development. *What stage is the Computer Team based on the Tuchman model of group development?*	Full classroom	Never got past the forming stage.
IV	25 -30 minutes (5)	*Q2. Under what conditions might the leaderless group idea have been more successful?* Note: Professor can refer to "self-managed" teams or groups for further insight about leaderless groups.	Small groups	• John needed to teach them to lead themselves. • Members needed to learn how to praise each other for good results. • Members needed to learn how to judge how well they were doing. • Members needed to expect high performance from themselves and the team. • Members needed to learn how to set their own performance standards. • Members needed to learn to be critical of their own poor performance. • Hold the two-day off site training that focused on TQM techniques at a later date once the team was clear about its goals.
V	30 –35 minutes (5)	*Q3. Why did the team do so poorly in responding to the mandate to become an integrated team?*	Small groups	• You cannot mandate that the team become an integrated team and expect it will happen. • There must be a need for interdependence among the members for the team to work.
VI	35 – 40 minutes (5)	*Q4. If you were Barbara, the new manager, how would you handle the situation with the team (right after she got the new assignment)?*	Small groups	Answers will vary. See answers to Question 4 for some ideas.
VII	40 – 50 minutes (10)	Report back on small group discussion.	Entire classroom. Each group select a spokesperson.	Instructor points out agreement and disagreement.
VIII	50 – 60 minutes (10)	*Q5. What did you learn from this case that might apply to your work life?*	Entire classroom	Answers will vary. The idea is to get students thinking about generalizations beyond the case.

<u>25-minute teaching plan on Integrated Teams</u>

Pre-assignment: Read case before class (10 minutes)

Activities. Do activities II, V, and VI in the 60-minute plan.

Discussion questions and answers

Question 1

Evaluate Williams' leadership of the team. What went wrong?

<u>Diagnostic question</u> (probes motives or causes)

Answer

William didn't do well as the leader.

Students may mention some of these reasons:

- William had no experience or training as a leader. And no one (John) to develop him.
- He didn't have any basis of power or authority.
- Team members didn't need him to help them do their jobs.
- The former leader of the team was still a member and in the middle of grievance proceedings.
- Team didn't really accept him.
- Team may have believed that leaderless group meant that they shouldn't allow any emergent leadership.

Leadership is the ability to influence a group toward the achievement of goals (Robbins, 1998: I-23). Based on this definition, William wasn't very effective. Is it different being a leader on a "leaderless team?" Perhaps, but likely informal leadership must still emerge, the members must accept the informal leader's suggestions and support, and goals must still be accomplished. By all accounts, the computer services team did not make any progress.

What went wrong? It is apparent that William didn't have any experience or training as a leader. He tried to educate himself by reading books on prize-winning teams, but he lacked confidence to apply the ideas. Instead, he tried to get members to read the book themselves so that they would share the same knowledge. William was not developed as a leader because John, the manager, cut the team loose, leaving them all to flounder. William had the interest to become a leader, but not the developmental support that he needed.

William did not have the benefit of a formal basis of power. He was not appointed supervisor and granted authority to act, review performance appraisals, or give rewards and punishments. Consequently, members didn't have a reason to follow him. He apparently didn't possess referent or expert power as well. By all accounts, he lacked power and authority.

Team members had no reason to depend on William to get their job done. He didn't provide any support to make their job easier. One important support a leader can provide a team is the opening of doors that can't otherwise be open. Since John was practicing a "hands off" approach, the team members were left to themselves to secure resources and support. William did not have any liaison role or network to help the team accomplish its goals.

It might have been difficult on William, and perhaps the whole team, to have Glen, their former supervisor, serving as a member of the team. We do not have enough information in the case to know what the members were thinking, but we can imagine that at least there would be some awkwardness about him being fired.

It is also apparent that the team didn't accept William as their leader. Without acceptance, a leader cannot lead. We do not know the reasons the team didn't accept him. Perhaps because they thought that a leaderless group meant that shouldn't allow any leader to emerge. Regardless of the reason, William was unable to influence the team to follow him and meet their objective of an integrative computer services team.

Question 2

Under what conditions might the leaderless group idea have been more successful?

<u>Hypothetical question</u> (poses a change in the facts or issues)

52

Answer

- John needed to teach them to lead themselves.
- Members needed to learn how to praise each other for good results.
- Members needed to learn how to judge how well they were doing.
- Members needed to expect high performance from themselves and the team.
- Members needed to learn how to set their own performance standards.
- Members needed to learn to be critical of their own poor performance.
- Hold the two-day off site training that focused on TQM techniques at a later date once the team was clear about its goals.

It is hard to know what the team needed to be more successful. Students' answers will likely widely vary.

While self-managed work teams or leaderless groups have emerged in recent years, they still have a long way to go. Self-management leadership is the process of leading others to lead themselves (Kreitner and Kinicki, 1995, p. 357). The definition alone helps us see part of the problem. John did not lead the team to lead themselves. Instead he cut them loose. Self-managed teams will likely fail if team members are not expressly taught to engage in self-management behaviors. It was unreasonable to assume that the members who were accustomed to being managed and led would suddenly manage and lead themselves. Transition training is required. While John did offer a two-day off-site training session, it was not enough and the team was unable to master the skills necessary to lead themselves.

What could John have done? According to researchers Manz and Sims, there are six behaviors he could have exhibited:

1. Encouraged self-reinforcement (getting members to praise each other for good work and results).
2. Encouraged self-observation/evaluation (teaching members to judge how well they are doing).
3. Encouraged self-expectation (members expect high performance from themselves and the team).
4. Encouraged self-goal-setting (encouraging the team sets its own performance standards).
5. Encouraged rehearsal (getting members to think about and practice new tasks).
6. Encouraged self-criticism (encouraging members to be critical of their own poor performance).

Finally, the team might have been more successful if the timing of the TQM training had been when the team needed the tools. At the early stages of its development, it was more important that the team become clear about its tasks.

Question 3

Why did the team do so poorly in responding to the mandate to become an integrated team?
Analysis skills (breaking a concept into its parts and explaining their interrelationships, distinguishing relevant from extraneous material)

Answer

- You cannot mandate that the team become an integrated team and expect it will happen.
- There must be a need for interdependence among the members for the team to work.
- Certain criteria are helpful (Tompkins, 1997):
  Pre-conditions
  1. Compelling reason to work together – usually interdependence
  2. Support from upper management
  3. Appropriate team member skills
  Conditions necessary to get the team to agree on their goals and process
  1. Emergence of leadership, which the team accepts
  Conditions to move the team to better performance

1. Methods established to resolve interpersonal conflicts
2. Emergence and acceptance of members who seek higher performance
3. Tools and techniques, such as the ones John taught at the off-site training session. The training came too early and the team was not yet ready for it.

One of the important lessons that can be drawn from this case is that you cannot mandate integration unless there is a need for interdependence. The team members on the computer services team had separate jobs. Their clients were other individuals who needed computer support. They felt extreme pressure to meet the requests of their clients in a timely manner. They did not feel any extreme pressure to meet the needs of the other team members. Meeting was a waste of their time because they had so many other pressing jobs to do.

Results from Tompkins study on this team and others at AVIONICS helps to see some other reasons the team did so poorly. First, it is helpful if there are certain pre-conditions for a team.

- Compelling reason to work together – usually interdependence
- Support from upper management. It was missing in this case.
- Appropriate team member skills. The members on this team had technical skills, but not interpersonal skills.

Second, there are conditions that help a team agree on its goals and processes.

- Emergence of leadership, which the team accepts. In this case, the team leader was not accepted and, thus, not effective.

Finally, there must be conditions to move the team to better performance

- Methods established to resolve interpersonal conflicts (not vote taking, but actual dialogue that builds trust and commitment among the members).
- Emergence and acceptance of members who seek higher performance. Apparently there was no member on the team that urged the team to improve its customer service or try to solve common problems among them.
- Tools and techniques, such as the ones John taught at the off-site training session. The TQM training can be very useful, but the training came too early in the group's development so the team was not yet ready for it.

Question 4

If you were Barbara, the new manager, how would you handle the situation with the team (right after she got the new assignment)?
<u>Synthesis skills</u> (putting parts together to form a new whole; solving a problem requiring creativity or originality)

Answer

Student answers will vary.

- Some may argue that that integration was impossible because they didn't have enough interdependence. To keep them together as a team, despite the government mandate, was a waste of time and, therefore, she should put it back the way it was.
- Barbara might have approached things a little more slowly. She might have interviewed members individually or perhaps as a team to find out what the team members needed. She might have found that they were happier with Glen's guidance on continuous process improvement and that they thought they were making progress. She could have provided better managerial support than John did and perhaps results would have been better. If the team didn't improve the computer services function within an agreed amount of time, they could mutually agree to change the structure back or to something new. This might have helped the members get around the feeling expressed at the end of the case that support for teams was just "lip service."
- Some students might argue that the team needed to find out why the team wasn't integrating. Perhaps it didn't have a clear enough vision of why it should integrate. Members might have

needed to see some examples of integrated service teams, perhaps through visiting similar facilities in their region. Perhaps there were not enough support structures in place to encourage integration, such as rewards for team work, integrated communication systems, or measurement and feedback systems focusing on team performance.

References

Manz, CC.and Sims, Jr., H. P. (1987). Leading workers to lead themselves: The external leadership of self-managed work teams. Adminstrative Science Quarterly, 32 (1): 106-129.

Robbins, S. P. (1998). Organizational Behavior: Concepts, Controversies, Applications, 8th ed. Upper Saddle River, NJ: Prentice Hall.

Tompkins, T. C. (1997). A developmental approach to organizational learning teams: A model and illustrative research. In M. M. Beyerlein, and D. A. Johnson (Eds.). Advances in Interdisciplinary Studies of Work Teams (Vol. 4, pp. 281-302). Greenwich, CT: JAI Press.

Tuchman, B.W. & Jensen, M.C. (1977). Stages of small group development revisited. Group and Organizational Studies, 2: 419-427.

Epilogue

There is no epilogue for this case.

Teaching Note
COST AND SCHEDULE TEAM AT AVIONICS

Topics (* = Primary topic with teaching plan)
 *Group Development, successful
 *Leadership, formal/informal/poor
 *Chain of Command, violating
 *Team Learning and Organizational Learning
 *Cohesiveness
 Leadership of Groups
 Empowerment
 Interpersonal Relations
 Conflict, management of
 Teamwork
 Workspace Location
 Group Dynamics
 Organizational Change
 Large Corporation (non-banking) Context

Case overview

  This case traces the development of the cost and scheduling team at AVIONICS, a major defense industry contractor. As part of the defense contract that the team had been working on, the government mandated that the cost and scheduling functions, which were traditionally two separate units, be completely integrated.

  When the case opens the team has already been together for two and a half months. A number of problems exist for them: 1) lack of communication; 2) lack of resources—both people and computer hardware systems; 3) the team's supervisor, Dan, is a "working manager," busy with his own projects. He appears to lack managerial skills; 4) members were operating out of crisis management and there was lots of conflict among members.

  Two of the team members decide that they have to do something about the fighting and poor performance, so they go to the supervisor's boss, John Johnson (same manager as the <u>Computer Services Team at Avionics</u> case). John suggests a team meeting without the team's supervisor. After listening to their gripes (see 1-4 above), the team asks management to help them out in several areas. John helps in two of the areas and tells why he can't respond in two areas:

  Helps: 1) co-locates the two functions on the 2nd floor. 2) Initiates action to bring four of the five new members needed to handle the workload.

  Can't help: 1) Regarding Dan, the supervisor. John prefers a "wait and see" approach. 2) Due to financial constraints of the company's budget, many of the team members could not receive MAC computers that were needed to run the integration software, IJMPP.

  After the second team meeting a week later, the team discussed the problems they were having with their supervisor, Dan. Their biggest gripe was that he was overly critical and lacked managerial skill. The team decides to take on more of the leadership functions to relieve Dan of the stress. They also discussed the feeling each had of "lack of support" from other members. They agree to try and put their differences aside.

  During the third week, a member of the team lost the data for the weekly report to the military client when she was transferring it from DOS to the Mac program (remember this was in 1993). When

Teri C. Tompkins, University of Redlands prepared this teaching note. The case and teaching note were prepared as basis for class discussion rather than to illustrate either effective or ineffective handling of administrative situations. Suggestions for improvement of this note should be sent to Teri.Tompkins@pepperdine.edu. Credit will be given in the next revision.

she and several members of the team couldn't rescue it, most of the team stayed until 4 a.m. to re-input the data. Although they were tired, they felt good that they had worked together to meet their goals.

Over the next 5 months the team made significant headway.

- Two members learned a difficult software program and taught it to the other members.
- They learned to recognize the strengths and weaknesses each member of the team brought to the table.
- They found themselves discussing issues more thoroughly and sharing their mistakes more openly.
- They got better at making and improving forecasts.

The case closes at the nine-month mark with the team members ruminating after a very positive government audit. "Pressure is okay if success and praise go with it," commented one member.

Industry

This case takes place in a major defense industry firm. The company is primarily a sub-contractor for companies such as TRW, Hughes Aircraft, and Boeing. The division was roughly 1500 employees of a much larger national organization.

Teaching objectives

1. To analyze the factors that help the group develop.
2. To evaluate management's leadership style.
3. To understand the dynamics of group cohesion and interpersonal relations.
4. To analyze the factors that caused stress on the team
5. To analyze the factors that helped the team achieve success.
6. To learn one model of organizational learning and apply it to the case.
7. To recognize development of empowerment in the case.

Other related cases in Volume 1

A New Magazine in Nigeria (cohesiveness). A Team Divided or a Team United? (cohesiveness, empowerment, group dynamics, leadership of groups). Handling Problems at Japan Auto (group development). Julie's Call: Empowerment at Taco Bell (empowerment). No, sir, Sergeant! (empowerment). Temporary Employees: Car Show Turned Ugly (cohesiveness, group dynamics).

Other related cases in Volume 2

Groupware Fiasco (group dynamics). The Safety Memo (empowerment).

Intended courses and levels

This case works well during the group level of organizational behavior courses, and during the leading function of management courses. It is especially well suited for executive and graduate students.

Analysis

All analysis is imbedded in the discussion questions and answers section.

Research methodology

Data for this case were gathered during research studying the question of how collective learning occurs. All members were interviewed individually. The team was also interviewed as a group without Dan or John for the purpose of constructing an event history. The company and people are disguised.

Teaching plan

The teaching plan below addresses how groups develop, the outcome of good group development, and leadership. Executive students might enjoy Question #5, which is not addressed in this teaching plan.

1. First do the teaching plan and then ask:
2. Q5: If you manage a team, what lessons do you draw that would make you a better manager of teams? If you are a member of a team, what lessons do you conclude from this case that would make you a better member of a team?

Topic: Group development, leadership, and cohesion
60-minute teaching plan

Pre-assignment: Read about group development.

	Timing	Activity	Organization	Student Outcomes
I	0-15 minutes (15)	Read the case. Note group development over time.	Individually	Familiarity with case facts and timing.
II	15 - 20 minutes (5)	*Q 1. What were the factors that caused the team to be stressed during the first 3 months of the teams forming?*	In small groups	Students should note: • Limited resources • Team supervisor's lack of skill • Different work styles of the individuals • Different perspectives of the individuals
III	20-25 minutes (5)	*Q 2. Why was the team able to succeed by the end of the case?*	In small groups	Students might note: • Developed cohesiveness as they established common goals and values (norms). • Improved learning when 2 members took initiative to learn difficult software program.
IV	25 - 35 minutes (10)	*Q 3. Was it a good idea for John to meet with the group without Dan? Why or why not?*	In small groups	Student opinion will vary. • By going over his head, he sent a signal of non-support (due to violating formal chain of command) of the supervisor. • However, the team members outnumbered the supervisor and it appeared that their concerns were legitimate. • Executive and employed students will note that this is not a rare occurrence and that it is difficult to tell who lacks skill when conflict and poor performance happens at the same time.
V	35-55 minutes (20)	*Q 4. Chart the team's development over the course of the 9 months. Does Tuchman's model of forming, storming, norming, performing, and adjourning apply here? If so, what were the key transition points?*	Full-class discussion or remain in groups.	• See the timeline of the team's development in answer to Question 4. Tuchman: forming/storming up to 3 months. Storming/norming up to 5 months or so. Norming/performing up to 8 months. Performing at 9 months.

58

	Timing	Activity	Organization	Student Outcomes
VI	55 - 60 minutes (5)	Summary. What lessons did you learn?	Full-class discussion, popcorn style.	Student reactions will vary. Good question to broaden learning beyond the case to students' own lives.

25-minute teaching plan on group development
Pre-assignment: Read case before class (15 minutes)
Activities. Do activities V and VI in the 60-minute plan.

Discussion questions and answers

Question 1
What were the factors that caused the team to be stressed during the first three months of the teams forming?
Analysis skills (breaking a concept into its parts and explaining their interrelationships, distinguishing relevant from extraneous material)

Answer
Students should note:
- Limited resources
- Team supervisor's lack of skill
- Different work styles of the individuals
- Different perspectives of the individuals

The cost and schedule team members became stressed when too few resources were at their disposal to accomplish the task at hand. The team needed to integrate a weekly report on the cost and scheduling functions. Of the twelve members that were supposed to be on the team based on the project projections, only 7 were on the team. In addition, team members had mixed computer platforms. Some had DOS programs and some had MAC. To integrate their reports they needed to transfer data from one machine to another, which was stressful.

The team's supervisor, Dan, appeared to lack necessary skills to adequately support it. Likely, Dan was also working with too few resources, which would increase his stress level. Dan's management style was to yell and accuse members of poor performance, which increased team members' stress.

The members themselves had different work styles and perspectives. Yet it was difficult in the early stages for team members to accept these differences. In addition, members were located in various parts of the building, making it difficult to communicate with each other. The lack of easy access and interaction, combined with the multiple perspectives, and high levels of pressure to complete their weekly task, made stress an inevitable consequence.

Question 2
Why was the team able to succeed by the end of the case?
Analysis skills (breaking a concept into its parts and explaining their interrelationships, distinguishing relevant from extraneous material)

Answer
Students might note:
- Developed cohesiveness as they established common goals and values (norms).
- Improved learning when two members took initiative to learn difficult software program.

The key to the team's success was the members' willingness to communicate and express their differences openly. At the same time, they began to focus on their performance goals, letting that take precedent over their individual differences. Members' willingness to express their concerns and search for similar values (such as fair work loads), also contributed to their success. Cohesiveness increases when individuals increase their opportunity to interact (co-location on the 2nd floor and weekly meetings), have a common goal (weekly report), share common values (loyalty, fairness, and acceptance of each other's differences), and have a common enemy (Dan, the supervisor).

Also, as the team improved its ability to deal with their differences (handle conflict), and accept each other's strengths and weaknesses, their sense of commitment to the team improved and they were better able to discuss their performance objectives. Thus, the team became more committed to common goals and values.

A second key event was when two members of the team took the initiative to learn the difficult software program. The software program was critical in reducing the amount of time the team was spending each week to get their job done. Reducing the overtime helped reduce stress levels, which helped improve the feeling of success, which created a positive spiral of successful events.

Question 3

Was it a good idea for John to meet with the group without Dan? Why or why not?
Evaluation skills (using a set of criteria to arrive at a reasoned judgment of the value of something)

Answer

Student opinion will vary. Students might note:

- By going over his head, he sent a signal of non-support (due to violating formal chain of command) of the supervisor.
- However, the team members outnumbered the supervisor and it appeared that their concerns were legitimate.
- Executive and employed students will note that this is not a rare occurrence and that it is difficult to tell who lacks skill when conflict and poor performance happens at the same time.

Students' opinion will vary on whether it was a good idea to meet with the group without Dan, the supervisor. By going over Dan's head, John sent a signal of non-support to him. He violated the formal chain of command. This can undermine Dan's authority and make it difficult for him to do his job. Students might argue that Dan needed coaching and mentoring to be a better manager. They might say that it was short sighted of John to go around Dan because Dan could never become a better supervisor.

On the other hand, other students will argue that the results speak for themselves. Why sacrifice the entire team with only the possibility of Dan improving his skills? How would that help the team meet its weekly goals in the present? Some will say that Dan may have been a major problem and that poor supervision can hinder a good team. When John allowed the team to blow off steam about Dan's shortcomings, the team was able to proceed on its own by finding a way to work around them (take on more leadership of the team so he could work on his other duties).

Executive students will comment that it is not uncommon for the formal chain of command to be violated. They might say that when a team is in trouble and not meeting its goals that it is difficult to recognize who is at fault, the manager or the team. As a manager, John had to make an educated guess about what to do to improve the situation – which he might have defined as meeting the performance objectives mandated by the contract. At the same time, John appeared to have good interpersonal skills. It appeared that at the meetings, he provided a venue and a listening ear to already motivated team members. His signal of support allowed the members to take off on their own.

Question 4

Chart the team's development over the course of the 9 months. Does Tuchman's model of forming, storming, norming, performing, and adjourning apply here? If so, what were the key transition points?

Application skills (using information in a new context to solve a problem, answer a question, or perform a task)

Answer

- 0 to 2 ½ months = chaos, difficult task, dissatisfaction, poor performance, too few resources.

Transition I to II = two members initiated discussion with John, the manager.

- 2 ½ to 3 months = Beginning of discussions, some support from management, some decisions to put aside differences.

Transition II to III = data crash, everyone pitched in.

- 3 months to 5 months or so = conflict communicated openly, acceptance of members' strengths and weaknesses, shared value of "fair work load" and "loyalty to team."

Transition III to IV = two members learn difficult software program and share it with others.

- 5 months or so to 8 months? = team begins to rely on members' skills and avoid members' weaknesses, develop ability to predict patterns, determined to meet weekly Friday deadline.

Transition IV to V = success, praise from outside of the team.

- 9 months = team pride, satisfaction, high performance.

The five bullet points above, describe the teams development over the course of the 9 months and the key transition points. Tuchman's model is somewhat supported, as long as it is not seen as a linear progression. It is obvious that the team cycled back to various stages along the way before better achieving the next stage. From 0 to 2 1/2 months the team appeared to be forming and storming. From 2 ½ to 5 months, they appeared to be storming and norming. Somewhere around the 5th month or so, the team appeared to be norming and performing. By 9 months the team was performing well. Group development cannot be neatly regulated and processed. Tompkins research (1995; 1997; 2000) on organizational learning and team development shows that teams both progress in progressive stages of learning and development AND they cycle backwards. The cycling backwards helps the team pick up missing skills and values, or reorient new members. Cycling backwards can have a positive spiral, in which members continue to improve and learn. Or it can be a negative spiral, in which case the team becomes less capable, and unable to get the momentum gathered to achieve successive stages.

Questions 5

If you manage a team, given the answers to the first four questions, what lessons do you draw that would make you a better manager of teams? If you are a member of a team, what lessons do you conclude from this case that would make you a better member of a team?

Synthesis skills (putting parts together to form a new whole; solving a problem requiring creativity or originality)

Answer

Students' answers will vary. The point of this question is to encourage students to generalize from this case to their work lives. This deepens their personal learning, making it more meaningful, and, therefore, memorable. As the instructor, you can improve students learning by helping them connect the concepts specifically to their own lives. Ask clarifying questions when they make a statement to help the student become clear about the lesson for him or herself.

References

Tompkins, T.C. (2000). Developing mature teams: Moving beyond team basics. In M. M. Beyerlein, and D. A. Johnson (Eds.). <u>Advances in Interdisciplinary Studies of Work Teams</u> (Vol. 7). Greenwich, CT: JAI Press.

Tompkins, T. C. (1997). A developmental approach to organizational learning teams: A model and illustrative research. In M. M. Beyerlein, and D. A. Johnson (Eds.). <u>Advances in Interdisciplinary Studies of Work Teams</u> (Vol. 4, pp. 281-302). Greenwich, CT: JAI Press.

Tompkins, T. C. (1995). The role of diffusion in collective learning. <u>International Journal of Organizational Analysis, 3,</u> 69-84.

Tuchman, B.W. & Jensen, M.C. (1977). Stages of small group development revisited. Group and Organizational Studies, 2: 419-427.

Epilogue

There is no epilogue for this case.

GROUPWARE FIASCO

Topics (* = Primary topic with teaching plan)
> *Group Conflict
> *Leadership, absence of
> *Electronic Meetings
> *Group Decision-making
> *Use of Technology
> Group Development
> Group Dynamics
> Higher Education Context

Case overview

      Dr. Susan Pollard, Dean of Human Sciences and Humanities (HSH) at Southern University, wanted the HSH division office to operate smoothly with more efficiency. Since Dr. Pollard's role, as dean of HSH, demanded much of her time outside the office, she relied on Dr. Eve Gordon, the new associate dean, to manage the office for her. Although the dean depended on Dr. Gordon to manage the office and staff in her absence, Dr. Gordon was reluctant to make any sudden changes in the department, though several were desperately needed. Since Dr. Pollard's priority was to ensure harmony at the HSH office, she decided to bring in a third party, a computer programmer who would implement his department's groupware software to improve staff communication and resolve conflict.

      Groupware had been used successfully elsewhere. However, it required participation from all levels and competent leadership and facilitation. Some felt that the groupware project, to start, encompassed neither of these essentials. The facilitator was a computer programmer lacking expertise in organizational development.

      Groupware worked in the following way: the secretaries would sit at computer terminals positioned in the shape of a horseshoe with the facilitator and a large screen sitting at the open end. The facilitator would ask questions about the problems in the office and the secretaries would then type their answers anonymously. The facilitator would then compile the answers from the large screen and prioritize them. The participants then suggested solutions to these problems in the same manner. The results of the session were to be outlined in a formal report and given to the participants and to Dr. Pollard. The Dean felt that an environment that provided anonymity for airing complaints would help facilitate conversation and, possibly, unearth solutions for the group's interpersonal conflicts.

      Although the sessions seemed helpful initially, things quickly turned ugly. During a later session, the facilitator asked for possible solutions to the problems in the department. Someone typed, "We need a man to be in charge of the department." Danielle, the youngest and most progressive (some said brash), typed a question that asked what was meant by the comment. The respondent conveyed that men and women differed and that she preferred working for a man. At that point, Danielle was convinced that the groupware project had met its match. Furthermore, everyone deduced who input both messages and the veil of anonymity had been lifted.

      After the final report was handed over to the dean, a meeting was called. Concern over possible communication and teamwork problems was expressed, but the gender comment was sidestepped. Eventually, the report and its contents faded. People settled back into their old ways and tensions over the sessions soon cooled. The dean announced her retirement shortly after and all decisions concerning the groupware sessions were placed on hold until a successor could be found.

This teaching note was prepared by Diane Fiero, Jonnetta Thomas-Chambers and Teri C. Tompkins, University of Redlands. The case and teaching note were prepared as a basis for class discussion rather than to illustrate either effective or ineffective handling of administrative situations. Suggestions for improvement of this note should be sent to Teri.Tompkins@pepperdine.edu. Credit will be given in the next revision.

Industry

      Administration at a Texas University. Higher education context.

Teaching objectives

1. To recognize and analyze factors that contribute to group conflict.
2. To examine group decision making options and weigh the advantages/disadvantages of these options.
3. To evaluate the groupware experiment and identify its strengths and weaknesses.
4. To identify how laissez-faire leadership and ignoring organizational hierarchies can sometimes lead to dysfunctional behavior.

Other related cases in Volume 1

      <u>A Team Divided or a Team United?</u> (group decision making, group dynamics). <u>Julie's Call: Empowerment at Taco Bell</u> (group decision making). <u>Temporary Employees: Car Show Turned Ugly</u> (group dynamics).

Other related cases in Volume 2

      <u>Computer Services Team at AVIONICS</u> (absence of leadership, group dynamics). <u>Cost and Schedule Team at AVIONICS</u> (group dynamics).

Intended courses and levels

      This case is intended for undergraduate, graduate, and executive students in organizational behavior (group level) and management courses. The case fits in several different functional areas of management. See the introduction to this instructor's manual for several suggestions for placement in management courses.

Analysis

      All related analysis and references are embedded in the answers to the questions.

Research methodology

      This case reflects the recollections of the author. The case is a true story. The names and the university are disguised.

Teaching plans

      The second teaching plan on group decision making has a great exercise to help students examine group decision making. Alternatively, if a decision lab is available, the students can experiment with decision making in the lab. Decision labs can sometimes be found through academic computing or the decision sciences department.

Topic: Group Conflict and Leadership

60-minute teaching plan

Pre-Class Preparation: none

	Timing	Activity	Organization	Student Outcomes
I	0-1 minute (1)	1-minute introduction of class activity.	Case discussion format—full class. Alternative: form students into small groups of 4-5 students	Prepare students to discuss case.
II	1-15 minutes (14)	Students read case.	Individual	Familiarity with case facts

	Timing	Activity	Organization	Student Outcomes
III	15-25 minutes (10)	Q1. *Summarize some of the factors that might have contributed to the conflict among the staff at the division office of HSH department.*	Case discussion format, make list on board or transparency	A list similar to this: • Inattentive leadership from the dean. • Change in leadership (the associate dean). • Improper use of the organizational hierarchy (using the power of the associate dean to back up Martha) • Social loafing. • Perhaps, overworked and stressed staff with too few human resources available.
IV	25-40 minutes (15)	Q2. *What were some of the problems with Gordon's leadership style?*	Case discussion format, make lists on board or transparency	• New to her position. • Blake-Mouton's grid = authority-compliance. • Ignoring organizational procedures and hierarchy. • Low need for power, high need for affiliation, and low degree of self-control.
V	40-55 minutes (15)	Q3. *If you were the dean, what actions might you consider to reduce the conflict among the division office? Evaluate the pros and cons of your possible actions*	Case discussion format, make lists on board or transparency	A list similar to this with pro/cons: • Clarify the rules and procedures. • Support the hierarchy. • Search for common goals through planning. • Develop liaison roles among the groups. • Organize a task force to address specific task problems. • Team meetings.
VI	55-60 (5)	*What themes or lessons have emerged from your analysis of this case?*	Instructor facilitate discussion	Answers will vary, but look for group conflict and leadership topics to reinforce this section.

<u>25-minute teaching plan for group conflict and leadership case</u>
Pre-assignment: Read case before coming to class (15 minutes reading time).
Activities III (allow 10 minutes) and V (15 minutes) in 60 minute plan above

Topic: Electronic Meetings and Group Decision Making
60-minute teaching plan

Preassignment: Read the case before class (15 minutes).
For alternative activity IV: Instructor reserve group decision lab, if one is available, and schedule class to meet there.

	Timing	Activity	Organization	Student Outcomes
I	0-5 minutes (5)	Review the process of groupware procedure.	Full class discussion; could ask a student to summarize their understanding of how groupware works based on the case and their reading.	See case under subheading: <u>The Groupware Project</u>. Key points: Sit around horse-shoe shaped table Facilitator presents issues/question Participants type in answers anonymously and simultaneously

	Timing	Activity	Organization	Student Outcomes
II	5-20 minutes (15)	Q4. *How successful was the groupware experiment in improving interpersonal relations? What were the key issues that lead you to this conclusion?*	Small group discussion or case discussion format	See full answer in discussion section. Not very successful. Groupware is better for solving problems, not for improving interpersonal relations, except maybe as a first step to identify issues anonymously.
III	20-30 minutes (10)	*Based on your readings and the case, what are the advantages and disadvantages to group decision-making?*		Advantages: more complete information and knowledge, increased diversity of views, higher quality decisions, increased acceptance of a solution. Disadvantages: time consuming, conformity pressures, can be dominated by one or a few members, ambiguous responsibility. Reference: Robbins, 1998, pp. 267 & 268.
IV	30-35 minutes (5)	Exercise of group decision-making, A person bought a house (Source: Scannell & Newstrom, 1994, section: 2.581). Read the following to students. "A person bought a house in California for $60,000. But a year later, her company wanted to transfer her to Texas, so she sold her house for $70,000 and moved to Texas. One year later, she decided to move back to California and was delighted to find that she could buy back her old house for $80,000, which she did. After another year, she decided to move to a bigger house, so sold it for $90,000. What was her profit or loss just from the purchase and sale of the property?	Individually have students write down their solution. Alternative: If a group decision lab is available, consider reserving it for this class session and doing this problem solving exercise (or another discussion issue such as, was Congress correct when they impeached President Clinton, why or why not?	If your students ask for clarification, you can tell them to ignore closing costs, moving expenses, and any other fees. Alternative: Students get an experience of what the author of the case experienced and can evaluate first hand, the advantages and disadvantages of using electronic meetings to problems or discuss "hot issues."
V	35-45 (10)	Solve problem as a group.	Groups of 5-7 students	Animated discussion about the correct solution and framing. [Don't try to solve the problem for the groups, let them frame the problem themselves]

	Timing	Activity	Organization	Student Outcomes
VI	45-50 minutes (5)	Ask for answers. How many groups thought? ▪ $20,000 profit ▪ $10,000 profit ▪ Break-even ▪ $10,000 loss ▪ $20,000 loss	On board or transparency, write the five potential solutions and then record how many groups (and individuals) thought it was the correct solution.	It is likely that there will be disagreement on the solution. However, there usually are more people who agree to the correct solution after the group has discussed the problem.
VII	50-55 minutes (5)	Provide the students with the correct solution. The key is to not use the investment and sales numbers more than once. Investment: $60,000+ $80,000 = $140,000. Sales: $70,000 + $90,000 = $160,000. $160,000-$140,000 = $20,000 profit.		Even after you provide the students with the correct answer, some will argue their solution is correct. Point out that decisions are often based on perceptions and how we frame the problem can result in very different solutions. Who's to say that their framing is wrong and therefore their solution is wrong? It depends on the criteria we are using.
VII	55-60 minutes (5)	Discuss results of group decision-making.	Full group, instructor led discussion	Usually more individuals after meeting in groups come up with the correct solution than individuals before groups (but not always!).

<u>25-minute teaching plan for electronic meetings and group decision-making.</u>
Pre-assignment: Read case before coming to class (15 minutes reading time).
Activities II (allow 10 minutes) and III (15 minutes) in 60-minute plan above

Discussion questions and answers

Question 1

Summarize some of the factors that may have contributed to the conflict among the staff at the HSH division office.

<u>Analysis skills</u> (breaking a concept into its parts and explaining their interrelationships, distinguishing relevant from extraneous material)

Answer

The following factors contributed to the conflict in HSH:

<u>Inattentive leadership from the dean:</u> The dean was out of the office most of the time, and depended on Dr. Gordon to ensure the operation ran smoothly and the people were well managed. She was perceived as a laissez-faire leader, showing low concern for both people and tasks. Managers with this style turn most decisions over to the work group and show little interest in the work process or its results (Schermerhorn, 1999, 268). This proved to be an ineffective style for this group, especially in a collegiate setting.

<u>Change in leadership (the associate dean)</u>: In the midst of change, the associate dean was new to her position. Not only was she adjusting to her new role, but the secretaries were as well. As the case briefly depicts, it seems that the management styles of the prior associate dean and the current one were at opposite ends of the spectrum.

<u>Improper use of the organizational hierarchy</u> (using the power of the associate dean to back up Martha): It appeared that Martha received preferential treatment. The fact that the new associate dean supported her claim of being overworked was a decision the division secretaries had to deal with. Unfortunately, they were adversely affected the most—they were required to juggle more work. They

didn't perceive complaining as feasible, especially when their new boss supported the root of their problems.

Social loafing: *Social Loafing* is the choice by some group members to take advantage of others by doing less work, working more slowly, or in other ways contributing less to group productivity (Wagner & Hollenbeck, 1997, p. 316). In the secretarial group the social loafer was Martha. Her work was constantly being delegated to the other secretaries and this was the basis for a lot of resentment in the office. Martha appeared oblivious to the fact that she was causing this strife and therefore did little to change her behavior. This increasing tension and office animosity was the reason that the dean and associate dean decided to send all of the secretaries to the groupware session.

Perhaps, overworked and stressed staff with too few human resources available: As stated in the case, the secretaries' workload was extremely heavy. In addition, they were reassigned Martha's work, as well as supporting the suite secretaries' overflow. Work factors can potentially create job stress. Job-related stress, as illustrated in the case, can result from excessively high task demands, role conflicts or ambiguities, and poor interpersonal relations (Schermerhorn, 1996, 244).

Apprehension: The case also conveys that the secretaries were apprehensive about voicing their complaints to the dean, fearing she would view them as uncooperative and instigating. Therefore, the dean and associate dean were not aware of the real cause for problems in the office because the other secretaries did not complain directly to them. Instead they chose to grouse to each other about their plight. Therefore the deans chalked the unpleasant attitude up to interpersonal conflict and decided the groupware project might alleviate this problem.

Question 2

What were some of the problems with Gordon's leadership style?
Diagnostic question (probes motives or causes)

Answer

Dr. Gordon, prior to becoming the new associate dean, served as the chair of the humanities department. New to her position, Dr. Gordon was unsure of her ability to manage people and it showed in her uneasiness in assigning tasks and dealing with conflict. *Blake and Mouton* would put Dr. Gordon in *the Authority-Compliance* section of their grid which states that efficiency in operations results from arranging conditions of work in such a way that human elements interfere to a minimum degree (Wagner & Hollenbeck, 1997, p. 385). Dr. Gordon just wanted everything to run smoothly. Unfortunately, Martha used this opportunity to take advantage of Dr. Gordon's inexperience and pressured her, through extensive complaints of overwork, into delegating her tasks to the other secretaries.

Question 3

If you were the dean, what actions might you consider to reduce the conflict among the division office? Evaluate the pros and cons of your possible actions.
Action question (calls for a conclusion or action) and evaluation skills (using a set of criteria to arrive at a reasoned judgment of the value of something)

Answer

Students will propose a variety of solutions. Solutions that focus on the true problem (large work load, insufficient or inefficient staffing, division secretaries whose work is interdependent, suite secretaries whose work is more independent, and uninvolved leadership) should be encouraged.

Leadership might conduct a work audit or job assessment to examine the division of workload. Advantage: move beyond symptoms to real problems (including personnel); it is usually done by someone outside of the department, allowing for objectivity. Disadvantage: Time-consuming, the expense may not outweigh the cost savings.

Add an additional staff member: Advantage, assuming there is a true shortage of human resources, would be relieving some pressure on the staff to manage the workload. Disadvantage: doesn't solve the way conflict is handled in the division, though it may reduce it as work stress is reduced. Another disadvantage is that the work problems may be due to inefficiencies or Martha's social loafing and not due to the shortage of staff.

Groupware Fiasco

The most simple and least costly method of managing inter-group relations is to establish rules and procedures (Robbins, 1998, 461). Most universities are bureaucratic in culture. In light of this, HSH needed a strong leader with clear communication and people skills who was not afraid to use his/her authority.

A set of formalized rules and procedures set the tone and boundaries in which a group should interact with one another. One disadvantage is that this approach works "best" when inter-group activities are projected ahead of time, allowing an opportunity to make the rules in advance (Robbins, 1998, 461). However, the advantage of this method requires all group members to play by the same rules. This leaves little room for preferential treatment or exceptions to these rules.

Question 4

How successful was the groupware experiment in improving interpersonal relations? What were the key issues that lead you to this conclusion?

Evaluation skills (using a set of criteria to arrive at a reasoned judgment of the value of something)

Answer

Groupware was not very successful. Groupware is better for solving problems, not for improving interpersonal relations, except maybe as a first step to identify issues anonymously. The groupware experiment only compounded problems. Instead of improving interpersonal relations, the groupware project's detached facilitator utilized a process that actually prevented effective group decision-making.

First of all, the facilitator of this project was actually a computer software designer. The only goal of the meeting stated by the facilitator was to come up with a list of prioritized problems and some possible solutions for each problem. Once the group members figured out how to enter their responses they were able to clearly communicate their thoughts and suggestions. One of the inherent problems with the groupware system was that it encouraged a large quantity of ideas, but did little to evaluate the quality of those ideas. It was up to the facilitator to transform the input into meaningful output. However, the facilitator was unfamiliar with HSH and had little concept of the problems plaguing their office. Therefore, he had little idea of what was important or what was just secretarial venting.

The rational decision making model involves choosing the final decision, implementing it, and later evaluating the decisions made. This is where the groupware project really fell short. The group was able to come up with general solutions to some of their problems. Once the report was given to the dean, there was no evaluation of the implementation and little feedback was collected from the participants regarding their perceptions of the groupware project itself. In part, this can be attributed to the fact that Dr. Pollard had announced her retirement and, until the new dean was in place, all changes were placed on hold.

Question 5

Suppose you were one of the secretaries in the pool, how might you try to effectively cope with the conflict and stress on the job?

Hypothetical question (poses a change in the facts or issues)

Answer

There are many ways in which the groupware activity could have been more effective. Perhaps an experienced facilitator with expertise in a university environment would have been more effective. If the groupware software had some way of delaying the entries, or scrambling them, it would have increased the chances of preserving anonymity.

The Delphi Technique, where each member of the group is interviewed individually, may have worked better for this particular group. Even within the groupware setting, all of the participants may not have felt free enough to say what was really on their minds, mainly that Martha was the major source of the conflicts in the office. At least in the Delphi technique, talking one-on-one with an impartial individual, there's a more significant chance of speaking freely.

Another way the group could have coped would have been to behave more empathetically towards one another. They should have considered the differences in their values as an opportunity to learn from each other. Indeed, they may have realized that the reasons their opinions differed, especially in regards to preferring a male/female boss, were related to work style/approach or personality traits. It is okay to "agree to disagree" and maintain respect for each other.

In retrospect, the biggest problem the group had was avoiding face-to-face communication. In the workplace, effectiveness is at its peak when open communication, honesty, trust and respect prevail. The groupware project undermined all of these essentials. Hiding behind a wall of anonymity portrayed that the group did not harbor enough respect, trust or honesty to feel comfortable enough to participate in open communication. Ironically, they were comfortable enough to gossip with one another, but when it was time for the moment of truth, their behavior proved the weaknesses of their relationships.

References

Robbins, Stephen P. (1998). Organizational behavior, 5th Edition, Upper Saddle River, NJ: Prentice Hall.

Scannell, E. E., and J. W. Newstrom (1994). The complete games trainers play: Experiential learning exercises. New York, NY: McGraw-Hill.

Schermerhorn, Jr., John R (1996). Management and organizational behavior essentials, 1st Edition, New York, NY: John Wiley and Sons.

Schermerhorn, Jr., John R. (1999). Management, 6th Edition, New York, NY: John Wiley and Sons.

Wagner III, J.A. and Hollenbeck, J.R. (1997). Organizational Behavior: Securing competitive advantage. Upper Saddle River, NJ: Prentice Hall.

Epilogue

Danielle's final comment, "Well, there went another great idea for open communication that proved difficult to apply to the real world." Danielle went on to graduate school to work on her masters in human resource development. She has now graduated, recently married, and is working in her chosen field.

INCIDENT ON THE U.S.S. *WHITNEY*

Topics (* = Primary topic with teaching plan)
*Power and Organizational Structure
*Authority, acceptance of
*Norms
*Bureaucracy: its functions and dysfunctions
*Transactional and Transformational Leadership
*Role Conflict
*Multiple Viewpoints for Considering a Case
Hierarchical Leadership
United States Military
Interpersonal Conflict
Government Context

Case overview

The incident takes place on a naval vessel, the U.S.S. *Whitney*. A young ensign, Jeff Beck, who is on his first assignment, goes against normal Navy hierarchy when he challenges his superior in order to get a clear accounting for merchandise from the ship's store that he is responsible for. He obtains approval from the ship's captain, but is dressed down by his superior officer, the ship's chief supply officer; nevertheless, the case shows that in informal terms he gains organizational power.

Working on a pre-commissioning vessel being prepared for Navy service, Ens. Jeff Beck has the job of accounting for merchandise that is being distributed free from the ship's store by the head of the supply department (the Suppo) who is Beck's supervisor, Lt. Cdr. Fuller. Fuller is a generally effective veteran officer, but he is known for his stern, overbearing style. Inability to account for the merchandise (while of minor value) might harm Beck and has created an accounting (paperwork) nightmare for him.

After being goaded by another officer, Lt. Wilson, Ens. Beck decides to test the chain of command by telling Fuller that he will request that the ship's captain as well as Fuller sign off on the list of free items. While Beck is within Navy rules, he is outside norms of usual behavior by a subordinate. Unexpectedly, Fuller agrees to let Beck take his request to the captain, who signs the list, appears to side with Beck in a kind of joke, and sends back a mild needling note to the Suppo.

The incident results in a demonstration of informal norms (respect for rules, deference, needling) and power within the ship's hierarchy of authority. It also displays significant role conflict for several of those involved. While Lt. Cdr. Fuller has the power to deny Beck's request to go above him to the captain, he does not. Instead he smugly approves the request, in effect daring Beck to go ahead. When Beck appears to have received a favor from the captain or, at least, when the captain seems to side with him against Fuller, Fuller blasts out angrily and publicly dresses down Ens. Beck. In the background of the case are Lt. Wilson, a mentor to Ens. Beck and a wily Navy veteran, and Lt. Smith, a female officer with little sea experience; both are informed of and encourage Beck's action, although their motives are never fully clear. The two officers provide immediate support to Ens. Beck after the Suppo yells at him. Twenty-minutes after the yelling episode the Suppo apologizes to Beck in an almost pleading tone of voice.

The epilogue states that Ens. Beck experienced a greater sense of power after this incident. His supply accounts were not questioned by Fuller, and he felt he understood the organizational politics of the ship much more. Discussion of the case focuses on leadership styles, authority in a bureaucracy, informal and formal norms and bases of power and the effects of role conflict.

This teaching note was prepared by Jeff Balesh, Kathryn S. Rogers, Pitzer College, and Teri C. Tompkins, University of Redlands. The case and teaching note were prepared as basis for class discussion rather than to illustrate either effective or ineffective handling of administrative situations. Suggestions for improvement of this note should be sent to Teri.Tompkins@pepperdine.edu. Credit will be given in the next revision.

Industry

US Military; Naval vessel

Teaching objectives

1. To distinguish between transactional and transformational leadership
2. To identify which basis of power is used by each character
3. To explore the roles and role conflict

Other related cases in Volume 1

A New Magazine in Nigeria (power). No, Sir, Sergeant! (acceptance of authority). Shaking the Bird Cage (power). Temporary Employees: Car Show Turned Ugly (power).

Other related cases in Volume 2

Saving Private Ryan and Classic Leadership Models (leadership). The Volunteer (acceptance of authority). Unprofessional Conduct (leadership). Your Uncle Wants You! (U.S. military).

Intended courses and levels

This course is intended for undergraduate, graduate, and executive students in organizational behavior, management (leading), and leadership courses. The topics include leadership, transactional and transformational leadership, French and Raven basis of power, role and norms.

Analysis

All related analysis and references are embedded in the answers to the questions.

Research methodology

This case reflects the recollection of the casewriter. No other people were interviewed for this case. The case is a true incident. Names and the ship have been disguised, but the organization has not been disguised.

Teaching plan

The USS *Whitney* is a rich case that can be used in a number of ways. Five possible teaching configurations (up to 120 minutes of class time) are suggested depending on different timeframes and teaching objectives. If a two-day discussion is desired, either Plan A or Plan B can be used first.

For executive teaching where there may be a heavy emphasis on skill development, the 25-minute session on leadership may be combined with the 25-minute session on bureaucracy and power for a (packed) 50+ minute class. It will introduce briefly both the power and leadership aspects of the case, but subtler points such as informal rules, coalitions, and the role of Wilson will need to be omitted.

USS *Whitney* Plan A

Topic: Power and organizational structure, norms, bureaucracy and its functions and dysfunctions

60-minute teaching plan

Pre-assignment: Read the case before class and consider how their sources of personal and organizational power influenced the people in the case.

	Timing	Activity	Organization	Student Outcomes
I	0-5 minutes (5)	Review and break in. Who are the key actors in the case? What type of organization is this? Who are the major (formal) power holders?	Ask for or appoint a volunteer for answers. Write names on board or overhead in hierarchical order.	Orientation, opening of discussion, introduce topics, warm up.

	Timing	Activity	Organization	Student Outcomes
II	5-15 minutes (10)	*Ask Q 3. Distinguish between personal and organizational power* Show slide with French and Raven's taxonomy of types of power	Full class identifies people in case who have different power sources. Fill in names from case in column next to each category; discuss emphasis on legitimate power and rules in a military hierarchy, chain of command.	Applying abstract classification to case facts.
III	15-25 minutes (10)	*Ask Q 4. Consider informal power sources* (link to Q 7 if it comes up.)	Full class discussion. Additional, if time: Ask for personal experiences.	Extend analysis skills, conceptualize power of "lower participants" in organizations; personalize case situation
IV	25-30 minutes (5)	Professor asks for or defines the concept of norms (ask students to note violation of chain of command in case). *Why is accountability so important in this organization? Is it really very important in this case?*	Mini-lecture	Students recognize organization as a system that depends heavily on conformity and clear expectations, but allows leeway. Suggest formal vs. informal rules of behavior. Introduce coalitions, sabotage, jokes as informal behavior, that illustrate power
V	30-50 minutes (10)	*Ask Q5, Q7 Why was Beck's action unusual?*	Divide class; have one side say why Beck was justified/ other why he was not justified in how he acted. [If time, *Ask Q 6. How might role conflict explain the Suppo's anger?]*	Application skills: using information in a new context; listening to alternate viewpoints; link data to organizational structure and role concepts.
VI	50-55 minutes (5)	Read epilogue to class; *Ens. Beck says that in retrospect he probably overreacted; but that in fighting his boss he gained more political savvy. What did you learn about the dynamics of organizational politics and power from this case? Do you think Beck gained or lost power? Do you think that testing of rules usually results in greater or less respect/power for a subordinate? What factors influence this?*	Question can be used for brief wrap-up or as writing assignment to prepare for a second discussion on this case.	Develop inferences, extend concepts.

<u>25-minute plan:</u> Power and organizational structure, norms, bureaucracy and its functions and dysfunctions
Pre-assignment: Read case
Do activities I, II, III from the 60-minute plan.

USS *Whitney* Plan B
Topic: Transactional and transformational leadership, role conflict, and multiple viewpoints for considering a case
60-minute teaching plan

Pre-assignment: Read case and consider the leadership exhibited in the case. Do you consider this leading effective or ineffective, why?

	Timing	Activity	Organization	Student Outcomes
I	0- 5 minutes (5)	Review observations of leadership behavior. Ask students *who are the primary leaders in the case?*	Discussion	Orientation, refresh names. Note the style and expectations of Fuller and Beck.
II	5 - 15 minutes (10)	*Q1: Is Lieutenant Commander Fuller primarily a transactional or transformational leader?* Review leadership reading. Link leading to motivating others.	Define concepts, show slides or write behavioral characteristics of different leadership patterns on the board.	Identify key concepts relevant to case; use specific case examples as illustration. See answers to Q1.
III	15 - 25 minutes (10)	*Q2: How would the situation be different if Lt. Cdr. Fuller were a transformational leader?*	Choose one or two pairs of students to demonstrate. Role-play transformational leading. Or, have all class members role-play in dyads and observe carefully themselves and their reactions/motivations	Application and practice of managerial skill; making behavioral concepts concrete. See answers to Q2.
IV	25 -30 minutes (5)	Get group to critique demonstration; tell their own feelings and consider long term organizational outcomes.	In groups above (III).	Practice giving critique/refine self-observation skill
V	30 - 40 minutes (10)	Develop and discuss a new concept. *Q 6. What might explain the Suppo's anger with Ens. Beck? Why didn't Fuller stop Beck from going to the captain? What did he expect as an outcome? What did Beck expect?*	Full class discussion, speculation	Extend causal analysis of case facts
VI	40 - 55 minutes (15)	*Would the outcome of the case have been different if Lt. Wilson had not been in the case? How do norms explain the captain's behavior? The Suppo's? Beck's? Wilson's to Beck? Which norms (of the Navy) supported each person to resolve the conflict or make it more severe?*	Use groups above or divide class into at least four group to discuss Q 5. Q 7 in groups of 4-6. Each group picks a primary character to focus on.	Reinforce concept of informal norms; extend analyses; develop inferences; enrich understanding of different viewpoints in a case

	Timing	Activity	Organization	Student Outcomes
VII	55 - 60 minutes (5)	*How did role conflict affect specific individuals in this case?*	Full class discussion.	Debriefing from groups.

25-minute plan on transactional and transformational leadership, role conflict, and multiple viewpoints for considering a case.
Pre-assignment: Read case
Do activities I (2min), II, III (use the role-play in dyads) , IV(3 min) from the 60-minute plan

Discussion questions and answers

Question 1
Is Lieutenant Commander Fuller primarily a transactional or transformational leader?
<u>Application skills</u> (using information in a new context to solve a problem, answer a question, or perform a task)

Answer
Lt. Cdr. Fuller's (Suppo) relationships with his subordinates were predicated on a "quid pro quo" philosophy. That is, if one performed the functions that he desired and accomplished the results he wanted, he would reward a person with positive reinforcement—through praise, recognition (e.g., by awarding one with a medal after a significant duration of time), or the simple attainment of the status of "being in his favor;" or through negative reinforcement—by a subordinate's avoiding the deleterious effects that accompany an unfavorable perception of him or her. Of course, any unfavorable attitude the Suppo may have had toward a person had the likely probability of resulting in punishment if the undesired performance continued beyond a reasonable amount of time. Furthermore, he had engendered neither feelings of commitment to his philosophy as a manager nor a grander sense of purpose.

In a transformational leadership situation, the leader's and follower's purposes become conjoined to form one higher purpose which then functions as a primary motivation for performance. However, in the narrative, Ens. Beck and the Suppo were working at cross-purposes: They were both trying to save their own professional reputation at the expense of the other's. Lt. Cdr. Fuller, then, was a purely transactional leader as he functions on a basic social exchange level. By being a transactional leader, situations like this one are not rare, as relations between leader and follower remain on a fundamentally superficial level. Neither person is intrinsically aligned with a common purpose beyond that which brings him or her personal gain. Thus, Lt. Cdr. Fuller, it can be argued, had only himself to blame for Ens. Beck's bold actions.

Question 2
Would the situation be different if Lt. Cdr. Fuller were a transformational leader?
<u>Evaluation skills</u> (using a set of criteria to arrive at a reasoned judgment of the value of something) or <u>hypothetical question</u> (poses a change in the facts or issues)

Answer
If Lt. Cdr. Fuller were a transformational leader, it would be improbable that this situation would have occurred. First, the way merchandise was given away would have been handled much differently. Because both he and Ens. Beck would be working towards the same, higher purpose, their interests would have been aligned on this issue. A couple of possibilities are obvious. Since the Suppo would have acknowledged that the giving away of merchandise could affect the ensign's performance of his job, he would have either not offered anything for free, or, if he absolutely had to give items away, he would have worked together with Ens. Beck in devising a system that worked for both of them. This system would have been one where Fuller kept a complete itemization of items with a listing of to whom each piece was given. The transformational Suppo would have appealed to the ensign's understanding that the Lt. Cdr. absolutely had to give the merchandise away and that they would work together in ensuring that Ens. Beck would not be hurt by any of these actions.

Another scenario can focus on the events after Lt. Cdr. Fuller had returned from the trip. If Ens. Beck had come to him with the itemized list for both the Suppo and captain to sign (which would have been highly unlikely if Fuller were a transformational leader), he could have gone through the ramifications of obtaining the captain's signature and how this action would probably not be beneficial for either of them. The key variable in any scenario is that both leader and follower are working together to promote a common purpose. By merely inputting this factor into the narrative, all relationships (including Lt. Wilson's and Ens. Beck's relationship, as Wilson would probably not have been as strong an influence if there wasn't the need for him to act as a buffer) would radically change.

Question 3

Using French and Raven's taxonomy of power, what were the bases of interpersonal power that Lt. Cdr. Fuller possessed over Ens. Beck?

Application skills (using information in a new context to solve a problem, answer a question, or perform a task)

Answer

Lt. Cdr. Fuller possessed all three of the organizational bases of power over Ens. Beck. Due to his position as head of the supply department, he had ample amounts of legitimate power. However, in this case, he neglected to use it *before* Ens. Beck took the itemized sheet to the captain to sign. He could have easily told the ensign that he did not want Ens. Beck to take it to the captain and Ens. Beck would have had to obey his wish, as the force of legitimate power in the military is probably the greatest of the five bases of power. By the very nature of the Navy's structure of chain of command and its strict requirement to show respect for those with higher rank and their commands, all the Suppo had to do was refuse Ens. Beck's desire to go to the captain. But he didn't. The reasons why can only be based on conjecture, but an argument can be made for the case that he was challenging the ensign (hence the condescending body language when Lt. Cdr. Fuller told the ensign to "Go ahead."). He most likely didn't expect the captain's reaction to the sheet or he wouldn't have gladly sent the ensign up to him. Instead, he could have been sending the ensign (1) to see if he would go through with the "threat" of approaching the captain, and (2) if Ens. Beck did go, to have the captain swiftly dismiss him—and, in so doing, justify the Suppo's position. Although one can surmise why his legitimate power was not used, it is clear that it wasn't, and his allowance of the ensign's maneuver turned out to be a significant turning point (or lack thereof) in the case.

Although the Suppo possessed reward power, this base of power did not come into play during the case. Ens. Beck did not use the possibility of being rewarded by Lt. Cdr. Fuller as motivation for his actions. However, coercive power surely came into play both in overt and covert forms. When the ensign decided to take the sheet to the captain, he also decided to put himself in Suppo's line of fire. The threat of this type of power really hung over the ensign's head throughout the entire narrative, and it was finally realized at the climax of the case during the browbeating. This type of conclusion, although the ensign didn't necessarily expect it, was certainly deemed as possible given the perceptions of Lt. Cdr. Fuller by his subordinate officers.

Lt. Cdr. Fuller obviously did not have much referent power, if any at all. If he had, the event would probably not have taken place, as the communication would most likely have been better between the ensign and him. Expert power also did not come into play as expertise, of which the Suppo did not have much in Ens. Beck's area, was not necessary or in demand in the case. Thus, the Suppo only possessed the organizational determinants of interpersonal power and not any of the personal forms, a prescription that doesn't make for subordinates who have much respect for a superior but will do what he or she demands because of the potential negative consequences associated with not obeying orders.

Question 4

What type of power, if any, did Ens. Beck possess?

Analysis skills (breaking a concept into its parts and explaining their interrelationships, distinguishing relevant from extraneous material)

Answer

It is obvious from the above analysis of French and Raven's understanding of interpersonal power that Ens. Beck did not possess any of these types of power. However, there must have been some sort of power that Ens. Beck enjoyed. Without *any* type of power, it is highly unlikely that he would have been able to go up to the captain with a note that obviously had the potential for creating harm for the Suppo. It was previously mentioned that the Suppo could have easily used his legitimate power to halt any further action.

While this is true, it would have to counter one type of power that the ensign did possess. This type of power is, according to Morgan's (1997) description of the 14 most important sources of power, a use of organizational structure, rules, regulations, and procedures. Since Ens. Beck was, throughout the narrative, technically correct in his concern over his accountability for the lost merchandise, he was entitled to a signature of a superior to absolve himself of the responsibility for it. The fact that he asked for the captain's signature as well as the Suppo's, while being slightly unorthodox, was fully within Ens. Beck's rights under the Navy's regulations that governed the sale of ship merchandise. The Suppo knew better than anyone the importance of maintaining accountability at all times, so he could not simply disregard this regulation and risk the loss of respect by his subordinates. Thus, the ensign's power resulting from his invocation of rules enabled him to go up to the captain and was a sufficient counter to the legitimate power that the Suppo had.

Question 5

How did implied norms account for the behavior noted in the narrative?

Application skills (using information in a new context to solve a problem, answer a question, or perform a task)

Answer

Implied norms failed in this case to provide for a mutually desired course of action because a couple of norms were at conflict with each other. The one well-entrenched norm of respecting one's chain of command and especially one's superior provided some difficulties for Ens. Beck in this case. Anytime one goes beyond his or her supervisor to levels further up the chain of command there has to be a good reason for it. Ens. Beck did follow the procedural norm of informing his superior that he was intending on going up the chain. If he hadn't, it would have certainly been much more disastrous than what had transpired.

Another way in which chain of command played an integral role in the case was Suppo's regard for the captain and his power over him. This respect for and perhaps even fear of the captain essentially accounted for the Suppo's outburst. The amount of respect and/or fear appears to be great: What else could explain how words written on a nonofficial form (not a counseling sheet or performance evaluation, for example) done in somewhat of a teasing manner, could incite such a response? In this context, the yelling is understandable. The ensign had not only just gone against the norm of respecting the chain of command, but he had also upset the relations between the powerful captain and the deferent Suppo.

In order for Ens. Beck to be able to circumvent the norm of not going up the chain of command, there had to be a substantive reason for it. This reason was found in the aforementioned rules of guarding one's accountability. The fact that regulations superceded an established norm is indicative of the relationship between rules and norms on the ship. Rules can always be invoked to support someone's position. However, if group norms are extremely well established, the incentive to invoke a rule will be significantly lessened. In this case, although the norm was well established, Ens. Beck's incentives came from not only the desire to protect his accountability, but also his disregard for the Suppo.

Question 6

Was there any role conflict that can be identified in this case?

Analysis skills (breaking a concept into its parts and explaining their interrelationships, distinguishing relevant from extraneous material)

Answer

Intra-role role conflict is defined as occurring when different individuals define a role according to different sets of expectations, making it impossible for the person occupying the role to satisfy all of them (Gibson et al., 1997). Intra-role conflict was at work in the narrative as Ens. Beck and the Suppo had different expectations regarding the ensign's role. Lt. Cdr. Fuller thought that the ensign's role was to take care of the rudimentary tasks of accounting for merchandise and trusting the Suppo's judgment if there was any difficulty, as giving away items presented. Basically, his role was to obey the Suppo, but staunchly observing the requirements of this role was made difficult by the tense relationship they shared. Thus, it is no surprise that Ens. Beck found it relatively easy to supercede the filling of this role by playing one that would serve his purposes better.

Ens. Beck perceived his primary role as being more concerned with his accountability than anything else. While obeying the Suppo was accepted, albeit begrudgingly, by the ensign as one of the roles he had to fill, trusting him was not. He did not want to trust someone like Fuller with effectively guiding him through these dubious situations, as he saw Fuller as one who would surely take care of himself before anyone else, especially a subordinate like Beck. Thus, conflict resulted and was eventually resolved when the Suppo berated Ens. Beck. This yelling fit effectively communicated where the ensign's priorities were supposed to lie, according to Fuller, and at least temporarily resolved the conflict.

Question 7

What roles did Lt. Wilson play in this case and how did they influence what happened?
<u>Synthesis skills</u> (putting parts together to form a new whole; solving a problem requiring creativity or originality)

Answer

Lt. Wilson, as Ens. Beck's mentor and friend, played the role of influential advisor. As such, he was able to offer the impetus necessary for the ensign to carry through the plan of protecting his accountability even though it was a bold one. After the Suppo berated Ens. Beck, Lt. Wilson took on the role of supporter. In performing both functions, he was obviously integral to defining Ens. Beck's outlook on the *Whitney*. That is, he not only advised him on appropriate or desirable action, but he also provided the support when things did not go as planned.

The latter factor is telling of their relationship. Lt. Wilson was obviously not correct in all of his decisions, but when he was wrong in his analysis of a situation, at least he was available to help pick up the pieces. Without Lt. Wilson's advice to write up the itemized sheet to present to both the Suppo and captain, it is doubtful whether Ens. Beck would have followed through with such a plan. As he played the aforementioned mentor role, Lt. Wilson may have advised such a course of action not only to satisfy the personalized motive of "getting back at" the Suppo, but also to see the ensign assert himself to achieve some measure of autonomy that was being usurped by the Suppo's disregard. Thus, Lt. Wilson, in performing the duties that his mentor role demanded, substantially influenced the events of the case to the ultimate betterment of Ens. Beck's position. Although there was an unexpected short-term result, the long-term benefited the ensign and his standing in the department.

References

Bass, B. M. (1985). <u>Leadership and performance beyond expectations</u>. New York: The Free Press.

Burns, J. M. (1978). <u>Leadership</u>. New York: Harper and Row.

Gibson, J. L., Ivancevich, J. M., & Donnelly, J. H. (1997). <u>Organizations: Behavior, structure, processes</u>. Chicago: Irwin.

Morgan, G. (1997). <u>Images of organization</u>. Thousand Oaks: Sage.

Epilogue

That was the last time Ens. Beck took anything of this sort up to the captain for his signature. The Suppo was now willing to sign <u>anything</u> without so much as a question. He even told the ensign that he didn't have to worry about his not agreeing to sign any of these "write-off" sheets. As time went on, Ens. Beck developed more political savvy and, looking back months later in hindsight, realized that he really did make a big deal out of this situation. That day's events weren't necessarily about a threat to his accountability, he knew later. After all, the Suppo's signature would have been sufficient to absolve Ens. Beck of any responsibility for the lost inventory. Rather, what happened that day was more about control and the reaction to being controlled.

Of course, there was a definite risk involved with fighting his boss on this issue. He knew at the time that Lt. Wilson was using him to fight back as well. Because the ensign was in total agreement with the lieutenant, and as a result of the mentor-mentee relationship that had been built between them, Ens. Beck, while knowing of the risk involved, trusted Lt. Wilson and his advice. He knew he had to fight back against Suppo's willingness to flaunt his accountability and, in no small way, had to assert his place in the department.

From that point on, Lt. Cdr. Fuller seemed to have a greater respect for the ensign's position. They came to something of an understanding, at least on this issue, as the Suppo didn't abuse his power in this arena anywhere near as much as he had been. The risk that had accompanied the struggle for what small slice of autonomy Ens. Beck had achieved had paid off.

INSUBORDINATION OR UNCLEAR LOYALTIES?

Topics (* = Primary topic with teaching plan)
*Problem Analysis and Solution Alternatives
*Authority, acceptance of
*Organizational Structure, dysfunctional
Interpersonal Relations
Leadership vs. Career Choice
Decision Case
Non-profit Organizations

Case overview
Ellen, the program director of Omega House, a hospice, was wondering how to deal with the new development officer, George. He reported to her and was also part of a cross-program task force on fundraising within the Social Action Consortium (SAC), the umbrella organization for a variety of service agencies, including Omega house, located in the Midwest. Ellen was accustomed to working with her team and found George's non-communicative approach disconcerting. Although George worked for both SAC and Omega house, his salary was drawn from Omega house's budget; however, George seemed to focus his energies on SAC's cross-program task force for fundraising as opposed to committees, which would benefit Omega house alone. When Ellen voiced her concern about Omega house's fundraising to George, he tersely replied, "I'm part of SAC's cross-program task force. I had a few conflicts and I had to decide where to focus my energies. I felt I had to do what SAC wanted." She was puzzled as to how to deal with the situation. Was the problem with George structurally rather than individually? George's structural place within SAC seemed unclear, with him seemingly reporting both to her and the SAC development office chief, who headed the task force. Thus, she asked herself, "Is the problem George's irresponsible and non-communicative behavior or is it confusion over who is to direct his efforts or both?"

Industry
Not-for-profit hospice care and its parent organization.

Teaching objectives
1. To practice identifying the key problems in the case and potential solutions to solve them.
2. To give students a feel for the structural difficulties one can encounter in managing a service program that is part of a larger agency.
3. To provide an example of one source of tension a former service provider, such as Ellen, faces as she makes the transition from professional service provider to manager.
4. To understand how today's team environments add complexity to the former chain-of-command orientation of classical administration.
5. To exemplify the complexity of supervising someone who answers to several parts of the organization (matrix vs. functional organizational structure).

Other related cases in Volume 1
A New Magazine in Nigeria (acceptance of authority). Costume Bank (career fit). Donor Services Department in Guatemala (career fit, organizational structure). No, Sir, Sergeant! (acceptance of

This teaching note was written by Asbjorn Osland, George Fox University, and Shannon Shoul. The case and teaching note were prepared as basis for class discussion rather than to illustrate either effective or ineffective handling of administrative situations. Suggestions for improvement of this note should be sent to tompkins@uor.edu. Credit will be given in the next revision.

authority). Shaking the Bird Cage (organizational structure). Split Operations at Sky and Arrow Airlines (organizational structure). Unmovable Team (career fit).

Other related cases in Volume 2

Angry Branch Manager (decision case). Incident on the USS *Whitney* (acceptance of authority). Reputation in Jeopardy (acceptance of authority). The Volunteer (acceptance of authority, career fit). Unprofessional Conduct (career fit). When Worlds Collide (organizational structure).

Intended courses and levels

The case is directed at students studying organizational behavior, nonprofit management, management for nurses, or social service administration. The case is ideal for an introduction to case problem analysis.

Analysis

The case deals with issues of organizational structure that impact communication and supervision. Students should have a moderate level of familiarity with the construct of organizational communication and structure to successfully analyze this case.

Overall, structure is a set of characteristics comprised of employee interactions with one another and management, standards of conduct embodied in the group, systems of rewards and punishments, and the system of communication (Goldhaber, 1993; Harris, 1993). Structure, as defined by Harris (1993), is the type of organizational system employed to get things done and should reflect the organization's strategy and goals; form follows function and structure follows strategy (Chandler, 1962). Goldhaber (1993) argued that structure is "done" by communication and that organizational structure is the network of relationships and roles that define an organization (p. 53). This organizational communication perspective is focused on the process of interaction rather than a rigid structural form appearing in an organizational chart.

George's communication patterns are altering the structure that Ellen perceives. The academic term for this interaction between process and structure is structurationism (Giddens, 1979). Structurationism is the on-going interaction of structure and process where both continue to be complemented by the other in an evolutionary cycle. Gioia and Pitre (1990) describe it in the following manner:

> "In brief, structuration theorists focus on connections between human action (in the form of structuring activities) and established organizational structures (cf. Riley, 1983). Proponents of this theory do not treat structuring as separate from structures; they consider social construction processes together with the objective characteristics of the social world (p. 592)."
> The tension between Ellen and George indicates a lack of clarity regarding structure (Daft, 1998). If it's a functional structure where George reports to Ellen, as Ellen seems to believe, then George is clearly mistaken. If it is a functional structure, then one of the weaknesses that is apparent is poor horizontal coordination (Daft, 1998, p. 215). However, if it's a matrix, as far as fund raising is concerned, with George reporting both to Ellen and the head of fund raising for SAC, then George, Ellen and the head of the fund raising unit at SAC need to communicate more clearly and discuss mutual expectations regarding George's performance. One of the weaknesses of the matrix is confusion regarding loyalties (Daft, 1998, p. 229). However, both Ellen and George should be able to see George's work as a horizontal linkage (Daft, 1998, p. 212) used to enhance the communication process.

Research methodology

 Both authors used participant observation. Shannon Shoul did her honors thesis at Omega house and later went on to work for SAC. Asbjorn Osland worked as a volunteer at Omega house for over 100 hours. Shannon interviewed people extensively and worked with George. Asbjorn interviewed Ellen and observed staff interaction. The organization and the names have been disguised.

Teaching plan

 There are several options for teaching this case. The discussion questions could be addressed. This case could also be used as a written assignment or to teach students how to do a problem analysis of a case. The author's method for doing case analysis begins on page 211 of this manual. He has used this case to help students identify situations, problems, solutions, and anticipated consequences. He also suggests the theory that might apply.

Topic: Teaching problem analysis and anticipation of consequences; Organizational structure
60-minute teaching plan

Pre-assignment: None

	Timing	Activity	Organization	Student Outcomes
I	0-15 minutes (15)	Students read case.	Individually	Familiarity with topics.
II	15-20 minutes (5)	Brief lecture on differences between situation and problem analysis.	Instructor lecture	Situation is the behavior observed (the symptoms). Problem is the real issue the key player(s) face.
III	20-30 minutes (10)	Students identify the three to five situations in the case	Individually or in small groups	A list of situations such as in the table below.
IV	30-40 minutes (10)	Identify problem (root cause of the situation).	In small groups or as a whole class.	See Analysis Table below
V	40-50 minutes (10)	Identify potential solutions, related to appropriate theories.	In small groups or as a whole class.	See Analysis Table below
VI	50-60 minutes (10)	Identify anticipated consequences.	In small groups or as a whole class	See Analysis Table below

25-minute teaching plan for problem analysis and solutions
Pre-assignment: Read case before coming to class (15 minutes); identify three to five situations from the case (10 - 15 minutes).
Do activities IV (5minutes), V (10 minutes), VI (10 minutes) in 60-minute plan above.

Analysis Table: Insubordination Or Unclear Loyalties?

Situation Analysis	Problem Analysis	Theory Application	Solution & Implementation	Anticipated Consequences
1. Ellen is the program director at Omega house, and George's supervisor.	1. Ellen is not sure if the problem is structural or personal, because George reports to the SAC development chief as well as to her.	1. Organizational structure and strategy (Daft, p. 202).	1. Make sure there is a clear distinction in the line of direct reporting. George will be responsible for following that line of report.	1. It may be necessary to change individual roles when the reporting structure becomes clearer. This may cause a problem for George if he does not want to do the work for the Omega house.

Situation Analysis	Problem Analysis	Theory Application	Solution & Implementation	Anticipated Consequences
2. George's salary is paid by a grant through the Omega house, but he also does work for SAC.	2. George is not spending very much of his time working for Omega house, even though his salary is paid through it.	2. Cooperative model of organization (Daft, p. 494).	2. Set different goals for the Omega house and SAC. George should be held responsible for making both targets and will be reviewed accordingly.	2. If the problem is personal, George and Ellen may end up not being able to work together effectively and then something else will need to be done.
3. George seems uncommunicative with Ellen and as far as she's concerned, the numbers say he is not doing his job at the Omega house.	3. Ellen is not sure of her management skills and thus, may not be communicating clearly what her expectations are of George.	3. Power sources for management (Daft, p. 444).	3. Have Ellen attend some management training classes so that she gains some confidence when dealing with subordinates.	3. Ellen will become more confident when dealing with people and issues in her job.

Discussion questions and answers

Question 1

How do hierarchical, autocratic systems work against cross-program task forces?

Analysis skills (breaking a concept into its parts and explaining their interrelationships)

Answer

First, one should analyze why autocratic systems may exist. The reasons are many but let's look at a few:

- Usually, people like Ellen have been taught to manage in hierarchical settings such as hospitals. Physicians tell nurses what to do and nurses then tell one another, based on their position in the hierarchy.
- Nonprofits may spend too little on management training and leave new managers to fend for themselves, with a tremendous range in abilities and resulting consequences.
- Ideologically-driven managers may sometimes be autocratic because they feel the mission to be all-important and the people working for them less so.
- Because of the emphasis on hierarchy in autocratic systems, fiefdoms tend to develop. Ellen is both immature as a manager and seemingly unaware of the cross-program needs that require George's attention.

Question 2

What do new managers need to develop into competent managers?

Synthesis skills (putting parts together to form a new whole; solving a problem requiring creativity or originality)

Answer

New managers like Ellen need training in management. Ideally they would be able to learn from their bosses as well as attend evening programs in management. All too often they emulate that which has been modeled for them (often autocratic, as mentioned above).

Question 3

To what extent is the problem with George personal and to what extent is it structural?

Evaluation skills (using a set of criteria to arrive at a reasoned judgment of the value of something)

Answer

The problem is both personal and structural. On the personal level, George is abusing the resources of the institution by making personal copies. Also, his record appears tarnished by an indiscretion at his previous place of employment. Additionally, he seems ill equipped to deal with the political sensitivity of working in several locations for several bosses since he has alienated Ellen.

At the structural level, Ellen has adopted a myopic focus on her own program rather than appreciating the need for the SAC task force. This may be justified since programs sometimes suffer within SAC due to seemingly arbitrary decisions by the autocratic executive director. However, Ellen should try to understand George's role in serving both Omega and SAC.

Question 4

What should Ellen do?

Action question (calls for a conclusion or action)

Answer

Ellen might proceed at several levels:

- George needed to be disciplined for the personal use of the copier. However, she has already taken the first step, a verbal warning. If he were to continue, then she could follow a progressive procedure (i.e., verbal warning, written warning, suspension, and termination), depending on the severity of the infraction.
- She needs to work with George to get him to appreciate the need for their own fundraising efforts as well as the cross-program needs of SAC. She should work with the leader of the cross-program task force at SAC to clarify George's role there as well as make her own needs explicit. Such confusion is common when subordinates divide their loyalties between two bosses, in this case, Ellen, the program head, and the cross-program task force leader.

Question 5

What should George do?

Action question (calls for a conclusion or action)

Answer

He needs to consider at least the following:

- Communicate better with Ellen on the needs of Omega house.
- Work with Ellen to make the Omega house fundraising committee more effective.
- Get Ellen and the task force leader at SAC together to clarify his role.
- Obviously, avoid using organizational resources for personal needs.

References

Albrecht, T.L. & Ropp, V. A. (1982). The study of network structuring in organizations through the use of triangulation. Western Journal of Speech Communication, 46, 162-178.

Chandler, A.D., Jr. (1962). Strategy and structure. Cambridge, MA.: MIT Press.

Daft, R. L. (1998). Organization theory and design. Cincinnati, OH: South-Western College Publishing.

Giddens, A. (1979). Central problems in social theory. Berkeley, CA: University of California Press.

Gioia, D.A. & Pitre, E. (1990). Multiple perspectives on theory building. Academy of Management Review, 15. 584-602.

Goldhaber, G.M. (1993). Organizational communication. Madison, WI: Brown & Benchmark.

Harris, T.E. (1993) Applied organizational communication: perspectives, principles, and pragmatics. Hillsdale, NJ: Lawrence Erlbaum Associates.

Monge, P., Edwards, J., & Kirste, K. (1978). The determinants of communication and communication structure in large organizations: A review of research. In B. Rubin's (eds.), <u>Communication yearbook</u> (pp. 1-21). New Brunswick, NJ: Transaction.

Riley, P. (1983). A structurationist account of political structures. <u>Administrative Science Quarterly, 28</u>, 414-437.

Epilogue

Omega house and SAC continue to provide valuable service to the community. Ellen still continues her management role, but George has left the organization.

LEADERSHIP OF TQM IN PANAMA

Topics (* = Primary topic with teaching plan)
*Hofstede's Cultural Dimensions
*High Power Distance
*Latin Collectivism
*Leadership
*Organizational Change
Innovation (TQM)
Culture (Latin)
Restructuring
International, Panama
Large Corporation (non-banking) Context

Case overview
       Jim had returned to Panama, where he had worked the previous two years (1990–1992) as the company HR manager, to conduct some interviews to better understand his research. Jim wondered how the latest company-change program, TQM, would fare. There were two different sites, Punta Blanca and Palo Amarillo, where Julian and Robert, respectively, served as general managers. Though not explicitly stated, the case illustrates behaviors that demonstrated that Julian was knowledgeable about the culture and wanted to see TQM succeed, whereas Robert saw TQM opportunistically as a means to help him further his agenda.

       The central question for Jim was, "How can TQM be adopted in these old, company-town operations of the Tropical Export Company? How can one expect participation to flourish when the leaders are so autocratic?"

       The production divisions mentioned above were part of the Tropical Export Company, a family controlled North American-based multinational corporation with very extensive production operations in Latin America that produce a labor-intensive tropical export product for industrialized markets, mainly North America and Europe. There are a number of production divisions spread throughout Central and South America, but Punta Blanca and Palo Amarillo are the ones Jim had served.

Industry
International agricultural commodities, characterized by intense cost competition and economies of scale production facilities

Teaching objectives
1. To familiarize students with the importance of the cultural context for managerial innovations.
2. To understand the implications of high power distance and collectivism in the Latin American context.
3. To appreciate how to implement organizational change in a cross-cultural context.

Other related cases in Volume 1
Julie's Call: Empowerment at Taco Bell (organizational change, TQM). Problems at Wukmier Home Electronics Warehouse (Hofstede's cultural dimensions). Split Operations at Sky and Arrow Airlines (organizational change). Unmovable Team (innovation).

Other related cases in Volume 2
A Selfish Request in Japan (Hofstede's cultural dimensions). Computer Services Team at AVIONICS (innovation, TQM). Insubordination or Unclear Loyalties? (leadership). Saving Private Ryan and Classic Leadership Models (leadership).

Intended courses and levels

This case is directed at undergraduate and graduate level human resource, organizational behavior/development/theory, total quality management and international business/cross-cultural management courses.

Analysis

Since culture reputedly accounts for more than 50 percent of the variance in managerial behavior (Hofstede, 1980), a leader must build on the cultural contingencies of the organizational setting when implementing organizational changes (Schein, 1992), such as TQM. In the Central American context, two cultural contingencies are particularly important: in-groups within Latin collectivist societies (Triandis et al., 1988) and high power distance—the acceptance of unequal distribution of power within social institutions (Hofstede, 1980).

Many Latinos feel a strong sense of belonging to a group (e.g., family, clan, and so forth). The strength of such in-groups is the foundation for the strong departmental loyalty. However, the "we–they" attitudes foster friction with other departments (out-groups). Such organizations often experience turf battles and inter-group tension that hamper cross-functional teamwork. Since Punta Blanca had been in existence for 70 years and Palo Amarillo for a century, many of the employees were from multigenerational families who felt a very strong bond to the organization and community. Organizational commitment was very high. In-groups in this context, particularly those within the production division where the team leader of the quality action team worked, took on a clan-like quality that made the bonds very powerful. Thus, the clan-like group feeling could serve as a cultural foundation for TQM in terms of group problem solving for those who belong to the group. On the other hand, it could work against TQM in the case of cross-functional teams imposed on an organization characterized by departmental or functional turfism.

Similarly, high power distance is another cultural characteristic that could aid the TQM process in terms of providing direction. Or it could inhibit the participatory process if subordinates are too fearful of reprisals from their leaders. Nevertheless, since TQM is predicated on high levels of employee involvement (Juran and Gryna, 1993; Ishikawa, 1985), the organizational implications of high power distance must be understood. At first glance, high employee involvement, or participation, seems to be in conflict with high power distance norms, where both leaders and subordinates expect that only leaders will have the unquestionable power to make decisions. Employees will find it more difficult to express their views as equals with management, and leaders will often find sharing power to be uncomfortable. For example, the autonomy of quality councils, which provide guidance and support for the TQM intervention (Scholtes, 1988), is sometimes threatened by the physical presence of top-level leaders in a high power distance setting. Though they may understand the importance of granting autonomy to a quality council, they are likely to assume control, be it direct or unobtrusive (Perrow, 1986), when the participants flounder or move in a direction unanticipated by the leaders.

As TQM generally entails changing the organizational culture, the role of the leader is crucial to the success of the intervention (Deming, 1986; Ishikawa, 1985; George, 1992; Juran and Gryna, 1993). Within this context, leaders must develop clear strategies for implementation. Ishikawa (1985) refers to this as TQM policy deployment—that is, consistent, explicit and concrete quality policies diffused to all levels of the organization. TQM policy deployment is based on the leader's perception of the contingencies affecting the implementation of TQM.

The conceptual implications for practice point to the necessity of acknowledging and building upon cultural and organizational contingencies. If high power distance is prominent, one cannot expect a quality council to assume an autonomous role if the general manager or leader is present—even as a silent observer. On the other hand, relatively leaderless groups were also incapable of functioning effectively. In the Punta Blanca case, using the second-in-command to lead the quality council seems to satisfy the need for leadership as well as allowing the quality council members to feel relatively free to express their views, thereby fostering a measure of autonomy essential to the quality council within TQM.

As indicated previously, Punta Blanca initially followed conventional TQM methodology and assigned cross-functional teams. In-groups and "turfism" hindered the effectiveness of these groups, so they resorted to functional teams, much like quality circles. When Julian realized that many organizational problems were of a cross-functional nature, he encouraged the quality council to have respected managers lead the quality action teams and choose their own members. This solution is consistent with both high power distance and in-groups, in that a recognized leader is free to choose members from his or her in-group. Such an in-group may reflect personal loyalties from various departments rather than functional area loyalties, thereby permitting a cross-functional approach to operate. This may be a way to avoid the resistance initially faced when cross-functional groups are imposed on organizational systems susceptible to turfism; one achieves cross-functional problem solving and communication, but in a culturally sensitive manner. In contrast, Robert described the TQM council as a "manager's council." Robert limited membership to department heads who "understood the way things work" (i.e. people who accept the command and control managerial orientation that had been in place for the century of Palo Amarillo's existence). Robert felt that participation was not appropriate. According to Robert, if he even asked a question, the subordinates were trying to guess what was on his mind. Perrow (1986) would refer to this as control over the cognitive premises for action, a powerful indirect control. Robert dealt with the one exceptional case, the young supervisor who challenged him, by removing him from the council.

Julian realized he had to withdraw himself, if any participation was to occur. He assigned the second-in-command to head the group. This still gave the council the leadership it lacked, and encouraged a more participative attitude on the council's part.

In both cases, Julian and Robert attempted to do what they felt was culturally appropriate to make the new TQM process work, yet remained consistent with their individual personalities. Thus, the initial action steps one might suggest, in regard to cultural contingencies, when implementing TQM, are for the leader to first interpret the organizational and national culture (Schein, 1992). Leaders should be sensitized to the culture of the specific location. The next step is to realize that cultural continuity can be a foundation for innovation while providing a satisfying environment for the employees (Salipante, 1992; Fry and Srivastva, 1992). This involves looking for solutions that incorporate cultural contingencies in a way that promotes rather than hinders the implementation process; the leader needs to make effective use of unobtrusive controls (Perrow, 1986) based on culture (e.g. Julian's cross-functional teams) in the implementation process. The leader also must understand that the innovation needs to be modified during the adoption process (Lewis and Seibold, 1993); an off-the-shelf or cookie cutter approach to innovation is especially risky when dealing with cultural contingencies.

Research methodology

The author was the human resources manager for the company at the time TQM was implemented. He worked at both production facilities with the two general managers, Julian and Robert. The author later wrote his dissertation on the TQM intervention.

Teaching plan

The various points that typically surface are listed in the following table. However, prior to or after the case analysis, you may wish to spend 30 minutes on a discussion of the cultural context in terms of Hofstede's dimensions. Students need to understand high power distance and the Latin version of collectivism before analyzing the case. The professor could also discuss the introduction of innovations to an organization. The actual discussion and analysis of the case should take 25-30 minutes.

Topic: Case Analysis
60-minute teaching plan

Pre-assignment: The entire class should have read and prepared the case. Individual reading and analysis of the case can take from 45 minutes to much longer, depending on the skills of the individual student. I tell students that I strongly prefer that they analyze the case as a group because I find that their group analyses are superior to ones prepared by individuals, as I mentioned in How one professor does in-depth case analysis (see page 211of this book). I find that individuals have a greater tendency to get off track on minor issues or come up with extreme, what I call "hormone-driven," solutions. As a group they prepare a spreadsheet such as that which follows. In my syllabus I allow students to choose to write up an analysis of a given case. Typically, they do five per semester but many more cases are assigned, usually one per week. Hence I ask for hands to see which students wrote up the case. I then select a volunteer to facilitate and another to serve as a scribe. I prefer student facilitation of cases because it gives them practice at facilitating a group and also provokes better dialogue, in that communication patterns are more likely to go from student to student within the audience. With an instructor leading the discussion, there is a tendency for communication patterns to go back and forth from the instructor, and in many cases, for the instructor to dominate the discussion. The preceding method works well with both adult students and juniors and seniors.

	Timing	Activity	Organization	Student Outcomes
I	0-15 minutes (10)	Situation analysis: summarize pertinent facts.	Student facilitated discussion with student scribe listing outcomes on white board	See "Typical Student Spreadsheet" that follows.
II	5 – 15 minutes (10)	Problem analysis: list those considered but not solved as well as developing clear problem statement.	Same as above	Same as above
III	15-25 minutes (10)	Theory application: must apply at least two and discuss.	Same as above	Same as above
IV	25 – 30 minutes (10)	Solution analysis: includes implementation plan.	Same as above	Same as above
V	30-45 minutes (5)	Anticipated consequences: Often overlooked and crucial to highlight.	Same as above	Same as above
VI	45 – 60 minutes (15)	Wrap up by instructor to emphasize points and cover additional points not mentioned by students.	Instructor leads discussion.	Student questioning and discussion, lead by instructor.

25-minute teaching plan:
Pre-assignment: Read case before class (45 minutes or more, depending on skills of student, plus one or more hours working in a group to develop the spreadsheet that follows.)
Activities. Abbreviate the previous plan but have instructor lead entire discussion, or simply lead students through Q & A of discussion questions with a wrap up at the end.

Typical Student Spreadsheet
(Either attached to the case write-up or generated on a white board in class)

Situation Analysis	Problem Analysis	Theory Application	Solution and Implementation	Anticipated Consequences
Long established machine bureaucracy production facilities; US multinational with quasi-neocolonialist orientation High power distance Latin collectivism Julian had extensive knowledge of culture. Robert used TQM in opportunistic manner	How to implement TQM in a strong organization culture characterized by high power distance and collectivism?	Hofstede's cultural dimensions with special emphasis on high power distance and collectivism. Jick's discussion of managing change.	Communicate change clearly. Train extensively. Be patient with pace of change. Build on existing cultural contingencies. Push for change. Evaluate progress; conduct post-mortem analyses of interventions.	Change could prove successful. Headquarters could lose interest in TQM and move on to something else. Manager could be transferred resulting in a loss of momentum for the change. Julian's approach worked whereas Robert's did not.

Discussion questions and answers

Question 1

How would you describe and contrast the different implementation processes in each location?
Analysis skills (breaking a concept into its parts and explaining their interrelationships, distinguishing relevant from extraneous material)

Answer

Initial focus:
• Robert's initial focus in Palo Amarillo was on alignment of the TQM process with his objectives. He referred to the quality council as a manager's council.
• Julian, in Punta Blanca, chose to wait for the quality council to develop its group identity, which it failed to do. He then imposed his solution: he assigned leadership to the second-in-command and

insisted that the council work with him. He believed in training, while simultaneously pushing persistently but patiently.

Strategy:

• Robert co-opted the council into a "manager's council."

•Julian allowed the council to flounder while pushing TQM downward. Julian tried to establish participation yet it failed without leadership. However, Julian was able to build on cultural contingencies to make cross-functional teams effective.

Question 2.

Was the way the two leaders implemented TQM culturally and functionally appropriate?
Evaluation skills (using a set of criteria to arrive at a reasoned judgment of the value of something)

Answer

Julian's solution built on high power distance. He named the second-in-command to head the quality council, who would provide leadership but yet be approachable enough to enable council members to participate. In the case, reference was made to the plastics company parallel; please recall that this was a subsidiary in the capital city that used the second-in-command to lead the quality council and didn't allow the general manager to be present when they were discussing issues. The second-in-command from the plastics company knew that the quality council members would defer too much to the general manager if he were present.

Julian's approach to the quality action teams (i.e., naming a respected team leader who then named his own team) also reflected the cultural value of high power distance and the in-group feeling prevalent in Latin America (i.e. the team leader named the members of the team).

Robert's approach was culturally appropriate in terms of how the organizational culture, as well as high power distance, permitted the general manager great leeway. However, though acceptable, this failed to produce the attitudinal change that was needed for TQM to become a part of the way the Tropical Export Company conducted its business.

References

Crozier, M. (1964). The bureaucratic phenomenon (trans. M. Crozier). Chicago: University of Chicago Press. (Original work published in 1963).

Deming, W.E. (1986). Out of the crisis. Cambridge, MA: MIT Press.

Fry, R. and Srivastva, S. (1992) in S. Srivastva and R. Fry (eds) Executive and organizational continuity: Managing the paradoxes of stability and change. San Francisco: Jossey-Bass.

George, S. (1992). The Baldridge quality system: The do-it-yourself way to transform your business. New York: John Wiley & Sons, Inc.

Hofstede, G.H. (1980). Culture's consequences in work-related values. Beverley Hills, CA: Sage.

Ishikawa, K. (1985). What is quality control? The Japanese way (trans. D.J. Lu). Englewood Cliffs, NJ: Prentice Hall, Inc.

Jick, T.D. (1993). Managing change: Cases and concepts. New York: Irwin McGraw-Hill.

Juran, J.M. and Gryna, F.M. (1993). Quality planning and analysis. New York: McGraw-Hill.

Lewis, L.K. and Seibold, D.R. (1993). Innovation modification during intraorganizational adoption, Academy of Management Review, 18:322–354.

Osland, A. (1996). The role of leadership and cultural contingencies in total quality management in Central America, Journal of Business and Management, 3:64–80.

Perrow, C. (1986). Complex organizations: a critical essay (3rd ed). New York: Random House.

Salipante, P.F. (1992). Providing continuity in change: the role of tradition in long term adaptation. In S. Srivastva and R. Fry (eds), Executive and organizational continuity: Managing the paradoxes of stability and change. San Francisco: Jossey-Bass.

Schein, E.H. (1992). Organizational culture and leadership. San Francisco: Jossey-Bass.

Scholtes, P.R. (1988). <u>The team handbook: How to use teams to improve quality.</u> Madison, WI: Joiner.

Triandis, H.C., Bontempo, R., Villareal, M., Asai, M. and Lucca, N. (1988). "Individualism and collectivism: Cross cultural perspectives on self–in group relationships," <u>Journal of Personality and Social Psychology, 54</u>: pp. 323–338.

Epilogue

Five years later, in 1997, Jim telephoned the organizational development manager of the company at his corporate office to inquire about the fate of TQM in both locations. He said that they were implementing a new approach entitled Operational Excellence, which focused more on the regional diffusion of specific production techniques. Though TQM was no longer in vogue as a formal approach, there had been some residual impact, such as the on-going existence of problem-solving teams, some use of statistical process control, and a more empowered workforce.

"Plus ça change, plus c'est la même chose"—the more things seem to change, the more they really remain the same. This saying is often used in reference to the resilience of social systems. Cultural foundations underlying social systems provide continuity to organizations (Fry and Srivastva, 1992; Salipante, 1992). They grow and change but all too often at a glacial pace. Faced with uncertainty, due to environmental competitive threats, managers deploy policies that are destined to enhance quality, empower previously passive subordinates, and so forth, all sincerely designed to enhance the competitive position of the organization in the marketplace. Then, when the managers later find that progress has been painfully slow or inadequate, they all too often jettison the particular change effort and embrace another without fully appreciating the foundation of continuity. People who are part of the cultural system of an organization usually do not or cannot perceive the basic foundation of continuity. One such underlying basic assumption is the power enjoyed by the elite, or high power distance, as conceptualized by Hofstede (1980).

The company's historical emphasis on command and control as expressed by the American and Central American managers and supervisors led the company to revert to its cultural foundation—power. Though vestiges of TQM remain, the shift to another managerial approach (i.e. "Operational Excellence") reflects the enduring foundation of power in the command-and-control orientation of the company and its managers. When the author asked one of the middle managers, who had successfully led a number of TQM teams, if he was more of a facilitator than a manager, he said: "I'm a boss." Being a boss is hard to let go of.

Teaching Notes
NEGOTIATING WORK HOURS

Topics (* = Primary topic with teaching plan)
*Communication
*Negotiation
International, Canada
Perception
Inter-group Conflict
Higher Education Context
Labor/Management Context

Case overview
       This case was developed to highlight effective communication skills. It can be used within a general business negotiation framework or to highlight the more specific labor/management negotiations. The case is taken from an actual labor/management negotiation at a Canadian university some years ago. The case is designed to demonstrate: (a) how initial assumptions of negotiators can limit the exploration of underlying interests; (b) how defensive communication tactics limit the exchange of information; (c) how effective questions can lead to a positive outcome. The case is broken into three sections, with group analysis and discussion occurring after each section. The first section, describing the background to the union and management perspectives, highlights how assumptions and lack of preparation limit the identification of underlying interests. The second part, which provides the dialogue that occurred during an initial negotiating session, reflects the defensive communication that often occurs within a negotiation session. Finally, the last section, which again is given in dialogue form, demonstrates the value of effective questions and appropriate responses. There are two potential handouts included with the case—"Effective Communications in Negotiations" and "Effective Listening" (see Appendices 1 and 2).

Industry
       University. Labor union. Canada.

Teaching objectives
1. To understand the importance of effective questioning in clarifying and obtaining information, and leading to the identification of acceptable alternatives.
2. To understand how defensive communications can limit the exchange of relevant information.
3. To understand how erroneous assumptions can limit the exchange of relevant information.

Other related cases in Volume 1
       A New Magazine in Nigeria (International case). Donor Services Department in Guatemala (International Case). Pearl Jam's Dispute with Ticketmaster (negotiations). Problems at Wukmier Home Electronics Warehouse (Unions). Split Operations at Sky and Arrow Airlines (intergroup conflict).

Other related cases in Volume 2
       A Selfish Request in Japan (International case, negotiations, Unions). Leadership of TQM in Panama (International Case). Violence at the United States Postal Service (Unions).

This teaching note was prepared by Loren Falkenberg, University of Calgary, and D. Ronald Franklin, University of Calgary. The case and teaching note were prepared as a basis for class discussion rather than to illustrate either effective or ineffective handling of administrative situations. Suggestions for improvement of this note should be sent to Teri.Tompkins@pepperdine.edu. Credit will be given in the next revision.

Intended course and levels

This case has been successfully used in undergraduate, MBA courses and in an executive program on business negotiations; it has specific relevance to courses in labor-management negotiations. In these programs it has followed sessions on preparation and planning for negotiations.

Analysis

Part 1

Susan has received the union's proposals for the upcoming bargaining of the current collective agreement, and one of the proposals that has been contentious in previous rounds of bargaining has been included. The proposal states that employee work hours are to be regulated to 40 hours a week performed between 8:00 a.m. and 4:30 p.m., Monday to Friday. Work performed outside of these hours is to be compensated at double the regular rate of pay. Susan is irritated that the union does not realize the proposal is unworkable within a university setting. Susan is very frustrated because the union has raised this issue in previous rounds of bargaining, and she thought it had been resolved by increasing the penalty payment for overtime work and by the addition of evening and weekend premiums for straight-time work. She did not want to have to address the issue again, particularly when it was costing the university more in compensation because of the last set of negotiations over this issue. In addition, Susan erroneously assumes that the National Federation of Public Service Union has encouraged the local union, which represents the employees, to include the "hours-of-work" model clause during this round of negotiations. She believes the National Federation wants to see this clause in every collective agreement to increase the amount of overtime pay. She also assumes that the National Federation is unaware or possibly ignoring the fact that the wording does not reflect the working conditions of non-office employees. On the basis of these assumptions, she prepares for the upcoming negotiations. She is not willing to make any further monetary concessions on this issue.

The union, on the other hand, is frustrated because the university has been unresponsive to an important issue to a small group of their membership (i.e., the electricians): how overtime payments can be avoided by the scheduling of weekend duties into the regular work schedule. The union assumes that the university is ignoring the arbitrary and unfair changes made to the assignment and compensation of overtime hours. They feel their only option is to submit the proposal again and force the issue with the university.

Part 2

As the bargaining begins, posturing and arguments ensue, following a traditional distributive format. The discussion focuses on positions rather than underlying interests and very little information is exchanged, with typical examples of defensive communication. At the end of the bargaining session, emotions are high and very little progress has been made. Susan realizes that the relationship is deteriorating without any advancement on the issue of overtime hours and, thus, requests closing the negotiations for the day.

Part 3

Susan has spent the evening and early morning assessing the stalemate and attempting to identify why it has occurred. She realizes that she does not understand the history of the proposal; that is, why it was first put forward four years ago. She also realizes that before progress can be made, she needs to understand which particular group of employees perceive that they have been "unfairly treated" and what specific changes they believe are needed. She decides that she must identify some very specific questions that will not create defensiveness in the union.

Once the negotiations move away from the wording and/or appropriateness of the proposal, more information is exchanged. Susan begins the negotiations in an open and trusting communication style and George reciprocates. Once the discussion is directed to the specific issues, a solution to the problem is identified. The rationale for the proposal, and the accepted solution, have nothing to do with the initial assumptions of the negotiators. In addition, both negotiators have had to move away from the stereotypical negotiation styles and enter a problem-solving mode. Part of the reason the two negotiators were able to do this was that trust had been established over the years and the union was willing to trust the university would correct the problem without changing the wording of the collective agreement.

In the past, it has been useful to provide students with the two handouts (see Appendices 1 and 2) to assist them in their analysis and answering of the questions.

Research methodology

This case reflects a true incident at a Canadian university. Names have been changed.

Teaching plan

A suggested pedagogy is to have the students work in groups of three or four, analyzing and answering the questions following each part of the case. Ideally, approximately 30 minutes is required for the analysis, group discussion, and class discussion for each section; in total, approximately 90 minutes works very well. The following 60-minute schedule has been used successfully.

Topic: Negotiations, including Effective Listening and Identifying Interests
60-minute teaching plan

Pre-assignment: None

	Timing	Activity	Organization	Student Outcomes
I	0 - 1 minute (1)	Introduction	After introduction, form students into groups of 4-5 members.	Prepare to discuss questions and answers.
II	1 - 10 minutes (9)	Students Read Part 1—Case In groups, students read and answer questions to Part 1.	Small Group Discussion	Students have learned the background of the negotiations.
III	10-20 minutes (10)	Whole class. Ask the whole class to identify appropriate negotiating strategy.	Large Group Discussion	Students review answers and hear others' opinions.
IV	20-30 minutes (10)	Mini-Lecture: Effective Listening	Whole Class. See Appendix 1 as a teaching tool.	Students have knowledge of effective listening skills.
V	30-40 minutes (10)	Students Read Part 2—Case In groups, students read and answer questions to Part 2.	Small Group Discussion	Students now read about the initial negotiations.
VI	40-50 minutes (10)	Students Read Part 3—Case In groups, students read and answer questions to Part 3.	Small Group Discussion	Students learn how the negotiation strategy has changed and the outcome.
VII	50-60 minutes (10)	Class Discussion. Summarize.	Students remain seated in small groups.	Realization of how assumptions influence negotiations—see Appendix 2.

25-minute teaching plan for Negotiation (two 25-minute plans to be completed over two days)
Pre-assignment: 1) Read Part 1 before coming to class (5 minutes reading time). 2) Write answers to the four questions in Part 1.
Mini-Lecture: Effective Listening (Appendix 1) (not included in 25 minutes). This lecture could be done between Part 1 and Part 2.
Day 1: Activities I, III (allow 10 minutes) and V (10 minutes) in 60 minute plan above.
Day 2: Activities VI, and VII (15 minutes)

Discussion questions and answers: Part 1

<u>Question 1</u>
What are Susan's assumptions as she enters the negotiations?
<u>Diagnostic question</u> (probes motives or causes)

<u>Answer</u>
Susan assumes that the overtime issue can be resolved through monetary means rather than a review of work scheduling. Thus, she believes that this issue was successfully resolved in the last round of negotiations at a significant financial cost to the university. Susan also assumes the union's proposal is based on the goals of the National Federation; that is, to have collective agreements contain provisions defining regular hours of work between 8:00 a.m. and 4:30 p.m. Based on these assumptions, Susan treats the union's proposal as inappropriate for an organization that requires employees to work in shifts or on the weekend and a waste of bargaining time. She believes it is an impossible position and wants to remove the proposal from the bargaining table.

<u>Question 2</u>
What are the union's assumptions as they enter negotiations?
<u>Diagnostic question</u> (probes motives or causes)

<u>Answer</u>
The union assumes management wants to maintain and/or increase control of scheduling and to find new ways to reduce compensation (i.e., not have to pay overtime). The union also assumes that management wants to eliminate overtime throughout the university.

<u>Question 3</u>
How do these assumptions influence their behaviors during negotiations?
<u>Cause-and-effect question</u> (asks for causal relationship between ideas, actions, or events)

<u>Answer</u>
Both parties believe the other party is not interested in addressing their specific needs or listening to their concerns; thus, they fail to openly communicate.
In the end, both parties adopt distributive tactics and end up with threats and a lack of movement on either side. In the previous four rounds of collective bargaining, neither side had been happy with the outcome. The union employees did not have the protection they wanted and management was paying more in compensation.

<u>Question 4</u>
What are the interests underlying the union's proposals (i.e., why is the union putting this proposal on the table)? What are the university's interests?
<u>Diagnostic question</u> (probes motives or causes)

<u>Answer</u>
The electricians, a small component of the union, are unhappy because they are working weekends (during the month of May) at straight time and have lost control over their work schedules.
The university needs to have the flexibility to schedule different groups of workers according to the needs and demands of operating a university. The university must manage a diverse range of operational details and keep compensation costs low.

Discussion Questions and Answers: Part 2

Question 1

Why did the negotiators fail to exchange any information?

Diagnostic question (probes motives or causes)

Answer

There are a number of points that can be raised here, such as a lack of appropriate questions and poor listening habits. However, a key point is the assumptions each negotiator had going into the negotiation. These assumptions led both negotiators to anticipate the other party's viewpoint and answers. In other words, Susan assumed that the problems were a) a monetary issue, b) the union responding to pressure from the National Federation, and c) the union not trying to understand the limitations management had to work under. In contrast, George was assuming that Susan would not listen to him and that management was only interested in the impact on the bottom line. Unfortunately, Susan's comment about contracting out only reinforced George's beliefs and George's comments about fairness and overtime compensation reinforced Susan's belief about the union's position.

Question 2

What specific communication mistakes were made by the negotiators? Provide examples.

Analysis skills (breaking a concept into its parts and explaining their interrelationships, distinguishing relevant from extraneous material)

Answer

Focusing on what you are going to say next—After George's response to Susan's opening question, she suggested that the university would have to contract out if they accepted the union's proposal; she did not respond to the issue of shift work or weekend work. At another point, when Susan asked why such a restrictive clause was necessary, George responded, "You know why—your managers don't know how to treat people fairly".

Did not respond in a supportive manner—At different points, both Susan and George responded with threats, such as the union going on strike or the university contracting out.

Inaccurate inferences were made—George asked, "Why are you unwilling to give our people decent working conditions?" and "Other employers seem to manage why can't the university?"

Questions were close-ended and emotional—George asked, "Why can't you treat the staff decently?" Susan asked, "Now, who is making threats?"

Positions were taken at the beginning of the discussion—Both parties stated that the other party had to move and give concessions; they would not move. Susan noted, "Your proposal is still not acceptable," and "You know we can't accept your proposal." George ended the session with, "When you come back tomorrow, be prepared to make some real concessions on this issue."

Question 3

When are breaks effective in a negotiation? Comment on the use of breaks in this negotiation.

Application skills (using information in a new context to solve a problem, answer a question, or perform a task)

Answer

Breaks often are needed to reduce emotional tensions and allow the parties to review their positions. If the parties take the time to rethink the issue under discussion and identify questions that will address the underlying interests, a break can be effective. Also, if emotions are dissipated to the point where the parties can discuss the issue without threats, a break can be effective.

Susan recognized that the relationship was deteriorating, particularly with threats being made, and that little progress was being made on resolving the overtime issue. She also believed a good relationship was critical to this set of negotiations and to the university in general. Thus, it was appropriate to ask for the breaks. However, it is also important to reflect, check assumptions, and identify how to get the negotiations back on track.

Question 4
What needs to be done to get the negotiation back on track?
<u>Action question</u> (calls for a conclusion or action)

Answer
Away from the negotiating table, the parties should:

- Identify the assumptions they are making and check them for accuracy.
- Identify questions that will clarify interests and identify alternative actions.
- Try to develop different perspectives that reflect the other party's views.
  At the negotiating table, each party should:
- Review the history behind the proposal (why did it initially become part of the bargaining?).
- Ask for specific examples of shift scheduling problems.
- Identify the groups experiencing shift scheduling problems.
- In general, ask specific questions and probe for specific responses.

Discussion Questions and Answers: Part 3

Question 1
Why did this interaction produce a better outcome? What were the turning points?
<u>Cause-and-effect question</u> (asks for causal relationship between ideas, actions, or events)

Answer
Susan was asking very specific questions and George was providing specific examples in his answers to the questions. There was probably more than one turning point. The first was at the beginning of the negotiation session when Susan opened in a less confrontational manner and George responded in a supportive manner. The second was when Susan recognized that both parties shared a mutual goal, getting the maintenance work done in May. A final turning point was when George was willing to trust Susan and accept the university's guarantee that it would no longer make seasonal changes in the electrical crew's schedule.

Question 2
How did the initial assumptions of the negotiators impact the exchange of information in the first session? How did they affect the exchange of information in the second session?
<u>Summary question</u> (elicits syntheses)

Answer
The questions and answers asked in the first round of discussions focused on (a) management's inability to provide further premiums for overtime and weekend work, (b) the scheduling limitations the university must work under, and (c) the lack of sensitivity of management to the needs of the members of the bargaining unit. The discussion did not change the assumptions of either party, nor did it improve the flow of information. During the break, both parties undertook activities that led to a change in assumptions. Once the parties looked to identify the information that was needed to clarify the issues and checked with constituents, assumptions were modified and more information was exchanged.

Question 3
Identify the elements of positive communication in this discussion.
<u>Application skills</u> (using information in a new context to solve a problem, answer a question, or perform a task)

Answer

Specific questions were asked—Susan opened with, "What incident or issue made your members believe that they needed a restrictive hours-of-work clause to protect them?"

Probes were used for elaboration—Susan asked, "Why are the shifts changed each year?" or "Why did the crew prefer the longer working hours?" George asked, "And they will be paid for the weekend work at the overtime rates, just like the collective agreement says?"

Paraphrasing went beyond repetition—Susan asked, "Then am I correct in assuming that you don't disagree with the need to get the work done on weekends in May?" or "Are you saying that the crew members preferred the seven-day shifts?" George asked, "You're saying that if we drop our hours-of-work proposal, you'll promise not to change the electrical maintenance crew's shift schedule for the month of May each year?"

Focus on what is being said and on the problem—George identified the specific issues surrounding the May schedule for the electrical crews—some wanted overtime pay compensation and others wanted time off. He moved from the vague response of protecting workers' rights to the specific issues.

Being sensitive to the speaker's needs—At the end of the dialogue it would have been easy for Susan to become angry with George for questioning the trust that she felt was in place; however, when he asked for time to check with his membership, she agreed to a fifteen-minute break.

Separated facts from inferences—George made a strong inference that management couldn't be trusted and employees needed formal protection through the collective agreement. Susan responded by saying, "We've always kept our word. We've never let you down before. George, we could spend weeks trying to come up with some wording that would satisfy both of us or we can agree to our proposal and get on with other matters."

Question 4

Which questions were the most effective? Why?
Summary question (elicits syntheses)

Answer

This is a summary question and opens a discussion for the learning points highlighted previously in these teaching notes. In addition, the following are summary learning points:

- Good negotiators continually check the accuracy of their assumptions.
- Effective questions acknowledge what has been said.
- Effective questions are aimed at identifying the underlying interests and needs of the other party.
- Effective questions reduce ambiguity and uncertainty.
- Effective questions help the parties focus and reexamine positions.
- Effective questions encourage communication.

References

Fisher, Roger, and Ury, William, (1991). Getting to yes: Negotiating agreement without giving in. Penguin.

Ury, William. (1993). Getting past no: Negotiating your way from confrontation to cooperation. Bantam Doubleday Dell.

Walton, Richard E., Cutcher, Joel E., McKersie, Robert B. (1994). Strategic negotiations: A theory of change in labor-management relations. Harvard Business School.

Epilogue

The changes were implemented and the hours-of-work proposal was never raised again. Susan and George continued as head negotiators for the next four sets of negotiations.

APPENDIX 1
Effective Listening

Skills Needed for Effective Listening	Diagnostic Questions to Evaluate Your Skills	Comments
Focus attention on speaker.	• Did you shift from being speaker to listener? • Did you interrupt the speaker? • Were you distracted? • Did you hear the speaker out or did you fill in gaps and listen selectively? • Were you sensitive to the speaker's needs. • Did you listen openly or defensively?	• Avoid "pseudo" listening—"hearing" is not "listening". • Focus on listening—not what you are going to say next. • Eliminate physical and mental distractions. • Do not mentally interrupt, anticipate, criticize or disregard what is said. • Withhold judgments. • Focus on problem.
Listen to understand.	• Did you listen actively? • Did you mentally organize what is said? • Did you respond in a supportive manner? • Did you pay attention to non-verbal cues?	• Active listening requires physical and mental attention (including eye contact). • We listen with only 25% to 50% efficiency. • Acknowledge what is said. • Watch facial expressions, body movements, and posture. Listen for tone and voice inflection.
Listen critically.	• Did you separate facts from inferences? • Did you evaluate inferences?	• Inferences are drawn from facts. • Inferences are often wrong.
Talk less.	• Did you listen as much or more than you talked?	• Listening should occupy more than 50% of our time.

APPENDIX 2
Identifying The "Real" Interests

	SUSAN	GEORGE
ASSUMPTIONS	• Union's position is driven by the National Federation. • Union is ignoring the variations in working conditions across the university. • Union just wants to find another way to get more money.	• University wants to save money at the expense of employees. • University wants more flexibility in work assignments. • University not concerned about the personal consequences for work schedules.
POSITION	• No more concessions on this issue—status quo remains.	• Any work done outside of regular work hours (8:30 a.m. – 4:30 p.m., Monday to Friday) to be paid at an overtime rate.
INTERESTS	• Flexibility in scheduling. • Control compensation costs. • Not unreasonable for electricians to return to previous work schedules in May.	• For electricians to regain some control over work schedules.

Teaching Note
PREFERENTIAL TREATMENT?

Topics (* = Primary topics with teaching plan)
   *Discrimination
   *Attractions
   *Power/Authority
   *Equity Theory
   *Motivation
   Interracial Differences and Conflict
   Poor Communication
   Interpersonal Conflict
   Higher Education Context

Case overview

     Paul was a Korean American student in his junior year at the Upland University. When he began his educational career, he had intended to become a doctor. However, he had tremendous difficulty during his sophomore year with several of the courses necessary to complete this major. During this difficult time he had sought the council of a respected professor and academic advisor, Dr. Richard David. Although he did not receive any significant support or encouragement from Dr. David, there was no reason to attribute the reasons behind his lack of enthusiasm to anything other than a shortcoming in his personality. That is, not until after his final meeting with the professor.

     Paul has just finished another relatively unproductive consultation with Dr. David, regarding his options after graduation, when he discovered he had forgotten his cap. When he returned to retrieve it, there was another student in consultation with Dr. David. Paul did not want to disturb them so he waited patiently in the hallway outside the open office door. Neither of the participants in the consultation was aware of his presence and Paul could not help but overhear their conversation. The other student had much in common with Paul's situation and was also looking for advice regarding what to do after graduation. However, this student was a Caucasian female and the difference in Dr. David's treatment of her and his treatment of Paul was astounding. Dr. David spoke animatedly with the student regarding her options, which was very different from the cold, removed attitude his used with Paul.

     After the lengthy consultation was finally over Paul entered the office, snatched his cap off of the desk and walked out without saying anything to the professor. He wondered what he should do.

Industry

     A medium-sized university. Traditional, quantitative grades are not given, only written, qualitative evaluations. Relationship building between faculty/staff and students is encouraged and expected.

Teaching objectives:

1. To introduce students to the concepts of discrimination, power/authority, and equity theory.
2. To teach students to explain "why" people behave as they do in the case; that is, to link case facts to course theories.
3. To recognize how symptoms of behavior can point to the real problem.
4. To decide what steps are appropriate if you were in Paul's position.
5. To recognize appropriate procedures in discrimination.

This teaching note was prepared by Brian Park and Teri C. Tompkins, University of Redlands. The case and teaching note were prepared as a basis for class discussion rather than to illustrate either effective or ineffective handling of administrative situations. Suggestions for improvement of this note should be sent to Teri.Tompkins@pepperdine.edu. Credit will be given in the next revision.

Other related cases in Volume 1

A New Magazine in Nigeria (authority, equity). Donor Services Department in Guatemala (equity). Fired! (motivation). Handling Problems at Japan Auto (motivation). Heart Attack (interracial differences and conflict). La Cabaret (interracial differences and conflict). Problems at Wukmier Home Electronics Warehouse (interracial differences and conflict). Unmovable Team (motivation).

Other related cases in Volume 2

Angry Branch Manager (interracial differences and conflict). Cafe Latte (equity). Reputation in Jeopardy (authority). Then There Was One (motivation). The Safety Memo (authority). Unprofessional Conduct (interracial differences and conflict). Violence at the United States Postal Service (interracial differences and conflict).

Intended courses and levels:

This case looks at individual perceptions, attraction, and discrimination. It fits at the individual level of organizational behavior, primarily at the undergraduate level. It is also appropriate for a human resource class in discrimination.

Analysis

All related analysis and references are embedded in the answers to the questions.

Research methodology

This case reflects the recollections of Paul in the case. The case is a true incident. The university and people have been disguised.

Teaching plan

Topic: Discrimination, Equity, and Attraction

60-minute teaching plan

Pre-assignment: Read case (15 minutes)

	Timing	Activity	Organization	Student Outcomes
I	0-5 minutes (5)	Summarize the case facts.	Ask or appoint a "volunteer".	Orientation and refresher on case.
II	5-15 minutes (10)	Ask: What is discrimination?	Full class discussion.	Knowledge of key issues: <ul><li>Discrimination: specific behaviors toward members of that group which are unfair in comparison with behaviors toward members of other groups.</li><li>Prejudice refers to an intolerant, unfair, or unfavorable attitude toward another group of people.</li><li>Racism is any attitude, action, or institutional structure that subordinates a person because of his or her color.</li></ul>
III	15 – 20 minutes (5)	Define equity.	Mini-lecture	Knowledge of key concepts: Equity—judgments about relational fairness based on the ratio of perceived inputs (I) and perceived outcomes (O) compared to a similar ratio of other person.

	Timing	Activity	Organization	Student Outcomes
IV	20 – 30 minutes (10)	Ask: *How can Paul use equity to decide whether or not Dr. David discriminated against him?*	Class discussion	Analysis: 1. Paul perceives that his inputs are similar to the female student. 2. He perceives that he has been treated inequitably. 3. It is not clear how Dr. David or the other student perceive the situation.
V	40 – 50 minutes (10)	Define attraction.	Mini-lecture.	Knowledge of six bases to attraction: 1. Similar beliefs, values, and personality characteristics. 2. Satisfies our needs. 3. Is physically attractive. 4. Is pleasant or agreeable. 5. Reciprocates our liking 6. Is in geographical proximity to us.
VI	50 – 60 minutes (10)	Ask: *Using attraction as a factor, how did Dr. David's behavior towards the female student differentiate from his behavior towards Paul?*	Full class discussion. Encourage students to justify their suggestions.	Analysis: Dr. David <u>may</u> been more attracted to the female student than he was to Paul.

25-minute teaching plan
Preassignment: Read case before class
Use Activities I, V, and VI from the 60-minute plan.

Topic: Power and Authority

60-minute teaching plan

Pre assignment: Read the case before class. (15 minutes)

	Timing	Activity	Organization	Student Outcomes
I	0-5 minutes (5)	Summarize the case facts.	Ask or appoint a "volunteer"	Orientation and refresher on case
II.	5 – 10 minutes (5)	Ask: *What other factors, if not discrimination, attraction, personality differences, and personal circumstances could have affected Dr. David's behavior towards Paul?*	Class discussion.	Synthesis: Power and authority may be another framework for explaining the situation.
II.	10 – 20 minutes (10)	Define power and authority.	Mini-lecture.	Five sources of power: 1. Reward Power 2. Coercive Power 3. Legitimate Power 4. Referent Power

	Timing	Activity	Organization	Student Outcomes
				5. Expert Power Authority is power from legitimate sources, recognized by subordinates.
III	30 –40 minutes (10)	*Explain the relevance of power and authority to explain why Paul did not confront Dr. David.*	Class discussion.	As academic advisor, Dr. David had all five sources of power, but it was coercive power that was the main influence on Paul. He felt threatened by Dr. David and did not want to cross him by being confrontational about the perceived inequity.
IV	40 – 50 minutes (10)	Ask: *What would you do if you were Paul?*	Class discussion.	Paul's options include: 1. Report the incident to the university and file charges of discrimination. 2. Talk to the female student. 3. Write a petition to the school requesting that Dr. David be reprimanded. 4. Follow up on the school's investigation of possible discrimination and sexual harassment on the part of Dr. David. 5. Find another advisor. 6. Confront Dr. David. Paul could make another appointment and tell Dr. David that he could not help but observe that his interactions with the other student were much different that their interactions. He could ask Dr. David to explain why.
V	50 – 60 minutes (10)	Hand out or read epilogue found in this teaching note. Ask *reactions.*	Individual or full class reading, followed by full class discussion.	Student reactions will vary. Point out or ask for places where there was agreement and disagreement between student suggestions and Paul's actions.

25-minute teaching plan
Pre-assignment: Read case before class (15 minutes)
Activities. Do activities I, II, III in the 60-minute plan.

Discussion questions and answers

Question 1

What factors, attitudes, beliefs, and circumstantial predicaments affected Dr. David's behavior towards Paul?"

Analysis skill (breaking a concept into its parts and explaining their interrelationships: distinguishing relevant from extraneous material)

Answer

People do not always behave as their expressed attitudes and beliefs would lead us to expect. Therefore, people's assumptions about the motivations of other's behavior can frequently lead us astray.

Especially when communication is limited. Without exploring all the possibilities, we may never truly understand the true intent, beliefs, and attitudes of others we encounter. Such is the reason to explore the possible factors that dictated Dr. David's behavior towards Paul.

There are three main motivations or factors that could explain Dr. David's behavior: 1. personality differences/clash; 2. Apathy due to various circumstantial reasons: over-worked, personal problems, does not know Paul well; 3. Discrimination: racial discrimination and/or sexual discrimination.

Daryl J. Bem's self-perception theory suggests that many of our attitudes are based on "self-observation" (as cited in Carlson, 1990, p. 587-588). When individuals' motives are unclear, "they come to know their own attitudes, emotions, and other internal states, partially by inferring them from observations of their own overt behavior and/or the circumstances in which this behavior occurs" (Deaux & Wrightsman,1988, p. 69-70). For example, in one of Bem's experiments, "subjects who are paid $1 to persuade fellow students to perform a boring task have a more favorable attitude toward it than those paid $20, because genuine interest is a more likely explanation for their own behavior than the receipt of such a small sum" (Carlson, 1990, p. 600). Applying Bem's theory, Dr. David's perception of the situation constituted his behavior towards Paul. So, the question is, how did Dr. David perceive his encounter with Paul? What was his self-observation?

What Dr. David experienced and perceived is not clear, but we can speculatively say that his experience with Paul and his own observation of his behavior towards him was not positive. In contrast to his interaction with the female student, Dr. David and Paul's interaction was brief, concise, and formal. However, it is presumptuous to assume that he disliked Paul, or that he exhibited discriminatory behavior.

One possible interpretation is that Dr. David's personality clashed with Paul's. Paul and Dr. David came from different backgrounds and culture. They had a twenty-year age gap and they could have had different interests; the possibilities of their differences are endless.

"As social animals, each of us is part of an ongoing social process, an interaction between the self and others" (Carlson, 1990, p.600), and in these interactions we make choices whether to develop closer relationships. More often than not, each individual makes this decision depending on the level of differences and similarities they detect. One does not randomly choose to become closer to another, but rather, it is systematic. The measure of differences and similarities of personality, interests, and overall person is determined before making such a decision. Therefore, Dr. David observed reasons to choose not to become more closely acquainted with Paul; hence, his interaction was different in contrast to the interaction with the female student.

The second factor is Dr. David's personal circumstances. Was Dr. David going through some difficulties in his life? Was he overworked? These questions are important in understanding Dr. David's position.

Recently, industries all over the world began to realize the correlation between job performance and the quality of personal life of their employees. Contrary to the beliefs of the early 20th century industrialists, (Morgan, 1997, p. 33), people are not independent of their personal problems when it comes to work. Some may be able to detach themselves from thinking about the problems they face temporarily and accomplish the given task; however, the success of this tactic is questionable.

Understanding the implications of the affects of personal problems, it is easy to entertain the possibility that Dr. David was facing some problems of his own—he may have been overworked and/or facing personal crisis—and therefore could not perform his job properly as an academic advisor.

As much as these others factors are possible reasons for Dr. David's behavior, so is discrimination. Given his position as academic advisor to a portion of the student body at the Upland University, Dr. David was entrusted with the task of aiding each student, regardless of their differences, to better their academic experience. However, as far as professional conduct is concerned, he discriminantly treated one student more favorably than the other.

During his interaction with Paul, Dr. David was apathetic, reluctant to show a proper display of guidance to the concerns addressed to him. On the other hand, when the female student indicated a similar concern he went as far as offering her his home telephone number. Dr. David's behavior towards the female student might be defined as sexual harassment, and his behavior towards Paul might as easily be defined as discrimination.

Question 2

What is discrimination?

Knowledge skill (remember previously learned material such as definitions, principles, formulas). References, Deaux, 1988, p. 463-464, Carlson, 1990, p. 588.

Answer

To understand the definition of discrimination, one must also understand the definition of prejudice. Prejudice and discrimination, although the terms are often used interchangeably, are actually two distinct concepts. "Prejudice refers to an intolerant, unfair, or unfavorable attitude toward another group of people" (Deaux, 1988, p. 463). Typically, prejudice implies an emotional response to a particular group of people. Discrimination refers to "specific behaviors toward members of that group which are unfair in comparison with behaviors toward members of other groups" (Deaux, 1988, p.463). For example, refusing admission to a female student because of her gender while accepting an equally qualified male student would constitute discriminatory behavior.

The U.S. Commission on Civil Rights has defined racism as "any attitude, action, or institutional structure which subordinates a person because of his or her color" (Deaux, 1988, p. 464). Such a definition incorporates both negative attitudes and discriminatory behavior, and acknowledges that racism can exist on either an individual or an institutional level. Due to mandated laws and statutes, and because such behaviors are less socially acceptable to show, blatant racism, sexism, etc., are less prevalent than they once were, however, those underlying attitudes can still be expressed through "symbolic discrimination" (Carlson, 1990, p. 588).

"Symbolic discrimination is frequently covert and subtle," and is pervasive in many levels of society. It has its roots, Sears and Kinder argue, "in early-learned stereotypes and in fundamental feelings about certain social groups and its members" (Carlson, p. 588). Again, symbolic discrimination has replaced more overt forms of discrimination and prejudice. "Individuals who hold such deep-seated attitudes are likely to behave discriminantly, not because their personal self-interest is at stake but rather because of more general racist, sexist, and etc. attitudes; prejudice" (Carlson, p. 589).

Question 3

Define equity. Was Paul treated fairly by Dr. David?

Application skills (using information in a new context to solve a problem, answer a question, or perform a task).

Answer

Equity suggests that people can determine judgments about relational fairness by "forming a ratio of their perceived investments or inputs (I) and perceived rewards or outcomes (O)." They then compare this ratio to a similar ratio of some other person (Wagner and Hollenbeck, 1998, p. 170). The equity formula is stated as follows for a fair system:

Equity formula

$$\frac{\text{Your Input}}{\text{Your Output}} = \frac{\text{Input of reference person}}{\text{Output of reference person}}$$

The outcome need not be exactly the same to define fairness, as long as those receiving fewer desirable outcomes than someone else see themselves as contributing fewer inputs than the other person. The key element to equity is to fairly weigh and measure all inputs and outputs before inserting them into the formula. For instance, an individual measuring fairness must not subjectively view their input or output; they cannot manipulate the truth. Still, equity can be problematic; equity judgments are based on individual perceptions of inputs and outcomes, no matter how much one tries to objectively present the data.

Paul had no reason to believe he was being treated unfairly until he observed the professor with another advisee. To most accurately utilize equity and its formula, Paul's interaction with Dr. David must be equally and objectively compared to the interaction between the female student and Dr. David. But before comparing the outcomes of each interaction, each person's input must be compared:

	Paul's input	The female student's input
Number of sessions	7 meetings; including the last meeting with Dr. David	Unknown
Conversation topic	Graduate schools	Graduate schools
Age	Twenty/junior	Early twenties/junior
The urgency of the topic	Same	Same
Grade Point	3.6 Average	Unknown
Gender	Male	Female
Race	Korean	Caucasian
Inquisitiveness	Same	Same

The output is as follows:

	Output to Paul	Output to the female student
Time spent	15 minutes	30 minutes
level of friendliness	Very unfriendly	Very friendly
level of attentiveness	Completely lacking	Very attentive
level of talkativeness	Less than 6 retorts	More than 20
level of aid	One sentence assistance	References, lists, and personal opinion
Frequency of silence	Duration of 2-5 minutes	Almost none
Miscellaneous	None	Home phone number

According to the data gathered, Paul's ratio does not appear to match the female student's ratio. Therefore, Paul has concluded that his interaction with Dr. David was not equitable in contrast to Dr. David's interaction with the female student. Paul's observation is missing some key data, however, which could lead him to a false conclusion.

Question 4
Define attraction. Using attraction as a factor, how did Dr. David's behavior towards the female student differentiate from his behavior towards Paul?
Knowledge skills (remember previously learned material such as definitions, principles, and formulas)
Answer
"No man is an Island, entirely of itself; every man is a piece of the continent, a part of the main; if Clod be washed away by the sea, Europe is the less, as well as if a Promontories were, as well as if a Mannor of thy friends or of thine own were; any man's death diminishes me, because I am involved in mankind; and therefore never send to know for whom the bell tolls; it tolls for thee." John Donne

Sociologists, psychologists, anthropologists, physicists, and the rest of the world can attest to the fact that no one person is an island. Social comparison theory proposes that people seek out interaction with others because we, as people, look to other people as a way to evaluate our own attitudes and abilities (Deaux, 1988, p.86). Affiliation with others also provides each individual with comfort and safety, and fulfills other desires and needs we have as humans. With the understanding that people are social animals and that each person needs and chooses to affiliate with other people, attraction can be understood as being a reason or a component of the need of the individual to affiliate with others in the society.

What makes people attractive to us? According to several independent researches conducted by different psychologists and sociologists, there are six bases to attraction: 1. Similar beliefs, values, and personality characteristics; 2. Satisfies our needs; 3. Is physically attractive; 4. Is pleasant or agreeable; 5. Reciprocates our liking; and 6. Is in geographical proximity to us (Deaux, 1988, p. 247).

Dr. David was in his mid-forties and not married. However, it is crass to assume that Dr. David was attracted to the female student before evaluating the circumstance of their interaction. To entertain and evaluate the possibility of his attraction to the female student, we must parallel his interaction with the female student with the six bases of attraction.

First, the concept of similar beliefs, values, and personality characteristics; which explains that we like people whose attitudes and values agree with ours, and we dislike those who disagree with us. There is a distinct possibility that Dr. David found similarities with the female student (e.g. she may be pursuing an undergraduate degree in the same field that Dr. David once pursued, came from the same city, state, have similar taste in clothing style, etc.). However, this information can only be speculative because there is not enough information to come to an informed conclusion.

Second, satisfies one's needs; does the female student satisfy Dr. David's needs. It is hard to understand the various domains of needs and the resources each person brings to the relationship; however, there is a distinct possibility that she could satisfy his needs.

Third, was there a physical attraction? This is also subjective and relative to what physicalities Dr. David finds appealing; yet, it is a possibility. Fourth, was the female student agreeable to Dr. David? Universally, people like people who are nice or who do nice things, and when we receive such responses from others we are naturally placed in a jovial mood. Even though there may be other reasons for being in such a mood, in the case of Dr. David, he was laughing, making jokes, smiling at the female student, when little over 5 minutes earlier he displayed apathy and indifference during his interaction with Paul. Fortunately, happiness is somewhat quantifiable, and therefore Dr. David's behavior with the female student may indicate that he found her more pleasant and agreeable than Paul.

Fifth, was their reciprocal liking; was the female student reciprocating Dr. David's positive behavior? The observation of the interaction indicates that the female student was reciprocating Dr. David's behavior. The definition of reciprocating "like" is a bit unclear, however, in terms of reciprocating the positive behavior of Dr. David, the female student responded in the same manner as she was treated.

Sixth, propinquity; were Dr. David and the female student within a close proximity? Yes. There aren't clear indications that Dr. David was attracted to the female student, however, there also isn't a clear indication that he was not. If he felt attraction towards the female student, it is only obvious that Dr. David would have treated her differently, but if there was no attraction, the difference in his behavior lies in some other factor.

Question 5

What other factors, if not discrimination, attraction, personality differences, and personal circumstances could have affected Dr. David's behavior towards Paul?

Analysis skills (breaking a concept into its parts and explaining their interrelationships: distinguishing relevant from extraneous material)

Answer

Paul's records indicated to Dr. David that he did not perform well when he was majoring in biochemistry, and, prior to the last meeting, Dr. David had met with Paul several times regarding his academic standing which included possible suspension from school due to his performance. Due to the negative nature of his interaction with Paul, Dr. David may have formulated a negative image of Paul as a student. He may further conclude from his past experience with Paul that there is no reason to further aid a student who is doomed with underachievement. Regardless of Paul's academic standing as a psychology major, getting almost straight A's, Dr. David's impression of Paul may have remained the same.

Question 6

Define power/authority and explain its relevance when Paul did not confront Dr. David.

Knowledge skills (remember previously learned material such as definitions, principles, and formulas)

Answer

Power and authority go hand in hand. Without authority there can't be power and without power there can't be authority. Power and authority have many forms, shapes, and sizes, but universally, they have influence over people. People generally comply with the requests of people in authority, and such obedience is generally approved by society at large. However, power and authority can easily be abused. In Stanley Milgran's experiment, people sometimes obeyed authority figures to the point of doing something that they believed might hurt someone severely, or even causing their death (Carlson, 1990, p. 600). The influence of power/authority is immense and it can cause people to lose correct, rational judgment. This abusive quality of power expands many different contexts of human relationships. Authority is not only within the confines of politics, or only where people think it can exist, but it exists in various dimensions of social interactions.

John French and Bertram Raven further denote the universal existence and applicability of power and authority by identifying their major bases, or sources (Hollenbeck & Wagner, 1998, p. 247). French and Raven identify five components of power: 1. Reward power, based on the ability to allocate rewarding outcomes—either the receipt of positive things or the elimination of negative things; 2. Coercive power, based on the distribution of undesirable outcomes—either the receipt of something negative or the removal of something positive; 3. Legitimate power, based on norms, values, and beliefs that particular individuals have the legitimate right to influence others; 4. Referent power, individuals who are held in such esteem by others that they are given the right to influence; and 5. Expert power, based on the possession of expertise, knowledge, and talent.

According to French and Raven's identification of different sources and dimensions of power, one need not be a king, politician, or in any particular position to have power and authority. The power position is relative to the eyes of the person being influenced by it. In this case, Paul perceived Dr. David to be seated on the throne of "power." According to the five different bases of power, Dr. David held "reward power." As an academic advisor and also as a professor of the university, Dr. David had the power to reward his students in the form of praise, which boosts the fragile self-esteem of young college students. He could reward students with valuable advice regarding various aspects of the field of academia. Finally, he could reward students with potential recommendation letters. The negative consequences are, of course, eliminating the possibility of the above rewards.

In addition, there is the factor of intimidation. Just as in Milgram's experiments, power influences people to sometimes mindlessly obey and conform. Were the people in the experiment agreeing, regardless of the nature of request, based solely on the fact that the person instructing them is wearing a white coat? Most likely not. The subjects of the experiment were confounded by the intimidation of the authority figure; they could not possibly think of doing anything other than their instructions advised. Paul also fell victim to this gravity of intimidation.

Question 7

What would you do if you were Paul?

Synthesis skills (putting parts together to form a new whole; solving a problem requiring creativity or originality)

Answer

Paul could report the incident to the university and file charges of discrimination. Dr. David may easily be doing this to other students, so it is important to let him know that such behavior is not tolerated. However, the case will be Dr. David's words against Paul's unless other students decide to substantiate Paul's claim, and thus, Paul may have difficulty proving his case.

Pros: Dr. David may be legally reprimanded; other students of color might benefit from his suspension or change of behavior; Upland University could avoid possible future law suits; other faculty members may learn from the mistake of a fellow colleague; Paul will receive his justice.

Cons: The process would be a long one, thus it will take a lot of Paul's time; a possibility of being alienated by other professors; the school might not take immediate action due to the time it would take to process the case; Paul might not see a conclusion before graduation.

Paul could talk to the female student. She also may not understand what exactly happened to her and may be confused about her encounter with the advisor and possible sexual harassment. She could also verify Paul's speculations about Dr. David's discriminatory behavior towards him, and therefore strengthen his case against him. Measuring input and output using the equity theory could do this.

Pro: This could strengthen Paul's case; the female student will also be vindicated for the wrong done to her (assuming she might have felt sexual discrimination).

Con: The female student might not want to be involved in the situation; the school may not see the use of equity theory as valid.

Paul could write a petition to the school requesting that Dr. David be reprimanded.

Pro: Other students may well support Paul's case and the faculty members may also be supportive.

Cons: There also is a chance that the students will be insensitive to a predicament that does not personally affect them. The professors and other faculty members might take Dr. David's side and alienate Paul. This could cause other issues and problems to rise in Paul's interactions with other faculty, making his last year at school very difficult.

Paul could find another advisor. Paul may be able to select a new advisor who could better assist him. Better assistance, in the long run, could help Paul make better decisions, which could lead to a better future.

Pros: The new advisor could help Paul achieve his future goals; Paul wouldn't have to see Dr. David any more; this would take very little effort by Paul; he could avoid being involved in the long process of filing charges against Dr. David.

Cons: Paul may never see Dr. David reproached; other students may face more discrimination by Dr. David; Dr. David would never truly understand the extent of his wrongdoing, therefore, he possibly may never change.

Paul could confront Dr. David. Paul could make another appointment and tell Dr. David that he could not help but observe that his interactions with the other student were much different that their interactions. He could ask Dr. David to explain why.

Pros: Dr. David hears the complaint directly from Paul and has the opportunity to address it before Paul goes to the authorities. If Dr. David's response is unsatisfactory, Paul can still make a formal complaint, he can document that he already spoke to Dr. David without result. If Dr. David's response is satisfactory, then Paul has solved the problem for himself.

Cons: Given Paul's beliefs about power and authority, it is unlikely that he will choose this option because it calls for direct confrontation.

References

Carlson, Neil R. (1990). <u>Psychology: The science of behavior</u>. Neeham Heights, MA: Allyn and Bacon.

Deaux, K. and Wrightsman, L.S. (1988). Social psychology, fifth edition. Pacific Grove, California: Brooks & Cole Publishing Company.

Morgan, M. (1997). Images of organization, second edition. Thousand Oaks, London, New Delhi: Sage Publications.

Wagner III, J.A. and Hollenbeck, J.R. (1998). Organizational behavior: Securing competitive advantage, third edition. (1993). Upper Saddle River, New Jersey: Prentice-Hall, Inc.

Zaden, J.W.V. Sociology: The core, third edition. New York: McGraw-Hill, Inc.

Epilogue

Paul sought the advice of another advisor. According to this academic advisor, Dr. Smith, Paul's options were: he could pursue the situation with the school by reporting the incident and wait to see what happened, or, he could simply change advisors.

Paul didn't want to go through the trouble of pursuing anything with the school; he didn't want to involve himself in such an ordeal during his senior year of college. It seemed obvious to him that the process would take a long time. In addition, he wasn't sure that he had a case against Dr. David. Even though it seemed clear to him that he was treated differently, he wasn't sure the school would see it the same way. In Paul's mind, Dr. David was a respected professor and he was merely a student that had been on academic probation in the past. The school would not easily believe such an accusation.

Paul was also hesitant because of the possible consequences of accusing a professor. He was afraid that the other faculty members would find out and turn against him and he would not risk that.

Even though Paul wanted to see Dr. David reproached for treating him differently, he saw little positive consequences for himself. Sure, the school would be a better place for students of color with one less such person, but the problem was too big for him to deal with. Therefore, he decided to confront Dr. David when he felt ready to confront him. However, the chance to speak with Dr. David never occurred. Although Paul did not file a complaint, he did change advisors. His new advisor, Dr. John Smith, was a caring and attentive man. For the remainder of Paul's stay at Upland, Dr. Smith assisted him with his future plans. When Paul decided to apply to graduate schools, Dr. Smith was there to help him every step of the way.

In March of 1998, Paul received two acceptance letters: he was accepted into the masters program in Human Resources Design at Claremont Graduate University, and he was also accepted into the masters program in Personnel Psychology at New York University.

Teaching Note
REPUTATION IN JEOPARDY

Topics (* = Primary topic with teaching plan)
　*Interpersonal Conflict
　*Conflict Resolution
　*Organizational Culture
　*Communication
　Organizational Change
　Authority, acceptance of
　Management Functions
　Banking Context

Case overview

Home Savings of America and Washington Mutual, both large financial institutions, became involved in a battle to acquire another institution, Great Western, in early 1998. This case chronicles Home Savings ultimate loss to Washington Mutual and the effects of the loss on the strategic plans and the entire culture of the organization. It details Home Savings' cultural decline and the effects of that decline on four of Home Savings employees.

All of the key players in this case were located at Home Savings' corporate offices. The Corporate Meetings and Events Department consisted of Amber, Sarah and Beth who worked together to plan all Home Savings corporate functions, including the incentive program that was at the center of the conflict. Lydia was the manager of a support department that assisted the Meeting and Events Department in putting together this incentive program.

In March 1998, Home Savings announced that not only had they lost their bid to acquire Great Western, but that Washington Mutual was going to acquire Home Savings as well. This meant the closure of the corporate facility and large numbers of layoffs, which contributed further to the rapidly deteriorating attitudes of its employees. After this announcement was made, Lydia requested information regarding past incentive programs. Lydia was shorthanded and asked for Amber's assistance with her request.

Amber's supervisor, Sarah, did not agree with the request and did not allow Amber to assist Lydia. However, Sarah did not communicate her disagreement to Lydia, and Amber was repeatedly told to lie in order to get out of assisting her. Although Sarah was directing Amber's actions, Lydia was completely unaware of this and proceeded to make damaging comments about Amber, which threatened Amber's reputation with the company.

Industry

Regional Banking – Savings and Loan. No union.

Teaching objective

　1. To analyze the importance of corporate culture and its effects on employee behavior.
　2. To experience trying to resolve the conflict between Amber and Lydia.
　3. To recognize the advantages of communication during times of conflict.

Other related cases in Volume 1

No, Sir, Sergeant! (acceptance of authority, interpersonal conflict). Questions Matter (acceptance of authority, interpersonal conflict). Split Operations at Sky and Arrow Airlines (organizational change, organizational culture). The Day They Announced the Buyout (organizational change).

This teaching note was prepared by Amber Borden and Teri C. Tompkins, University of Redlands. The case and teaching note were prepared as basis for class discussion rather than to illustrate either effective or ineffective handling of administrative situations. Suggestions for improvement of this note should be sent to Teri.Tompkins@pepperdine.edu. Credit will be given in the next revision.

Other related cases in Volume 2

Computer Services Team at AVIONICS (interpersonal conflict). Cost and Schedule Team at AVIONICS (interpersonal conflict). Insubordination or Unclear Loyalties? (acceptance of authority). The Safety Memo (assessment of organizational culture, interpersonal conflict). The Volunteer (acceptance of authority).

Intended course and levels

This case is appropriate for undergraduate, graduate, and executive students. It is a useful discussion tool on the topics of communication and organizational culture in organizational behavior (systems or process level) or management (leading function).

Analysis

All related analysis and references are embedded in the answers to the questions.

Research methodology

This case reflects the recollection of one of the main characters in the case. The case is a true incident. The people, but not the organizations, have been disguised.

Teaching plan

Organizational Culture. The changes to organizational culture and behavior following the announcement of a merger can be addressed with the following questions. See question 2 for a sample of answers.

1. *What role did culture play in guiding performance and behavior before the merger?*
2. *Were there any heroes in the organization before the merger? If so, who were Amber's heroes?*
3. *What happened to Amber and her heroes' behavior and performance after the merger was announced?*
4. *Why did the W.E. C.A.R.E. document no longer guide people's behavior after the merger announcement?*
5. *What conclusions do you draw about the qualities of organizational culture after reading this case?*

Communication or Conflict. This case can be taught effectively with a role play to teach conflict resolution or communication. After the merger was announced, employees began to reduce their willingness to communicate and resolve differences, figuring that they would be laid off soon anyway. However, the avoidance of communication and handling conflict increased individual member's stress. The Computer Services Team at AVIONICS and the Cost and Schedule Team at AVIONICS demonstrate what can happen when conflict is avoided or embraced.

Topic: Communication or Conflict
60-minute teaching plan

Pre-assignment: None

	Timing	Activity	Organization	Student Outcomes
I	0 – 15 minutes (15)	Read the case.	Individually	Familiarity with case facts

	Timing	Activity	Organization	Student Outcomes
II	15 – 20 minutes (5)	Question for group with Lydia's perspective: *How do you see Amber? What is your perception of her?* Question for group with Amber's perspective: *How do you see Lydia? What is your perception of her?*	Divide the class into even number of groups, e.g. 2, 4 or 6 groups (with around 4-5 students per group). For each pair of groups, decide which group will take Lydia's perspective and which group will take Amber's perspective.	To identify with the character and to evaluate the other person's behavior and attitude.
III	20 – 30 minutes (10)	For each group: *How would you like to handle this situation?*	Discuss as a group. Tell them to prepare for a role play.	An action plan. Some may chose not to act. It might be interesting to match them up with a role play from a group that wants to confront.
IV	30-45 minutes (15)	Role play several rounds.	Select one Amber and one Lydia from the groups. Have them role play in front of the class. Alternative 1: pair up all the Ambers and Lydias and have them role play simultaneously. Alternative 2. All the Ambers and Lydias form a line. The first Amber faces the first Lydia, the rest stand behind their character. The first Amber and Lydia role-play for about 1 minute and then the person behind may tap the shoulder of the first Amber (or Lydia) and continue with the role-play (the first Amber or Lydia goes to the back of the line).	Opportunity to apply their ideas about how to solve the problem.
V	45 – 55 minutes (10)	Discuss the outcomes.	Can do this in small groups or as a whole class. Alternative: Have the small groups come up with another action plan after discussing the problems with the first role plays. Then have them role play their new strategies.	Points to make: *Conflict resolution requires both parties to be willing to communicate. *Often one person willing to initiate will then allow the other to decide to communicate. *Because of the likely layoffs, one or both parties have no significant long-term stake in resolving the conflict. Is it worth it to confront each other? *What are the advantages and disadvantages of not discussing the issue with each other?

	Timing	Activity	Organization	Student Outcomes
VI	55 – 60 minutes (5) or longer	Summary or mini-lecture.	Full class discussion.	Use this case to summarize or launch a lecture on effective communication or culture dynamics or motivation (is it worth dealing with the person).

25-minute teaching plan on Communication or Conflict
Pre-assignment: Read case before coming to class.
Activities: Do activities II (5 minutes), III (5 minutes), IV (10 minutes), VI (5 minutes).

Discussion questions and answers

Question 1

To what extent does the merger resolve the conflict?
Evaluation skills (using a set of criteria to arrive at a reasoned judgment of the value of something)

Answer

Sarah, Amber, Lydia and Beth would probably not be working together beyond the conclusion of the merger, and until that point it was not necessary for them to work together on further projects. The announcement of the merger removed the need for the relationships to be cultivated or maintained for ease of future dealings. Regardless of whether or not Amber decided to confront Lydia or Sarah and resolve the conflict, the outcome of the merger would remain the same.

In this scenario, it is critical to define the real problem in order to make an intelligent, valid decision about a solution. The problem is not simply Sarah's attitude or Lydia's comments. Amber attempted to avoid the conflict because at the beginning the issue seemed trivial and there was little chance of satisfying the concern due to the merger. Also she believed that the potential disruption outweighed the benefits of a resolution and addressing the problem might make matters worse. Home Savings would be closing its doors soon anyway so Amber might likely decide to let it go and not mention anything to Lydia or address the problem with Sarah.

Question 2 - Culture

What role did culture play in guiding performance and behavior before the merger? Were there any heroes in the organization before the merger? If so, who were Amber's heroes? What happened to Amber and her heroes' behavior and performance after the merger was announced? Why did the W.E. C.A.R.E. document no longer guide people's behavior after the merger announcement? What conclusions do you draw about the qualities of organizational culture after reading this case?
Analysis skills (breaking a concept into its parts and explaining their interrelationships, distinguishing relevant from extraneous material) and evaluation skills (using a set of criteria to arrive at a reasoned judgment of the value of something)

Answer

The emotional undercurrents caused by the merger announcement and subsequent decline in Home Savings' culture combined to create an atmosphere conducive to creating this conflict. Home Savings' culture was based on the shared philosophies, values, and beliefs that were reflected in the behaviors of the leaders and employees at every level. These values were the attitudes and mindsets that determined how work was accomplished and how employees interacted with one another.

To help you understand the importance of culture and its impact on performance, let's focus on one of its three components, heroes. Heroes provide role models and make attaining success and accomplishment possible. They are essential to a strong organizational culture and symbolize the values of the organization internally and externally. Heroes preserve what makes the organization special, but they also set high standards and are masterful at creating a motivating environment. Sarah and Lydia held such positions and were, by many, regarded as heroes. Mergers like this one, especially in which all employees in one location are being laid off, have a very negative effect on the attitudes of those heroes, which in turn affects the employees they inspire.

When the merger was announced the behavior and attitudes of Sarah and Lydia changed dramatically. Loyalty was gone and Home Savings' W.E. C.A.R.E. culture swiftly underwent a change. The culture, that took years to develop, was lost in a single strategic management decision. Now that we have knowledge of a probable cause of the breakdown we can better understand the reasons that human behavior can sometimes be unpredictable and irrational.

Human beings, even managers, often act from emotions rather than reason so it is possible that under the circumstances Sarah was acting out of personal frustration and culture shock. After being employed with the company for almost twelve years the sudden negative shift in direction could have caused a large amount of stress. The effects of Sarah's attitude, and the way she communicated it, influenced Amber's performance. One of the primary purposes of managerial motivation is to stimulate employees to produce or perform more effectively. This was not demonstrated in executive management or Sarah's actions. As stated earlier, the collapse of Home Savings' culture was a major contributor to the circumstances of this case. In most other situations, Sarah demonstrated the ability to understand and interact effectively with employees. Sarah had better than average human relations skills and utilized them in effectively leading, motivating, and communicating with subordinates and peers for the previous twelve years. Yet, in this situation, for all the reasons listed above, she abandoned Home Savings' We Care values and avoided communication with a co-worker.

Question 3
What are the essential management functions, and which ones were not demonstrated in this case?
Knowledge skills (remember previously learned material such as definitions, principles, formulas)

Answer
The essential management functions are planning, leading, organizing and controlling. First, leading is an important aspect of management and involves the leader's qualities, styles, and power as well as leadership activities of communication, motivation and discipline. Leading is getting employees to do what you want them to by example. It involves assigning tasks, issuing instructions, requesting cooperation and demonstrating a willingness to work toward the same objectives. Leaders are in influential positions because they have the power to influence ethical issues and decisions affecting many people. In this situation Sarah is not leading Amber toward one of Home Savings' cultural values, reaching to improve.

Sarah was also not exhibiting the organizing function of management; that is, she did not consider the resources and activities that were required in achieving the organization objectives in this case. Lydia was overwhelmed with work due to the loss of her administrative assistant so she asked for assistance from Amber, who states she could easily have spared the time it would have taken to carry out the assignment. Sarah did not consider the organizations overall objective to establish itself as one of the country's most profitable and admired financial service institutions. She did not consider the insignificance of the request when compared to the mission of the organization. Therefore, she was not demonstrating her ability to organize the resources of Home Savings to meet that objective.

Epilogue
Ultimately, Amber decided to let the issue drop. She felt that since everyone was being laid off anyway that it wasn't worth the complications a discussion would create. Lydia left the company soon

after Sarah left. Amber continued working with Home Savings and was offered a position with Washington Mutual. She decided not to take it and instead is pursuing her education and evaluating a number of careers, especially ones that might involve self-employment.

RICHARD PRICHARD AND THE FEDERAL TRIAD PROGRAMS

Topics (*=Primary topic with teaching plan)
   *Expectancy Theory
   *Goal Setting
   Self-efficacy
   Higher Education Context

Case overview

Richard was a hard working young executive assistant in a federal grant program at a university. The case describes the internal thoughts that Richard has as a worker on the program. Richard was dissatisfied with the input from the other team members on the project. He was frustrated that they came in late to work and didn't complete their tasks. Yet, Richard continually took over any task that was not completed by members of the team. He rationalized that it contributed to the program goals, which were paramount.

On Friday, at the end of another 50 plus hour week, Dr. Duncan, the director of the program, asked Richard to come in on the weekend to work on a grant. She told him that the other two office workers would be there. Grudgingly, he agreed. He was told to be at the office at 1 P.M. on Saturday. He arrived on the dot only to find the parking lot empty. Finally, at 2:15, Dr. Duncan and Dorthy (Duncan's daughter and a work-study assistant on the project) arrived with a simple "hello." A little while later, Stephen, the other office worker arrived. Richard was angry that they wasted more than an hour, but didn't say anything.

As they work on the project, Richard's anger subsided. He felt happy to see the amount of work they were accomplishing as a team. The stacks of paper and completed graphs looked good to him. By 8:30 P.M. Dorthy left for another engagement. At 11:30, Stephen headed home. Richard stayed behind to organize the paperwork. Finally, at 5 A.M. Richard headed for the door. Dr. Duncan came out of her office to thank him for his hard work. As he walked to the car in the early morning hours he was surprised how satisfied he felt. For once he wasn't the last to leave. It was good to get a simple thank you from Dr. Duncan and to watch the team work together to accomplish something, even if for one day.

Industry
Educational. University setting, grant program.

Teaching objectives
   1. Distinguish among positive, negative, and zero valence in expectancy theory.
   2. Define instrumentalities and apply the concept to the case.
   3. Describe how role perception and goal setting influenced the behavior in the case.
   4. Explain self-efficacy theory and show an example of self-efficacy from the case.

Other related cases in Volume 1
A New Magazine in Nigeria (goal setting).

Other related cases in Volume 2
Changing Quotas (expectancy theory). Groupware Fiasco (higher education context). Negotiating Work Hours (higher education context).

This teaching note was prepared by Earle Hall and Teri C. Tompkins, University of Redlands. The case and teaching note were prepared as a basis for class discussion rather than to illustrate either effective or ineffective handling of administrative situations. Suggestions for improvement of this note should be sent to Teri.Tompkins@pepperdine.edu. Credit will be given in the next revision.

Intended courses and levels

This course is intended primarily for undergraduate students in organizational behavior. It is best introduced during discussions of individuals, rewards, and motivations.

Analysis

All related analysis and references are embedded in the answers to the questions.

Research methodology

This case reflects the recollection of the casewriter. The case is a true incident. Names and the organization have been disguised.

Teaching plan

Topic: Expectancy Theory and Role Theory
60-minute teaching plan

Pre-assignment: none
Instructor preparation: Print copies of epilogue, if you plan to share it.

	Timing	Activity	Organization	Student Outcomes
I	0- 10 minutes (10)	Mini-lecture on expectancy theory. Use classroom environment as setting for illustration. E->P->O	Entire Class	Understand E - P P - O (instrumentality) Valence
II	10 - 20 minutes (10)	Students read case (Part A only)	Individually	Familiarity with case facts.
III	20 - 35 minutes (15)	Explore the likely scenario associated with Richard's decision. Map each scenario using e->p_>o.	Small groups. Some assigned "a", some "b" a) Richard gives in. b) Richard doesn't give in.	Apply expectancy theory to the case. See questions 1, 2, and 3 for possible answers (too complicated to list here).
IV	35 - 45 minutes (10)	Discuss which decision is more likely.	Full class	Students' opinion will vary. Some will respond by what "they" would do, others will respond by trying to put themselves in "Richard's shoes." Regardless, keep helping them clarify what the meanings of valence, instrumentality, and expectancy are, and how they apply to the case.
V	45 - 50 minutes (5)	Read rest of the case (B).	Individually	Learn what Richard did.
VI	50 - 59 minutes (9)	*Was this decision healthy or unhealthy for Richard? The work group? The organization? Why? Support your answer in terms of goals and roles*		Again, student opinion will vary. Some will think that Richard was a great team player. Others may think that he needs to improve his ability to say no, especially when they showed up over an hour late. Is it healthy for the work group? It is possible that Richard "enables" the work group to avoid their work, because he

	Timing	Activity	Organization	Student Outcomes
				picks up the slack? Thus, others are able to avoid negative consequences, and not see how their behaviors are a problem. See also answers to questions 4, 5, and 6.
VII	59 - 60 minutes (1)	Read epilogue.		

25-minute teaching plan on expectancy theory.
Pre-assignment: Read case A and B before class (15 minutes)
Activities. Do activities I, III, and VI in the 60-minute plan.

Discussion questions and answers

Question 1

The decision to be made in the case is whether or not Richard should come in to work on Saturday. Explore the two options available to Richard (Richard should go/Richard should not go). Tell whether the valence is positive, negative, or zero for each option and support your answer by listing the possible expectations resulting from each option.

Diagnostic question (probes motives or causes). Application skills (using information in a new context to solve a problem, answer a question, or perform a task)

Answer

If Richard decides to go in to work on Saturday, he has a positive valence. Although the case does not specifically mention what he hoped to gain from going in to work on Saturday, in order for him to decide that he would go in, he would have had to anticipate receiving some kind of satisfaction from his decision in order to say yes. A possible reason to go in on Saturday may be attributed to his view on teams and teamwork. Reference is made in the case to the fact that Richard often does work that is not his because of his commitment to the objectives of the team. He is asked to partake in an activity that is not directly related to his program, but seeing that his program does operate under the FEDERAL Program, he is a part of the FEDERAL team. His peers had also made a commitment to help and he may have been doing this out of loyalty to his peers having some idea of what a great deal of work this would be. Richard's expectations based on these reasons may have been due to the personal satisfaction that could be gained from contributing to a "team" activity, or simply from knowing that he helped his friends.

Some other expectations could be to obtain some kind of reward such as monetary compensation, a promotion, or something noting his contribution that would allow him to gain something tangible. He may also expect to avoid something negative by going to work on Saturday. He may feel that by not going his boss or his peers may look down on him for not contributing to the task. His desire in this case would be to avoid the negative perceptions or actions taken against him by his boss and peers. Whatever expectations he may have, the results from his course of action would be something desired enough to cause him to go in to work on Saturday. This would result in a positive valence.

If Richard does not decide to go in to work on Saturday, he has a negative valence. His expected gain would not be enough to make him want to go to work. Some reasons for this may be that he does not feel that his boss or his peers would act negatively towards him if he did not choose to go in to work on Saturday. Another reason may be that he believes that based on the current trends in his organization, the possibility of him gaining some kind of reward for the extra work would be very slim. Therefore, there is not enough incentive for him to go. The expectation that there is nothing in the situation to persuade him enough to go would result in Richard having a negative valence.

A measure of zero valence would imply that his expected gains or losses from choosing a particular option were equal. Therefore he could choose to either go or not go. Each option may result in the same things discussed in the above answers.

Question 2

What part do instrumentalities play in expectancy theory? Give some examples of possible instrumentalities leading to Richard's decision.

<u>Comprehension skills</u> (understanding the meaning of remembered material, usually demonstrated by restating or citing examples)

Answer

Instrumentality is a person's belief about the relationship between performing an action and experiencing an outcome (performance-outcome expectation). The concept of instrumentality can be seen as what a person feels they must do (performance) to achieve an outcome. This is linked to expectancy theory, along with valence and expectancy, because it helps to explain Richard's attitude and behavior.

If Richard based his decision on trying to please his boss, the instrumentality in that situation would be Richard's belief that by coming in to work on Saturday and doing what was needed (performance), he would be agreeing to her request which may be linked to remaining in a positive light with her (outcome expectation). This would be a satisfying outcome to him, causing him to exhibit the behavior.

If Richard based his decision on his belief that maybe she would change her mind about giving some kind of monetary compensation, the instrumentality would be doing what was required of him on Saturday (performance), which may be linked, at some point, to her rewarding him monetarily for his performance (outcome expectation). This would be a satisfactory outcome for him, causing him to exhibit the behavior.

If Richard based his decision on the fact that it was a long task, he may have sympathized for his coworkers and wanted to help them, or he could have been viewing the task as a team effort since his coworkers were involved. In this situation, the instrumentality would be Richard's belief that coming in on Saturday to support his coworkers in whatever way he could (performance) may be linked to alleviating the workload or helping his coworkers in a way that they would appreciate (outcome expectation). This would, in turn, satisfy him and cause him to exhibit the behavior.

If Richard decides not to go in to work on Saturday, the instrumentality may be that he does not feel that his boss or his peers would act negatively towards him (outcome expectation) if he did not choose to go (performance). Another instrumentality may be his belief that based on the current trends in his organization, the possibility of him gaining some kind of reward for the extra work would be very slim (outcome expectation). Therefore, there is not enough incentive for him to go (performance).

Question 3

Based on expectancy theory, is it possible for Richard to put forth an effort while having low valence, instrumentality and expectancy? Use facts from the case to support or refute your answer.

<u>Exploratory question</u> (probes facts and basic knowledge)

Answer

No. Expectancy theory states that valence, instrumentality, and expectancy must be high in order for effort to come about. While Richard was not enthusiastic about the idea of coming to work on a Saturday, he did decide to go. Seeing that effort came about, theoretically, one can conclude that valence, instrumentality, and expectancy were all high. This would mean that he saw the possibility of possibly gaining some kind of intrinsic or extrinsic reward (expectation) and the expectation of receiving the reward outweighed the expectation of not receiving the reward. Richard mentioned that in addition to Dr. Duncan waiting for his response as if she expected no less than a "yes," he hoped to help the team, which indicates that he expected to gain an intrinsic reward. Richard evidently perceived a clear link between exhibiting a certain behavior and receiving the reward for that behavior (instrumentality). This instrumentality would be his coming to work on a Saturday and helping out the group, being linked to receiving at least an intrinsic reward. As a result of high expectation and instrumentality, his valence was high, or positive, in favor of going to work on Saturday.

Question 4

Point out Richard's perception of his role in the organization as it relates to his goals and decision in the case.

Analysis skills (breaking a concept into its parts and explaining their interrelationships, distinguishing relevant from extraneous material)

Answer

It appears that Richard perceived himself as the "glue" of the organization. Richard had an idea of the organizational goals and how to go about accomplishing them, so he did not have a hard time doing what was necessary, with the exception of the workload. Richard perceived his actual role in the organization as one that extended beyond his organizational title. It was clear that he was strictly goal oriented when it came to his work and his role was to carry out the goal in whatever way he could. This did not mean that the organization could not function without him. Although it appeared that way, we see that in the aftermath of his decision (see epilogue), when the program coordinators believed that Richard could no longer perform the same job that he was doing before, they were compelled to step in and assume the responsibilities that came with their titles and the program continued to function successfully.

Question 5

Point out the importance of role theory and goals to explain why the coordinators possibly did not work as hard as Richard.

Analysis skills (breaking a concept into its parts and explaining their interrelationships, distinguishing relevant from extraneous material)

Answer

Role perceptions are people's beliefs about what they are supposed to be accomplishing on the job and how to go about accomplishing these tasks. A few problems were mentioned in the case that dealt with this theory. One is that coordinators placed a lot of emphasis on title. The grant clearly stated the jobs of each staff member, but by placing more emphasis on title than duty, coordinators would designate responsibilities to those lower in the hierarchy. This could have been done because the coordinators simply did feel like doing some of the "busy" work that came with their title, or it could have been attributed to "goal setting," as well as "goal commitment" issues.

Also, the Scholar Sustenance Program had three coordinators in the program as opposed to two, which was originally stated in the grant. This was due to the conflicts that arose between Mr. Adams and Mr. Butler. The case mentions that at times, these conflicts were due to unclear boundaries. Role perceptions should have been clarified at the point where it was seen as a problem. Bringing in a third coordinator may have made it more confusing given that the third counselor was said to have the same responsibilities as the Mr. Adams and Mr. Butler.

Dr. Duncan was mentioned as not being a "micromanager." Staff members knew the goals of their program and were left to do their jobs the best way they saw fit, while remaining within the parameters of the grant. Not setting specific goals may have made the coordinators feel as if the goals were more difficult than they really were. "Goal setting theory" states that goals seen as too difficult are typically met with less commitment. Based on "expectancy theory," a goal may be rejected when it is seen as impossible. Though commitment is important in increasing the effect of goals on performance, participation does not always guarantee commitment. The goals could have been made more concrete by practicing goal setting, such as establishing program and staff member specific goals. By doing this, responsibilities for each person could have been discussed and agreed upon in a more equitable manner.

Question 6

Suppose Richard made the decision of not going in to work, which may not have resulted in his role in the organization being changed by Dr. Duncan. Is there another way that he could have persuaded the coordinators to contribute more work to the program?

Hypothetical question (poses a change in the facts or issues)

Answer

Referring back to goal setting theory, it may have helped if Richard recommended that the program staff meet to discuss the program goals in detail. It was mentioned in the case that there was some conflict between Mr. Adams and Mr. Butler and this conflict was affecting program goals. This resulted in Ms. Sutton being hired, in part, to once again bridge the tutorial and counseling components of the program. Having three counselors, instead of two as stated in the grant, resulted in "boundaries being overstepped," as the case describes it. If boundaries were overstepped, some employees may have been under the impression that roles had changed because of the fact that the program was not designed to have three coordinators. At this point, there was a clear need to discuss the new organizational structure and strategy to achieve the program goals. Goals and strategies have been used to increase performance on a variety of jobs. One con of this is that developing strategies consumes time that might otherwise be devoted to task performance. Because of this, there may be situations in which goals actually hinder performance. Studies show that for complex tasks, the task strategies, or plans of action that people devise have a big impact on the outcome of their efforts. This impact can obscure or even wipe out the effects of goal setting.

The next step should have been to clearly map out what role changes were made and what responsibilities these changes brought about for each new role. This would have ensured that everyone understood the goals and how they were to be carried out, thus simplifying the tasks. Energy could then be devoted towards the right goals and outcomes. Determining "important goal attributes" has been shown to increase performance in a wide variety of jobs and has been most effective when accompanied by feedback so that progress can be monitored. According to goal setting theory, simplifying the tasks should improve the level of commitment among the staff members.

"Goal commitment and participation" is another factor that affects performance. Both specific and difficult goals lead to increased performance only when there is high goal commitment. When goals are too difficult, they are typically met with less commitment. Remember that based on expectancy theory, people may reject goals that they perceive to be impossible. One con of this is that although commitment is important to increasing the effect of goals on performance, participation does not always guarantee commitment. The rationale behind setting and defining goals, strategies, and responsibilities is that merely clarifying the ends sought is unlikely to enhance performance. This was evident because Mr. Adams and Mr. Butler knew the overall goals of the program, but with the change in structure, it was less clear on how to go about achieving them efficiently.

Question 7

Explain self-efficacy theory and show an example of self-efficacy from the case.

Comprehension skills (understanding the meaning of remembered material, usually demonstrated by restating or citing examples)

Answer

Self-efficacy theory refers to the judgements people make about their ability to execute courses of action required to deal with prospective situations. Self-efficacy determines how much effort people will expend and how long they will persist in the face of obstacles. When faced with difficulties, people who doubt their capabilities slacken or give up their efforts all together. Those with a strong sense of efficacy exert greater effort to master the challenges. Some sources of self-efficacy are past accomplishments, observation of others, verbal persuasion, and logical verification.

An example of self-efficacy is Richard agreeing to come in to help write the grant. Richard had little or no prior grant writing experience. He mentioned that the people in any of the programs at the coordinator level would have been better qualified to do the job because they had graduate degrees and more experience in grant writing. Even those coordinators who were not familiar with grant writing were extremely knowledgeable about the contents of the grants for their programs.

Question 8

What possible sources of self-efficacy may have lead Richard to believe that he could accomplish the task that was asked of him?

<u>Application skills</u> (using information in a new context to solve a problem, answer a question, or perform a task)

Answer

Richard was the last person to stay of the three people that Dr. Duncan had asked to come in on Saturday. Based on self-efficacy theory, Richard had a strong sense of efficacy that caused him to exert greater effort to master the challenge. This efficacy may have come from past accomplishments. Richard worked hard for the organization. His past experience in successfully overcoming obstacles and assuming responsibility for things that he had no experience with may have caused him to believe that grant writing would be like any of those other things that he did not have experience with but was able to do successfully. For example, he did not have experience at being a program coordinator, nor did he possess the educational background of the coordinators, yet he was able to take on the coordinators' responsibilities. This example could also be an example of the logical verification concept as a source of self-efficacy because he had already mastered tasks that he may have likened to the new task.

Richard may have also found efficacy by verbal persuasion. Richard wondered, "Why is Dr. Duncan asking me to come in on the weekend, of all the other people that she could ask?" This could be a form of indirect verbal persuasion. Dr. Duncan can be seen as a credible source of efficacy given her title, experience, and educational background. Her asking him to come in as opposed to some of the coordinators would imply that she trusted he could accomplish the task that was being asked of him. Dr. Duncan also mentioning that other coworkers would be coming in could be seen as a form of verbal persuasion. Dr. Duncan mentioned to Richard that Dorothy and Stephen (who are almost Richard's peers in age, work experience, and knowledge of the programs), would be coming in on Saturday. This could have also been an implication that "if they can do it, you can do it," falling in line with verbal persuasion concept.

The example of observation of others could have come from seeing the coworkers who came in to work that Saturday. Richard may have been able to reassure himself that he could do what was expected of him by watching Dorothy and Stephen do their jobs on Saturday. Once again, both could be credible sources because they are similar to Richard in many ways.

Question 9

What is the relationship between self-efficacy theory and the concepts of expectancy theory?

<u>Relational question</u> (asks for comparisons of themes, ideas, or issues)

Answer

Expectancy theory attempts to explain the determinants of workplace attitudes and behaviors through the concepts of valence, instrumentality and expectancy. Desire comes about only when both valency and instrumentality are high. Effort comes about only when the three variables of valency, instrumentality, and expectancy are high. It is possible to have low motivation when there is no expectation that a goal can be reached, even when valence and instrumentality are high. If Richard did not believe that he could accomplish the task for whatever reason, this indicates a lack of self-efficacy. Based on self-efficacy theory, we know that people with low self-efficacy may slacken or give up effort all together when faced with an obstacle. The result of no or low self-efficacy is no expectancy. No expectancy can be interpreted as not making an effort and having no anticipation of performing well. Going back to expectancy theory, Richard's motivation would then have been low, regardless of his valence and instrumentality.

References

Wagner III, J.A., Hollenbeck, J. R. (1998). <u>Organizational Behavior: Securing Competitive Advantage: 3rd. Edition</u>. Upper Saddle River, New Jersey: Prentice-Hall.

Epilogue

The Saturday episode turned into the start of a series of additional "favors" requested of Richard by Dr. Duncan. There were other grants to write and other projects to handle. Eventually, Richard unofficially became one of Dr. Duncan's personal assistants. He was constantly pulled from his daily program specific duties to tend to matters that she requested to be handled with top priority. This forced the coordinators to handle more of their own responsibilities because nobody was there to "pick up the slack" when they did not do their job. Richard was even able to turn down tasks that were assigned to him by his coordinator superiors because he had to tend to the other projects. Overall, accepting this initial Saturday task gave him some grant writing experience, and it placed him in high regard in the organization. He never did get any monetary compensation for any of his additional work, but he did receive compensatory time off whenever he wanted it. Also, his workload gradually decreased because people began to assume that he would not have the time to handle certain tasks. This was definitely pleasing for him. It also pleased him to see people who formerly did nothing now doing what they should. This made the program even more efficient because Richard never stopped putting in 100 percent.

SAVING PRIVATE RYAN VIDEO CASE: CLASSIC LEADERSHIP MODELS

Topics (* = Primary topics in teaching plan)
*Trait Theory of Leadership (Stodgill, 1974)
*Behavioral Models of Leadership (Kerr, Schreisheim, Murphy, and Stodgill, 1974)
*Contingency Theory of Leadership (Fiedler)
*Normative Theory (Vroon and Yetton)
*Path-Goal Theory (March and House, 1974)
*Transformational Leadership Theory (Burns, 1978)
Government Context
Stress
United States Military

Case overview
"*Saving Private Ryan*" tells the story of the D-Day invasion through the eyes of a schoolteacher turned warrior, Captain Miller. Its central story takes us on a journey that starts in a landing craft on Omaha Beach and ends with a pitched battle in a battered French village. Along the way, we meet paratroopers, glider pilots, and prisoners of war. A small platoon of soldiers are sent to rescue the last surviving brother in a family of four. The other three have died in the past week fighting in Europe and Asia. In its simplest interpretation, the mission to save Ryan is just a plot device to get us on the beach and then behind the lines to dramatize the way different groups of soldiers experienced the war. At a much deeper level, it asks us what risks we are willing to take to protect the things we hold dear.

Students will learn to apply classic leadership models to their lives as managers using leadership examples from the film "*Saving Private Ryan*" (Spielberg, 1998). Each theory can be taught using a different part of the film. Other leadership theories can be substituted at the instructor's discretion, but these six will be examined in this teaching note. While all six of the models confirm that Captain Miller is an outstanding leader, only the last gives us any insight on how he continues to influence Private Ryan fifty years later.

Industry
Military in battle. World War II.

Teaching objectives
1. To comprehend classical leadership theories.
2. To apply classical leadership theories to analyze situations under high stress and personal danger.
3. To evaluate the appropriateness of classic leadership theories to dangerous, high stress environments.

Other related cases in Volume 1
Julie's Call: Empowerment at Taco Bell (contingency theory). Questions Matter (leadership).

Other related cases in Volume 2
Computer Services Team at AVIONICS (leadership). Cost and Schedule Team at AVIONICS (leadership). Incident on the USS *Whitney* (transformational leadership). Leadership of TQM in Panama (leadership). Unprofessional Conduct (leadership).

This teaching note was prepared by Jim Spee, University of Redlands. The teaching note was prepared as a basis for class discussion rather than to illustrate either effective or ineffective handling of administrative situations. Suggestions for improvement of this teaching note should be sent to Teri.Tompkins@pepperdine.edu. Credit will be given in the next revision.

Intended Courses and Levels

This case is suitable for undergraduate and graduate courses that cover leadership as a major topic, such as organizational behavior and leadership. It has been classroom tested with great enthusiasm from graduate and undergraduate students.

Analysis

Analysis is embedded in the answers to the discussion questions.

Research Methodology

This is a film case. The author developed the analysis by viewing the film several times, reading secondary reviews, reviewing film clips, and researching books and articles about D-day and World War II.

Teaching Plan

Note: When making the assignment to watch the film out of class, it is helpful to give students permission to fast forward through the parts of the film that they find objectionable or too violent. Some students (and instructors) do not have an appreciation for violence in films and should not be made to watch the entire film. One instructor successfully taught this film even though she fast-forwarded through all the violent clips. The film was meaningful enough without watching the violent sections.

This teaching note accompanies the video *Saving Private Ryan* (DreamWorks Home Entertainment, 1999). The teaching note assumes that the video will be available for students to view outside class and for viewing during the class session. The teaching note is divided into six topics. You may use any or all of the segments, depending on which leadership model you are interested in. Another option is to use a clip from the film with a model not covered here.

You may choose to use the video for in class discussion, or assign students written work that analyzes the film using the six models presented here or other leadership models. Students may need to research the historical background of D-Day and World War II to appreciate the context of the film. The film could be used in conjunction with "Apocalypse Now, " "The Thin Red Line," or another war film to compare and contrast what they communicate about war and leadership.

Students will need to view the film before coming to class. The teaching plan is divided into six parts, one for each model you will use to analyze Captain Miller's leadership. You can use clips from the film for parts 2 through 6.

Alternative teaching plan to those below: This film was taught successfully in one graduate-level class session of 60 minutes covering all six of the leadership styles. Students were asked to view the film before coming to class. In addition, they were asked to read material on the six leadership styles in their textbook. When class began, the students were divided into six groups, each covering a different leadership style. Without viewing the film in class, they were asked to analyze a point in the film that illustrated the leadership model the group was assigned. They were to provide examples from the film and to outline on the board (or transparency) how the model applied. They were also asked whether the leadership model could explain Private Ryan's behavior at the end of the film, where he appeared to be seeking Captain Miller's approval (via the cemetery scene) for having conducted his life well. After spending about 20 minutes illustrating their leadership style with examples from the film, the group made presentations to the rest of the class describing the leadership style and providing the illustrations. At the end of each presentation, they were asked by the instructor whether the leadership model explained Private Ryan's behavior. Only the transformative leadership style explained Private Ryan's commitment to Captain Miller after a lifetime of living.

Topic 1: Trait Theories
60-minute teaching plan

Pre-assignment: View the film (2 hours 49 minutes). Search online for reviews of the film. Bring at least four reviews from a variety of sources, including newspapers and magazines.

	Timing	Activity	Organization	Student Outcomes
I.	0-10 minutes (10)	Use Stodgill's model to set up the discussion.	Mini-lecture	To comprehend classical leadership theories: Stodgill (1974) lists personality characteristics that make it more likely that someone will emerge as a leader. These include: • Achievement drive • Adaptability • Alertness • Ascendance • Attractiveness • Energy • Responsibility • Self-confidence • Sociability
II.	10-25 minutes (15)	Summarize the events of the film.	Ask or appoint a "volunteer."	Orientation and refresher on case.
III.	25-40 minutes (10)	Ask the students to look for references to Miller as leader in the reviews they collected before class.	Students work individually.	Students will begin to notice how many leadership traits are mentioned. (See table 2).
IV.	40-50 minutes (10)	Outline Stodgill's model and look for evidence that Miller exhibits the traits of a successful leader.	Group Discussion.	Discussion question: To apply classical leadership theories to analyze situations under high stress and personal danger, does Miller exhibit the traits listed above? What additional traits does he exhibit, according to reviewers of the film?
IV	50-60 minutes (10)	Students apply what they have learned to their lives as managers.	Group Discussion.	To evaluate the appropriateness of classic leadership theories to dangerous, high stress environment.

Topic 2: Behavioral Models of Leadership
60-minute teaching plan

Note: For video timing, set the timer to zero after the Paramount Pictures Logo, approximately 1:27 into the tape.

	Timing	Activity	Organization	Student Outcomes
I.	0-10 minutes (10)	Overview of the behavior model of leadership.	Mini-lecture	Comprehend classical leadership theories. Behavior theory examines two orientations: <u>Relationship Orientation</u> ▪ Listens to group members ▪ Easy to understand

	Timing	Activity	Organization	Student Outcomes
				▪ Is friendly and approachable ▪ Treats group members as equals ▪ Is willing to make changes (Forsyth, 1983, p. 215) <u>Task Orientation</u> ▪ Assigns tasks to members ▪ Makes attitudes clear to the group ▪ Is critical of poor work ▪ Sees to it that the group is working to capacity Coordinates activity (Forsyth, 1983, p. 215)
II.	10-20 minutes (10)	Show the segment that begins with Captain Miller in the landing craft.	Video clip from 00:03:47 to 00:05:56. First row of soldiers on landing craft are killed instantly.	Discussion question: Following the behavioral model of leadership, what should Miller do?
III	20-35 minutes (15)	Show the next segment that gets them to the foot of the hill on the beach.	Video clip from 00:05:56 to 00:15:34. "They're killing us, sir. We don't stand a ...chance. That ain't fair."	Discussion question: Based on the behavioral model, what should Miller do next?
	35-50 minutes (15)	Show the next segment that gets them to the top of the hill.	Video clip from 00:15:34 to 24:29 "Dog 1 is open!	Discussion question: Rate Miller's performance as a leader using the behavioral model.
IV.	50-60 minutes (10)	Students apply what they have learned to their lives as managers.	Individual reflection, choose a few to share with the group.	To evaluate the appropriateness of classic leadership theories to dangerous, high stress environment.

Topic 3: Contingency Model of Leader Effectiveness
60-minute teaching plan

Pre-assignment: None.

	Timing	Activity	Organization	Student Outcomes
I.	0-15 minutes (15)	Review Fiedler's contingency model of leadership	Mini-lecture.	To comprehend classical leadership theories. Fiedler's three factor contingency model of leadership describes when relationship motivated leadership or task motivated leadership will be most effective. The three factors are • Leader/member relations • Task structure • Leader position power Fiedler uses a measurement called the least preferred coworker (LPC) scale to determine whether a leader is primarily relationship motivated or task motivated.

	Timing	Activity	Organization	Student Outcomes
II.	15-20 minutes (5)	The platoon arrives in Neuville and meets the paratroops.	Video clip starting with 00:45:23 to 00:48:27. "Show me."	Discussion question: How should Miller get his men across the village, based on contingency theory?
III.	20-25 minutes (5)	Caparzo wants to save the little French girl who reminds him of his niece.	Video clip from 00:48:27 to 00:51:14. "Please, Captain, it's the decent thing to do!"	Discussion question: How should Miller deal with Caparzo, based on contingency theory?
IV.	25-30 minutes (5)	"We're not here to do the decent thing." Caparzo is shot.	Video clip from 00:51:14 to 00:52:18. French girl runs back to her father.	Discussion question: Rate Miller's leadership.
V	30-50 minutes (20)	Students apply contingency model to this situation.	Group Discussion.	To apply classical leadership theories to analyze situations under high stress and personal danger.
VI	50-60 minutes (10)	Students apply what they have learned to their lives as managers.	Individual reflection, choose a few to share with the group.	To evaluate the appropriateness of classic leadership theories to dangerous, high stress environment.

Topic 4: Normative Model of Leadership
60 minute teaching plan

Pre-assignment: None

	Timing	Activity	Organization	Student Outcomes
I.	0-15 minutes (15)	Outline the Vroom and Yetton normative model.	Mini-lecture.	To comprehend classical leadership theories. Review Vroon and Vetton.
II.	15-20 minutes (5)	Show the segment that begins when the group finds the German machine gun nest.	Video clip 01:22:37 to 1:24:20 "Seems like an unnecessary risk given our objective."	Discussion question: Should Miller stop and take the machine gun or not?
III.	20-30 minutes (10)	Show the segment in which Wade is killed and they release the German POW.	1:24:20 to 1:39:37	Discussion question: What should Miller do about Reiben's intention to desert the platoon?
IV.	30-40 minutes (10)	The segment ends with them burying Private Wade.	1:39:37 to 1:43:13	Discussion question: How did Miller resolve the conflict?
V.	40-55 minutes (15)	Students analyze Miller's decision to attack using the model.	Group Discussion.	To apply classical leadership theories to analyze situations under high stress and personal danger, evaluate Miller's leadership style with Reiben using the Vroon-Yetton model. A. Is there a quality requirement such that one solution is likely to be more rational than another is? YES

	Timing	Activity	Organization	Student Outcomes
				B. Do I have sufficient information to make a high quality decision? YES (Skip to D.) D. Is acceptance of the decision by subordinates critical to effective implementation? YES E. If Miller was to make the decision by himself, is it reasonably certain that his subordinates would accept it? NO F. Do subordinates share the organizational goals to be attained in solving this problem? SKIP G. (Is conflict among subordinates likely in preferred solutions?) Use Method Group II, consultation with the group to achieve consensus before proceeding.
VI.	55-60 minutes (5)	Students apply what they have learned to their lives as managers.	Individual reflection, choose a few to share with the group.	Evaluate the appropriateness of the Vroon-Yetton leadership theory to dangerous, high stress environments.

Topic 5: Path Goal Theory
60-minute teaching plan

	Timing	Activity	Organization	Student Outcomes

I.	0-15 minutes (15)	Review path goal theory.	Mini-lecture	To comprehend path goal leadership theories. The level of leader involvement that will result in the highest level of performance and satisfaction varies depending on:
				 • Subordinate expectations
				   • Autonomy
				   • Experience
				   • Ability
				 • Task characteristics
				   • Structure
				   • Difficulty
				 • Organizational structure and systems
				   • Work-group norms
				   • Organizational rewards
				 • Organizational controls

II.	15-20 minutes (5)	Show the conflict with Ryan over whether to stay or go.	Video clip from 1:46:10 to 1:50:50. Ryan says to Miller, "There's no way I'm leaving this bridge."	Discussion question: What should Miller do next?
III.	20-25 minutes (5)	Show Miller's decision and preparation for the battle.	Video clip from 1:50:50 to 1:55:30.	Discussion question: How would you rate Miller's leadership in this scene?

	Timing	Activity	Organization	Student Outcomes
IV.	25-50 minutes (25)	Students evaluate Miller's leadership from that perspective.	Group Discussion	To apply classical leadership theories to analyze situations under high stress and personal danger.
V.	50-60 minutes (10)	Students apply what they have learned to their lives as managers.	Individual reflection, choose a few to share with the group.	To evaluate the appropriateness of classic leadership theories to dangerous, high stress environment.

Topic 6: Transformational and Transactional Leadership
60-minute teaching plan

	Timing	Activity	Organization	Student Outcomes
I.	15 minutes (15)	Review the Burns and the Bass models of transformational leadership.	Mini-lecture	• To comprehend classical leadership theories. Transformational leaders define and articulate a vision for their organizations. • Followers accept the credibility of the leader (Tracey and Hinkin, 1998). • Transactional leaders emphasize work standards, assignments, and task-oriented goals based on bureaucratic authority and legitimacy within the organization. They focus on task completion and employee compliance and rely heavily on organizational rewards and punishments to influence employee performance.
II.	15 –30 minutes (15)	Show the first and last scenes in the film, which show Ryan as an old man, Miller's last words on the bridge in Romelle, and the final scene in the cemetery where we see Miller's name on the gravestone.	Video clips from 0:00:00 to 0:03:47 and from 2:34:20 to 2:41:42 (Fade out).	Orientation and refresher on case.
III.	30-50 minutes (20)	Students evaluate Miller's leadership using the transformational and transactional leadership models.	Group Discussion	To apply classical leadership theories to analyze situations under high stress and personal danger.
IV.	50-60 minutes (10)	Students apply what they have learned to their lives as managers.	Individual reflection, choose a few to share with the group.	To evaluate the appropriateness of classic leadership theories to dangerous, high stress environment.

Additional Theories

The six theories analyzed here are given as examples and launch points for discussion. Instructors could substitute their favorite theories for those suggested in this teaching note. Some suggestions include the servant leadership model suggested by Robert Greanleaf or Kathy Eisenhardt's model of strategic decision-making in high velocity environments.

Discussion questions and answers

Question 1

What traits does Captain Miller (Tom Hanks) display as a leader in the film <u>Saving Private Ryan</u>?
<u>Analysis skills</u> (breaking a concept into its parts and explaining their interrelationships, distinguishing relevant from extraneous material)

Answer

Early studies of leadership focused almost exclusively on traits that distinguish a leader from the other members of a group. While some personality factors are stronger than others, the correlations have been weak. Stodgill (1974) lists personality characteristics that make it more likely that someone will emerge as a leader. These include achievement drive, adaptability, alertness, ascendance, attractiveness, energy, responsibility, self-confidence, and sociability.

Film reviewers cite a range of traits that make up the character of Captain Miller. Some of them are there because of the way the role was written; others appear because of Tom Hanks, the actor playing the role. Table I shows a list of the traits ascribed to Miller in a few of the reviews.

Table 1 Captain Miller Leadership Traits

Trait	Source
Ability to improvise battle plans	Levy (1998)
Brave	Levy (1998)
Cool head	Levy (1998)
Decent	Maslin (1998)
Deliberate in separating his best memories and instincts from the grim realities of his duty	Levy (1998)
Earns the absolute trust and loyalty of his men	Levy (1998)
Fallible man	Maslin (1998)
Has survived experiences so unspeakable that he wonders if his wife will even recognize him	Ebert (1998) Maslin (1998)
He does his best because that is his duty	Ebert (1998)
Intensely decent	Levy (1998)
Intensely dedicated officer	Levy (1998)
Modest, taciturn brand of heroism	Maslin (1998)
Noble	Levy (1998)
One of those American hero types	Levy (1998)
Only complains to his superiors. ``I don't gripe to you, I don't gripe in front of you," he tells them. ``Gripes go up."	Graham (1998)
Smart	Levy (1998)
Stoic, cynical mask	Wilmington (1998)
Strong	Maslin (1998)
Sustains his courage while privately confounded by the extent that war has now shaped him	Maslin (1998)
Tad boyish	Levy (1998)
Tough	Wilmington (1998)
Unsung	Levy (1998)

Stodgill argues that more positive leadership traits a potential leader has, the more likely they are to take a leadership role. How does Miller come out on Stodgill's list of personality traits (i.e. achievement drive, adaptability, alertness, ascendance, attractiveness, energy, responsibility, self-confidence, and sociability)?

In achievement drive, Miller appears to rate high. He has risen to the rank of Captain rather than staying a lieutenant or going in as an enlisted man. He believes he should do his duty to the best of his ability and that makes him stand out.

Miller rates very high on adaptability. In the final battle scene, he is the only one who has read the Army manual on sticky bombs. He shows the other soldiers how to make them and together they devise a plan for defending a vital bridge from the Germans. On Omaha Beach, he is constantly developing new plans on the basis of the resources that he has available. Since these represent only five percent of the original force, he has to take what comes. When confronted with a German machine gun nest near a radar installation, he devises an attack plan on the spot.

Miller gets high marks on alertness as well. Although at Omaha Beach, he initially goes into shock from the sound and fury of the German defenses, he eventually gets his feet moving and exits the landing craft. From then until the end of the movie, he seems to be in some kind of hyper aware state that keeps him on track no matter how harsh the opposition. In the war as depicted by SPR, when you lose your alertness, you will probably die. The second time Captain Miller goes into shock, he does not recover.

By casting Tom Hanks in the lead role, director Steven Spielberg ensures that Captain Miller will rate very high on attractiveness. Hanks is one of Hollywood's top performing actors and rates high in attractiveness with both men and women. The men in his platoon are clearly attracted to him and interested to learn more about his past, although he keeps it closely hidden for most of the film. They like him, they want to know more about him, but they don't understand him.

Miller appears to be one of the most energetic characters in the film. Although at least one member of the group, Upham, is terrified under fire, Miller continues to function at a very high level. He gets by on very little sleep, but makes sure that the others get rest.

Captain Miller takes his responsibility seriously. He does not shirk the assignment to save Private Ryan, even though he sees it as more of a public relations move than anything that will contribute to winning the war. He puts his own spin on the assignment, however, by insisting that the platoon engage the enemy even when it is not exactly consistent with the primary assignment. "If we don't take out this machine gun nest, the next platoon will run into it. We have to take it out now," he tells the group. He understands the larger goals of reaching Cherbourg and eventually Berlin and takes responsibility based on his knowledge of both the short term and long term objectives.

Miller shows high levels of self-confidence in front of the other men, although we know from his moments in private that he has his doubts. "Gripes go up," he tells them. "I don't gripe to you, I don't gripe in front of you." Miller has enough confidence in his own leadership to accept a certain level of discontent within the group.

One trait where Miller does not rate as high is on sociability. He does not interact with the group. They have a pool going to see who will be the first to learn what he did back home. He keeps his private life very private. He does not participate in casual conversations with his subordinates, although we see that he is very relaxed with his peers when he meets with them. It is apparent, however, that the distance he has developed from the group is the result of his wartime experiences and not part of his normal personality back home. He may have been sociable when he joined the Army, but he has lost some of it due to the traumas he has experienced.

The reviewers also point out some traits that make Miller less likely to be the leader, as shown in Table 2. As the table shows, nothing in Miller's past suggested that he would be such a strong leader in combat. Even he is somewhat mystified by his success.

Table 2 Reviewer's comments on Miller's leadership traits

Traits	Source
Despairing about his role in leading men to slaughter	Turan (1998)
English teacher-turned-soldier	Wilmington (1998), Ebert (1998)
He's as far from John Wayne as imaginable	Levy (1998)
His hand, as if in revolt, is seized regularly with shakes and tremors. His hands tremble, he is on the brink of breakdown. The periodic trembling of one of his hands reveals he's dangerously close to coming apart	Wilmington (1998), Ebert (1998), Turan (1998)
Miller finally does tell his story, at a moment when his squad is on the brink of disintegrating. What is so moving is how ordinary it is.	Graham (1998)
Mystery to his men	Graham (1998), Maslin (1998)
Secretly vulnerable	Wilmington (1998)
Self-doubting and emotional	Levy (1998)
Self-enclosed	Wilmington (1998)
Slightly embittered and obsessive	Wilmington (1998)
Troubled at the person the war has turned him into	Turan (1998)

Based on these traits, we would not have identified Miller as a leader if we saw him in another situation. "Back home when people find out what I do, they say 'it figures.' But here it's a big mystery," Miller says when he finally reveals his past. The film confirms the weakness of trait theories—that we can't tell what traits will be needed until a particular situation arises.

Reviewing the trait literature, Stodgill (1974) suggested that dominance has a negative correlation with leadership emergence, while attractiveness, extroversion, emotional balance, and nurturance have no clear relationship. In general, Miller only gives direct orders when he knows the group has agreed to go forward. He knows that he cannot force someone to fight against his or her will, so he gives people alternatives. When Private Reiben (Edward Burns) wants to desert, he backs down and asks him to wait until he can submit the paperwork. His low level of dominance is consistent with Stodgill's approach.

While it could be argued that Miller shows a high level of attractiveness, a low level of extroversion, a low level of emotional balance, and a moderate level nurturance, these do not have a clear relationship to leadership emergence in the literature. They do have a relationship to survival, however. As Miller's stress level increases during battle, his emotional balance goes over the edge and he goes into shock.

In addition to personality traits, Stodgill examined physical and mental characteristics such as height, weight, age, intelligence, and task abilities. In height and weight, Miller cannot be distinguished from his subordinates. He is younger than Sergeant Horvath is but older than most of the group. His entire group appears highly intelligent so it is hard to distinguish him on that score. Miller does have some outstanding skills and abilities that increase the group's chances for survival. Just by surviving the blood bath at Omaha Beach, Miller has proven his survival skills, or at least his luck in not being one of the 95 percent casualties. Although not as highly skilled as some in the group like the sharpshooter, the group never questions his ability, only the wisdom of those higher in command.

One trait Stodgill fails to mention is that the leader usually has to be alive. Researchers might put this under the category of "participation rate." Stein and Heller (1979) found a high correlation between leadership emergence and the number of remarks a member makes. As leader, Miller has more interactions with the rest of the group because they all look to him for direction.

What applications can you make to your life as a manager?

The evidence against trait theories is as strong in *Saving Private Ryan* as it is in other studies. The film suggests that we should no longer look at leadership traits alone when trying to explain success or failure of our leaders. The response of the reviewers, however, shows how strongly the trait model is entrenched in our everyday way of thinking. We have to be careful not to stereotype people as leaders or followers on the basis of limited observations.

When we see the traits shown by Captain Miller we deem them heroic. These traits seem rare and admirable in today's world of downsizing and globalization. As researchers, we propose models that can describe and prescribe behavior. Do any of our leadership models explain what it takes to motivate the kinds of sacrifice we see in *Saving Private Ryan*? Do managers as leaders demonstrate any of the traits we admire in Miller? Sadly, none of these traits explain why Ryan would return to Normandy after fifty years to ask himself if he had earned Miller's sacrifice.

Question 2

Does Captain Miller exhibit the behaviors of a successful leader suggested by the behavioral model of leadership?

Analysis skills (breaking a concept into its parts and explaining their interrelationships, distinguishing relevant from extraneous material)

Answer

The weaknesses of the trait model led researchers to look for other indicators of leadership success. Krech and Crutchfield (1948) were quickly overwhelmed by the list of behaviors attributed to successful leaders. Kerr, Schreisheim, Murphy, and Stodgill (1974) created the Leader Behavior Description Questionnaire to assess leadership action. The LBDQ works along two dimensions, which they called relationship orientation and task orientation.

Captain Miller's leadership behaviors in *Saving Private Ryan* demonstrate behavior consistent with both a task orientation and a relationship orientation. These behaviors can be observed in the opening scenes on Omaha Beach.

Behaviors related to relationship orientation include:

- Listens to group members
- Easy to understand
- Is friendly and approachable
- Treats group members as equals
- Is willing to make changes (Forsyth, 1983, p. 215)

Listens to group members. From the first scene, Miller is constantly observing the troops under his command. When he sees the barrage of bullets that hits the men in the front of the landing craft, he orders the rest over the side. Things aren't much better under water, but at least they have a chance. Once on the beach, huddled behind the steel obstacles set by the Germans to slow their landing, Miller sees that the troops do not want move. "Where's the rallying point?" someone asks him. "Anywhere but here!" he answers. Next a demolitions expert comes along and wants to blow the obstacle so the tanks can land. "The tanks have all sunk in the surf, " Miller tells him. "I don't care, I am still going to blow this obstacle." Miller realizes he has to get the men off the water line and up to the base of the sand dune. Once there he asks the other survivors the situation. "Who's in charge here?" "You are sir." "Who is left?" Bits and pieces of several companies. They put together a working unit.

Miller is constantly exchanging information with everyone around. He confers with Sergeant Horvath and asks the sniper, Jackson, if he can get a clean shot. As they move forward under heavy fire, Horvath says to Miller, "If your mother saw you now, she'd be very upset."

Miller replies, "I thought you were my mother." Even in the heat of battle, Miller pays attention to what people say.

Easy to understand. Miller's commands in the first twenty minutes are confined to short bursts that the men can understand quickly. *"Over the side." "Dog 1 is now open." "Grab your weapons and move!"* The situation is life and death. He orders the medics to stop treating the wounded and move forward. Every order is clear and concise. The men are trained to understand what he means.

Is friendly and approachable. We do not see much in Miller's overt behavior that suggests he is friendly or unfriendly in the Omaha Beach scenes. We get a deeper message about him; however, as we see him repeatedly dragging wounded men off the beach, only to see them cut apart by machine gun fire.

He tries to help them, sees it is hopeless, and moves on reluctantly to save himself so he can rally the survivors to finish the attack. Sergeant Horvath notices his rush into the battle as they hide from German fire. His comment about his mother suggests that they have known each other for some time and that Miller can be approached under the right circumstances.

Treats group members as equals. Miller looks and acts like the other members of the company. If not for the captain's bars on his helmets, we wouldn't even know he was an officer. D-Day survivors say that this is historically inaccurate because officers never put insignia on their uniforms. In the film, it helps us to identify Miller as someone in authority amidst a totally chaotic scene. Miller does not behave like someone in a superior position, except to use his knowledge of the overall plan to give orders. Everyone knows in general what needs to be done and knows their specialties. They look to him to identify when and where they should put their skills to use. Being an officer appears to be another specialty, just like firing a machine gun, sharpshooting, or using explosives.

Is willing to make changes. Miller is improvising during the entire Omaha Beach scene. No one is where he is supposed to be. None of the companies have more than five percent of their men, but his job is to open up the beach. He uses the resources he has at hand and blows an opening in the dunes. Next, he takes out the first machine gun, clearing an open space less deadly than the water line. Finally, they climb the hill and take out the deadly pillboxes. He changes the plan but sticks to the mission, which is to open "Dog 1."

Based on the data in the Omaha Beach scene, it is hard to conclude that Miller has a strong relationship orientation. We need evidence of his behavior in a less stressful situation.

Behaviors related to task orientation include:
- Assigns tasks to members.
- Makes attitudes clear to the group.
- Is critical of poor work.
- Sees to it that the group is working to capacity.
- Coordinates activity. (Forsyth, 1983, p. 215)

Assigns tasks to members. Miller gives orders as soon as the landing craft hits the beach and continues giving them throughout the battle. As soon as he reaches the base of the cliff, he begins to assign tasks to other soldiers. "Grab your weapons and move," he tells them. Because the chain of command is clear, the soldiers next to him obey immediately, realizing that the units they came in with no longer exist due to the heavy casualties. He tells Medic Wade to move on to someone he can help. He orders the group into the trench with the phrase, "It's time to get into the war."

Makes attitudes clear to the group. Miller's behavior in the opening scene shows his attitudes in several ways. He wants to stay alive and to keep as many of his men alive as he can. He yells to another soldier who is hiding behind an obstacle on the beach that he has to move on: "Stay here and you're a dead man." He pushes the survivors who make it to the base of the dune to continue the attack even though they are scared stiff. As they are working to open an escape route off the beach, Miller uses a mirror to peek around the corner of a rock at a German machine gun. Miller says to the platoon: "Let's get into the war. Covering fire!" His attitude is clear; they can't just sit there, because they still have a job to do. Sergeant Horvath is not so sure: "It's a goddamn firing squad, just add a blindfold." Miller replies: "It's the only way to get everyone out of here." With this statement he reveals that his concern goes beyond the orders he has received from above. He major concern now is the welfare of his men, which is clearly not served by sitting as targets on the beach.

Is critical of poor work. Throughout the attack on Omaha Beach, Miller is critical of how the operation is going. He is upset because he is losing so many men and believes it may be his fault. He is angry because the tanks have foundered in the surf leaving them without the support of heavy weapons. He is critical of the medics who are dying to save the wounded instead of helping with the attack. "Get rid of that crap, finds some weapons, and follow me," he tells them. The task at hand, stopping the hail of fire from the cliffs, is so obvious to him he can't believe that anyone would try doing anything else, regardless of their previous assignment.

Sees to it that the group is working to capacity. Clearly, the second rangers are working way beyond their capacity when they attack Omaha Beach. Ninety-five percent of the troops were lost in the first wave. The remaining men were somehow able to succeed in the attack but only because the Germans had sent their reserves to Calais. In spite of these horrible odds, Miller manages to get outstanding performance from the surviving men and they succeed in securing the beach.

Coordinates activity. The first time you watch SPR, you do not realize how busy Miller is during these first scenes. He seems to be moving in slow motion and so much is happening around him that it all looks automatic. In the second viewing, you begin to notice that he is constantly giving orders to coordinate the work of the survivors who are from several different companies. It appears that from their training, they have skills that will help the attack succeed. Miller combines the work of the sharpshooter, Jackson, the demolitions man with the Bangalore pipe bomb, and the rest of the troops to take out the German's first lines of defense and open up an exit from the beach.

What applications can you make to your life as a manager?

Chris Argyris (1974) differentiates between espoused theories and theories-in-use when explaining our behavior in groups. Theories-in-use are the actions we take when we are under severe pressure, regardless of what we might say our preferred action would be.

Although we never hear Captain Miller espouse any leadership theory except the cryptic "gripes go up," we see him exhibiting leadership behaviors that are both relationship oriented and task oriented. The implication for leaders today is that they should consider both the people they are leading and the nature of the task the group must accomplish. Sadly, many managers ignore both. When managers fail to take into account the needs of their subordinates and are unable to give them any clues about the tasks that they will have to accomplish, their leadership is in doubt. It is so easy to get wrapped up in the day-to-day demands of any job that keeping track of where other people are in the process can be very difficult. If we add the complications of differing time zones and physical locations, today's managers face many obstacles to leadership.

We admire Miller as a leader in part because the objectives were clear and because his group exhibits a high level of camaraderie seldom seen in the workplace today. In our admiration, we should not ignore the pressure they withstood and the high casualty rate they faced in achieving their objective. We have to look to the leaders who are not in the film for an explanation of those casualties; the film does not depict them. We have to assume that they, like Miller, are willing to trade men for the mission. Do we expect leaders to do the same today? It often seems that way. When organizations place high demands on their members' time and energy with few rewards, the result can be illness, injury, or violence that sometimes matches the scenes in SPR. If such is the case, we have to ask, is the mission worth it? In *Saving Private Ryan* we believe that it is. The case for achieving the mission of most corporations is not as clear.

While Miller's behavior is consistent with both task oriented and relationship-oriented leadership, these models do not explain why Miller used one approach or the other in a given situation. Even if they did explain, they could not tell us why Ryan still felt Miller's influence fifty years later and still wanted his approval. To understand Miller's leadership at a deeper level, we will now analyze it using a model that explains when a particular style will be most effective.

Question 3

Does Captain Miller change his leadership style in different situations consistent with the recommendations of the contingency model of leadership?

Analysis skills (breaking a concept into its parts and explaining their interrelationships, distinguishing relevant from extraneous material)

Answer

Fiedler (1978) proposed a three factor contingency model of leadership that describes when relationship motivated leadership or task motivated leadership will be most effective. The three factors are leader/member relations, task structure, and leader position power. Fiedler uses a measurement called the least preferred coworker (LPC) scale to determine whether a leader is primarily relationship motivated or task motivated. To determine whether Captain Miller is an effective leader using Fiedler's model, we have to determine the characteristics of the situation and his primary motivational style.

To analyze Miller's leadership style using Fiedler's model, we will use evidence from the second battle scene, in the town of Neuville, where they meet up with a group of paratroops.

With only a few exceptions, Miller appears to have strong relationships with the members of the group. He treats them as reliable and trustworthy and they generally cooperate with him to get the job done.

Fielder suggests that an effective leader would change his behavior to meet the needs of the situation.

The structure of the task in saving Ryan is not clearly defined when they arrive at Neuville. This is not a step-by-step standard operating procedure. They must improvise as they go along. They never know exactly where the enemy or the rest of the American Army are precisely located. They create plans on the spot and restructure as needed. One characteristic of the American Army that stands out in the film is its ability to reform under new commanding officers whenever existing units are broken up due to casualties or lost troops. Miller is clearly a master of improvisation within a known set of objectives. In the village, the paratroopers are split. They want to join up with the other group to see if Ryan is with them. Miller makes calls like a football quarterback: "Try a left hook. Two of your guys, two of mine." The men always seem to know what he means.

As a leader in a military unit, Miller's position power is very strong. Although we do not see him do so, we know he controls rewards in the form of medal recommendations, punishments in the form of courts martial, hiring by choosing who will be in his unit, and task assignment by giving group members specific directions during their attacks.   The only kind of reward that matters to anyone, however, is going home alive. Miller does everything he can to protect them, but things do not always go the way he expects and men are lost. Caparzo is killed trying to do "the decent thing" by helping a little girl. "That's why we can't take children," Miller tells the others. In his position, he has to order people to do things that are fundamentally <u>not</u> decent, but that must be done to accomplish their mission, capture Berlin and go home.

According to Fiedler's model, when leader-member relations are good, Captain Miller's situation fits in the Octant III and calls for a leader who is task motivated.

Octant	I	II	III	IV	V	VI	VII	VIII
Leader/member relations	Good	Good	Good	Good	Bad	Bad	Bad	Bad
Task structure	Structured		Unstructured		Structured		Unstructured	
Leader position power	Strong	Weak	Strong	Weak	Strong	`Weak	Strong	Weak

(Source: Fiedler, 1978)

When leader-member relations are good, the other requirements of the situation mean that his high level of task orientation is very effective. The group gets along well, respects his authority, and looks to him to help structure the task. They seldom need his help to resolve their differences because they don't have many.

We have to look to another scene in the film to determine how Miller behaves when relationships deteriorate in the group. After the next battle at a German radar site, we see Miller change his behavior to a more relationship-oriented style, consistent with Fiedler's recommendations.

In order to rank Captain Miller on the LPC scale, we would have to have him complete Fiedler's instrument. Since that is not possible, we have to infer his motivation from his predominantly task oriented behavior, which appears to support the Fielder model.   He urges the men to rest when they get to the church but does not worry much about his relationship with them. He wants them ready to move on in a few hours. His concern always seems to be for the task. In a conversation with Sergeant Horvath, Miller explains how he is able to put task ahead of relationship:

"You tell yourself it happened so you can save the life of ten others. I've lost 94 men under my command. That means I saved ten, maybe twenty times as many. It's simple. That's how you rationalize the choice between the mission and the men."

The only problem is that this mission is not about territory, like their other missions. As Horvath points out, "Only this time the mission is a man." Miller replies, "This Ryan better be worth it. He'd better design a better light bulb or find a miracle cure because I wouldn't trade a hundred Ryans for Veccio or Caparzo." Miller faces a dilemma. He is a task-oriented leader in a situation that seems to call for it but where the sacrifices needed by his men are inconsistent with the purpose of the mission itself. His doubts about their purpose are shared by the men in the platoon and will have to be resolved before they can finish their mission.

What applications can you make to your life as a manager?

The Fiedler contingency leadership model does not have universal support in the literature (Forsyth, 1984). Researchers such as Ashour (1973) criticize it for being overly simplistic and methodologically unsound. As is obvious from the chaos we witness in *Saving Private Ryan*, some situations are so uncertain and equivocal that they defy our ability to analyze them, even if we were able to apply a model like Fiedler's with any consistency. Moreover, Fiedler's model still cannot explain how Miller is able to lead his men into battles where the odds for survival are very poor. For day-to-day tasks, Fiedler's model may have some value, but in extreme situations, leaders need better models to draw on. Once again, we cannot tell from the contingency model what makes Miller so inspiring to Ryan, who he only knows for less than a day.

Question 4

Is Captain Miller's behavior consistent with the decision making approach recommended by the Vroom-Yetton normative model of leadership?

Analysis skills (breaking a concept into its parts and explaining their interrelationships, distinguishing relevant from extraneous material)

Answer

In an attempt to resolve some of the difficulties with the contingency theory, researchers have proposed a normative leadership model (Vroom, 1974. 1976; Vroom & Yetton, 1973). In the normative leadership model, Vroom and Yetton (1973) propose several methods of leadership ranging from fully autocratic to fully participative. The methods include Autocratic I, Autocratic II, Consultative I, Consultative II, and Group II. In the heat of battle, it would be unrealistic to expect Captain Miller to actually follow such an elaborate decision making process. The purpose of this exercise is practice using the model as an analytical tool.

The model provides a decision tree based on the answers to seven questions. The decision tree results in twelve possible outcomes and suggests that one or more methods may be acceptable depending on the outcome. To determine whether Captain Miller was an effective leader based on the normative model, we need to analyze his decisions using the decision tree and determine whether he used an acceptable method to deal with the decision. The basis for the analysis will be the third battle scene in which the platoon attacks the machine gun nest next to a radar installation.

The crucial decision is whether or not to attack the German machine gun. The group disagrees about the wisdom of taking the risk, which may detract from their assignment to find Private Ryan. Miller overrules their objections and they attack, losing their medic in the process. Let's examine his decision using the normative model.

Is there a quality requirement such that one solution is likely to be more rational than another is?

It is hard to translate a wartime objective into the language of business decisions. The group had two "quality requirements." One was to survive long enough to find Private Ryan. If the Germans killed them while they were attacking the emplacement, they would not complete their assignment. The problem with this argument for not attacking was as follows: Miller knew that their commitment to saving Ryan was not very high. Everyone understood that the purpose of their mission was to improve home front morale and to create positive public relations for the Army.

Knowing this argument is weak, Miller reminds them of a higher order "quality requirement" that goes above their short term assignment: the Army must reach Cherbourg and drive out the Germans if they are going to succeed in the invasion and eventually reach Berlin. "Then we can all go home," he tells them. In doing so, he invokes a different measure of quality that requires risk and sacrifice beyond what it will take just to rescue Ryan. He uses the same argument with Ryan later on when Ryan refuses to leave the bridge his unit is committed to defending.

The quality requirement of contributing to eventual victory wins out against the quality requirement of saving their own skins so one solution becomes more attractive than another. The answer to question A is YES. Therefore, we go on to question B.

Do I have sufficient information to make a high quality decision?

Miller never has a lot of information about what is going on in the field. They must make decisions on the basis of quick observations and past experience. In this decision, though, the group and Miller have a pretty good idea of what it will take to take out the machine gun. The answer to question B is YES, so we can skip question C (Is the problem structured?) and go on to D.

Is acceptance of the decision by subordinates critical to effective implementation?

Miller cannot attack the machine gun nest by himself. He needs the rest of the group to carry out the plan. Their survival instincts tell them that their best move is to go around the emplacement and keep searching for Ryan. If Miller wants them to attack, he must have their acceptance. A direct order might be disobeyed. The answer to question D is YES. We now proceed to question E.

If Miller was to make the decision by myself, is it reasonably certain that his subordinates would accept it?

When they begin the discussion it is pretty clear that Miller's decision would not be accepted at first. He will have to persuade them to attack. They do not see how it could possibly be in their best interests or in the best interests of saving Private Ryan to take on this problem. The answer to question E is NO, so we go on to question F.

Do subordinates share the organizational goals to be attained in solving this problem?

One of the reasons the group questions Miller's decision to attack in the first place is because of his "gripes only go up" policy. Up until this time, he has not revealed to the group how he feels about the assignment to save Private Ryan other than a cynical statement that they know does not reflect his true feelings. For the first time we learn that while he has chosen to obey orders and take the assignment, he also has a higher order goal, which is to win the war so he can go home to his wife. Once he shares this information, the rest of the group agrees. They don't really care about saving Ryan either. They do care about winning the war. The decision to attack makes no sense if their goal is to save Ryan. It only makes sense if the goal is to guard the rest of the advancing army from potential danger and speed them to their objectives: Cherbourg and eventually Berlin. The answer to question F is YES, therefore we skip question G. (Is conflict among subordinates likely in preferred solutions?). The decision tree indicates that this is Problem Type 5 in the model. The acceptable method is "Group II" in the Vroon-Yetton model. Group II requires consultation with the group to achieve consensus before proceeding.

Question	Answer
A.	YES
B.	YES
C.	Skip
D.	YES
E.	NO
F.	YES
G.	Skip
Problem	5

Type	

Which of the methods, if any, did Captain Miller actually follow?

The Autocratic I (AI) method requires the leader to solve the problem alone based on the information available at the time. The Autocratic II method (AII) requires the leader to solicit information from the group and then decide on the solution alone. The Consultative I (CI) method requires the leader to share the problem individually with members of the group and then make the decision alone. The Consultative II (CII) method requires the leader to share the problem with the entire group, obtain their suggestions and then make the decision alone.

The Group II (GII) method requires the group to share the problem with the group. Together they should generate alternatives and attempt to reach agreement on a solution. The leader is more like the chairperson of a committee but does not try to influence the outcome of any particular solution.

Miller's decision method is a blend of Consultative II and Group II. He consults with the group and asks for their suggestions. They suggest going around and continuing the search for Ryan. He proposes another alternative: attack the German emplacement and take it out of the path of the advancing army. He listens to their reasons and gives his. He does not appear willing to change his mind but he does not rely solely on his formal authority to carry the decision. Even though Miller's behavior is not totally consistent with the model, it is believable and realistic. It may be the closest thing to group decision-making that we will ever see in a group behind enemy lines. From the perception of the viewer, it is clearly a dilemma for the group whether they should risk one of their lives to save the lives of the next platoon that comes this way. At this point they are no longer discussing whether they should save Private Ryan. They must decide whether it is worth the effort to save an unknown soldier in an unknown unit that chance will bring down the road next.

What applications can you make to your life as a manager?

One criticism of the Vroon-Yetton model is that it is too complex and time consuming to apply on a regular basis in day-to-day decision-making. When we see Miller, we have no expectation that he will analyze every decision using a complex, seven question, twelve outcome, five style normative model. We just want him to be an effective leader. As viewers, we believe that he is one. Does Miller's use of group or collaborative decision making techniques explain why the men follow him into battle? Once again, the scenes depicted in the film are two orders of magnitude more extreme than what most of us face in organizations. The model does not show us how Miller appeals to higher order goals in order to motivate their behavior on short-term tasks that are extremely dangerous. The model also gives us little insight on what gives Miller so much influence over Ryan in the short time they are acquainted.

Question 5

Does Captain Miller provide the level of leader involvement that will result in the highest level of performance of his subordinates, according to path-goal theory?

Analysis skills (breaking a concept into its parts and explaining their interrelationships, distinguishing relevant from extraneous material)

Answer

House and Mitchell's (1974) have proposed another model for understanding leadership, path-goal theory. Path-goal theory asks how much assistance a leader should provide subordinates in accomplishing their tasks. The model proposes that the level of leader involvement that will result in the highest level of performance and satisfaction should vary depending on subordinate expectations, task characteristics, organizational structure and systems. In this section, we will examine the final battle scene, defending a bridge from German attack using path-goal theory.

Subordinate expectations

According to House and Mitchell (1974) subordinate expectations are influenced by three distinct characteristics: autonomy, experience and ability. Individuals who prize autonomy will expect less involvement from their leaders. Individuals who are experienced will also expect less involvement. Individuals with high ability will expect lower involvement.

It is not clear how much the members of Miller's platoon value their autonomy. Army training has drilled into them the importance of the chain of command. While they may have valued it in a prior life, in this situation, they look to Miller for leadership. They expect his involvement. Once the soldiers decide not to leave the bridge, they give up a large portion of their autonomy. They know they may not be able to preserve their own lives in the face of superior German forces. They look to Captain Miller because his leadership offers them the best chance of success, but not necessarily the best chance of individual survival.

With the exception of Corporal Upham, all of the platoon members are highly experienced. In the Omaha Beach segment, we saw Sergeant Horvath scooping up a can of Omaha dirt and adding to a backpack with cans from Africa, and Italy. By luck and skill, Horvath survived several other amphibious landings. He does not want his commander giving him advice on how to save his skin, or ordering him to take unnecessary risks. Upham on the other hand, knows nothing about combat and looks to Miller and the others for direction constantly. He finally gains acceptance from the group when they explain the meaning of "FUBAR." Before his final confrontation with the Germans at the end of the story, it is not clear whether he is really learning anything from his experiences.

All of the members of Miller's group and Ryan's group are highly skilled. We see the sharpshooter using his unique talents to eliminate German threats one at a time. Ryan knows that bazooka ammunition can serve as a grenade. Mellish knows how to fire the large machine gun. Captain Miller is not a sharpshooter, bazooka specialist, or machine gunner. He does not bring those skills to the group, but he coordinates their work together so that they can apply their skills effectively. He also uses his knowledge to help them create new weapons such as sticky bombs from existing materials.

Overall, subordinates do not expect Miller to tell them what exactly what to do in every situation. They look to him to set them in place to do their specialized jobs. They have autonomy within their specialty but they expect Miller to take control over what happens to the group whenever possible.

Task Characteristics

Key task characteristics, according to House and Mitchell (1974), are structure and difficulty. A highly structured task does not require as much direction to perform. The task of defending the bridge is not structured at all when Miller arrives. What little structure exists is provided by Miller and by the formalities of rank that were drummed into every soldier in boot camp. The soldiers expect Miller to have a high level of involvement in problem solving. The paratroops in Ryan's unit have wired the bridge with explosives and are waiting for the Germans to advance. They meet up with Miller while on reconnaissance to see if the Germans are coming close to their town.

The task is extremely difficult and dangerous. Miller's approach makes it even more dangerous because he intends to make a contribution to the war at the same time he completes the assignment to find Ryan. As the level of difficulty ratchets up, those present become more dependent on Miller for leadership. When Ryan refuses to leave his unit with Miller, the crisis that began at the machine gun nest climaxes for Ryan. Private Ryan, who values staying with his friends above saving his own life, solves Miller's dilemma between the mission and the man. Miller is amazed when Ryan refuses to go: "Is that what they are supposed to tell your mother?" he asks Ryan. " Tell her I was with the only brothers I have left," Ryan replies. From this point on the focus of the mission is back on winning the war and, if possible, saving Ryan. The mission comes before the man and the man agrees.

Linderman (1997) suggests an alternative explanation. Linderman suggests that comradeship, the connection between the soldier and his fellows, was a major appeal to battle. "To a soldier, it was incontestable that the presence of comrades improved the odds that he would survive the war. (p. 265)." The mission is not to win the war, it is to stay and defend your comrades. Miller and his platoon have been together "since Anzio." They have met the comrade test by looking out for each other over numerous battles, including the ones we see in the film as they search for Ryan. Now Ryan must prove that he is also a comrade, a friend worth saving. The only way he can do that is by putting comradeship ahead of saving himself.

Once Ryan and Miller agree, Miller goes back to talk to Horvath. Miller tells him: "Sergeant, we have crossed some kind of boundary here. We are in the surreal. What do you think?" Horvath replies,

"You don't want to know what I think." Miller disagrees, "No, Mike, I do." Horvath sums up the theme of the film, "Maybe saving Private Ryan was the one decent thing we were able to pull out of this whole shitty mess. We do that, we all earn the right to go home." With that, Miller begins to structure their defense of the bridge by laying out the tactics they will follow and creating a structure where one did not exist before. The task is still difficult but it is no longer unstructured by the time the Germans arrive in Romelle.

Organizational Structure and Systems

Organizational structures may help or hinder leadership effectiveness. Structures such as work group norms, organizational rewards, and organizational controls can duplicate or complement the support leaders give to groups.

The norms of the "work group" in SPR are biased towards high performance. Low performance in this context can result in death, so that could be a motivating factor. Because the norms for performance are high, Miller does not spend much time dealing with opportunists and slackers. Quite the opposite, Miller must deal with Ryan's refusal to leave his unit when he is needed.

Organizational rewards are not much of an issue in the gritty battle-scarred world of SPR. The soldiers fight to survive, they fight to hold onto key resources such as bridges, they attack enemy strongholds and beat down resistance. We never see anyone get a medal. We never see anyone ask for one or get recommended. External rewards such as these seem trivial in light of the life and death struggles we see on screen. The greatest reward in this universe is to stand by your buddies and defend them when they need it. The greatest punishment is knowing you have let them down, as Upham does when he is frozen in fear on the stairs as two soldiers fight hand to hand in the next room. The group seems to have a tacit acceptance that if they are still alive at the end of the day they have done a great job.

We also see very little evidence of organizational controls in the final battle of the film. No one has to worry about his or her budget, other than running out of ammunition. Each soldier has his own measure of personal effectiveness: survival. He does not have to rely on the army to tell him whether or not he is doing a good job. The group is not in communication with the rest of the army. They choose to stay and fight. They choose to accept Miller's leadership both because of his rank and because of his expertise. Miller chooses to accept Ryan's refusal to leave even though it was not what the Army wanted in the short term. The group controls at this phase of the story are much stronger than those of the larger organization.

In Captain Miller, we see a leader who has a good fit with the expectations of the soldiers, with the nature of the task confronting them, and with the organizational systems that are in place to support their performance. Path-goal theory suggests that Miller will be an effective leader in this situation. We observe that he is very effective.

What applications can you make to your life as a manager?

Path-goal theory does not tell us what will happen if the situation changes, but it suggests ways that Miller could be effective in other settings, if he had survived. He does not. Sometimes leaders succeed at the mission but are casualties themselves. What motivates people to take on leadership roles under such conditions? What kind of leadership behaviors should they exhibit that will demonstrate their level of commitment to their followers? None of the models we have surveyed so far have given us much help, other than to confirm what we already know—that Miller is an effective leader. None of them help us understand his affect on Private Ryan.

In the next section, we will look for answers to these questions by examining the opening and closing of *Saving Private Ryan* using the transformational leader model proposed by Burns (1978).

Question 6

Is Captain Miller a transformational leader?
Analysis skills (breaking a concept into its parts and explaining their interrelationships, distinguishing relevant from extraneous material)

<u>Answer</u>

Burns (1978) defined transformational leadership and contrasted it to transactional leadership. Transformational leaders motivate followers by appealing to higher ideals and moral values. Transformational leaders define and articulate a vision for their organizations. Followers accept the credibility of the leader (Tracey and Hinkin, 1998).

Based on bureaucratic authority and legitimacy within the organization, transactional leaders emphasize work standards, assignments, and task oriented goals. They focus on task completion and employee compliance, and rely heavily on organizational rewards and punishments to influence employee performance (Tracey and Hinkin, 1998).

Miller seldom talks about higher ideals and moral values and ideals, but he does to Ryan. "James, earn this," he tells Ryan as he takes his last gasp. Ryan understands what he means. Miller stayed to defend the bridge because he respected Ryan's desire to stay with his unit. Ryan knows that Miller lost two men to save him and that those lives have to stand for something. With three words, Miller creates a vision in Ryan's mind that defines how he will spend the rest of his life. He has to be a good man to earn the sacrifice that Caparzo, Wade, and Miller made to bring him home alive.

Miller never uses his bureaucratic authority to order Ryan away from the battle. He realizes that he has no legitimate grounds for asking Ryan to leave. Although his mission is to save Ryan, completing that task will result in Ryan failing to complete his mission, which is to defend the bridge. No one cares about organizational rewards and punishments. They don't exist. The only reward is to survive the battle. The only punishment is to be killed by the enemy.

Clearly, with Ryan, Miller has adopted a transformational role, not a transactional one. Their relationship lasts less than a day, but it affects Ryan for the rest of his life. At this point in the film, it is clear that, like Ryan, we too must "earn this." We have an obligation to do something special with our lives to deserve the sacrifices that Miller and millions of others made so that we can live our lives in peace and freedom. Miller's leadership transforms us, too. It appeals to higher values and articulates a vision for a future in which everyone lives to their highest potential, "invents a miracle cure, or creates a longer lasting light bulb." In spite of the horrifying death and destruction, we are inspired to achieve more and justify their loss.

What applications can you make to your life as a manager?

Once we begin discussing transformation, we, like Miller, cross some kind of boundary into the surreal. Most leaders do not seek to transform their followers and those that do are immediately suspect. Most organizations do not strive to achieve higher ideals or moral values so the entire discussion seems moot. At the same time, we struggle with systemic changes in organizations that threaten the livelihood of their participants and cause untold confusion and misery. Although it may not be as devastating as a world war, it results in suffering, nonetheless.

Often, we like World War II movies because they harken back to a simpler era when good and evil seemed more clearly defined. Watching *Casablanca*, for example, you realize a strange irony. When the Germans are singing loudly in Rick's and Lazlo starts singing the Marsellaise, no one starts singing on behalf of the Moroccans. They are in Casablanca where the native language is Arabic and they are singing in French and German. This suggests that good and evil are never simple to define. In *Saving Private Ryan*, both sides commit atrocities and destroy each other mercilessly. Yet some strains of decency survive.

The question for managers is this: Will managers, as leaders, put their energy into missions that are worth the sacrifice? Will they inspire their followers to live better lives, not just by performing better in the organization, but by being better people? Some managers do, but they are rare.

References:

Brennan, J. I. (1998). 'Private Ryan': Rating the big one. <u>Los Angeles Times</u>. Wednesday, July 15. <http://www.hollywood.com/news/topstories/07-15-98/html/1-3.html>.

Burns, J. M. (1978). <u>Leadership</u>. New York: Harper & Row.

Ebert, R. (1998). Review of <u>*Saving Private Ryan*</u>. Chicago Sun Times, July 24. <<u>http://www.suntimes.com/ebert/ebert_reviews/1998/07/072404.html</u>>.

Fiedler, F. E. (1978). The contingency model and the dynamics of the leadership process. In Berkowitz (Ed.) <u>Advances in experimental social psychology.</u> (Vol. 12) New York: Academic Press.

Forsyth, D. R. (1983). <u>An introduction to group dynamics.</u> Belmont, CA: Wadsworth.

Fussell, P. (1975). <u>The great war and modern memory.</u> Oxford: Oxford University Press.

Fussell, P. (1989). <u>Wartime: Understanding and behavior in the Second World War.</u> Oxford: Oxford University Press.

Graham, B. (1998). War is hell: Spielberg and Hanks team for the extraordinary `*Saving Private Ryan*' and bring the dramatic battle back to life. <u>San Francisco Chronicle.</u> Friday, July 24. <<u>http://www.sfgate.com/cgi-bin/article.cgi?file=/chronicle/archive/1998/07/24/DD35860.DTL</u>>.

Gritten, D. (1998). When the going got tough for 'Private Ryan.' <u>Los Angeles Times.</u> Wednesday, July 15. <<u>http://www.hollywood.com/news/topstories/07-15-98/html/1-5.html</u>>.

House, R. J. and Mitchell, T.R. (1974). Path-goal theory of leadership. <u>Journal of contemporary business.</u> 3:81-97.

Levy, S. (1998). Steven Spielberg's World War II epic blows away all previous war movies 'Ryan': Blood and gore may overwhelm some viewers. <u>The Oregonian.</u> July 24.

Linderman, G. (1997). <u>The world within war: America's combat experience in World War II.</u> New York: Free Press.

Maslin, J. (1998) '*Saving Private Ryan*': A soberly magnificent new war film. <u>New York Times,</u> July 24. <<u>http://search.nytimes.com/search/daily/bin/fastweb?getdoc+site+site+4113+0+wAAA+saving%7Eprivate%7Eryan</u>>.

O'Sullivan, M. (1998). Spielberg wins battle, not war. <u>Washington Post.</u> Friday, July 24, 1998. <<u>http://www.washingtonpost.com/wp-srv/style/movies/reviews/savingprivateryanosullivan.htm</u>>.

Rozen, L. (1998) *Saving Private Ryan*. <u>People.</u> August 3. <<u>http://www.pathfinder.com/people/980803/picksnpans/screen/screen2.html</u>>.

Schickel, R. (1998). The reel war: Steven Spielberg peers at the face of battle as Hollywood never has before. <u>Time.</u> Arts/cinema 152 (4) July 24. <<u>http://pathfinder.com/time/magazine/1998/dom/980727/the_arts.cinema.reel_war19.html</u>>.

Shulgasser, B. (1998). Spielberg's "Private' matters: director takes his camera down in the trenches and produces his best work. <u>San Francisco Examiner.</u> July 24. < <u>http://www.sfgate.com/cgi-bin/article.cgi?file=/examiner/archive/1998/07/24/WEEKEND8689.dtl</u>>.

Siskel, G. (1998). Heroic 'Ryan' rings true. <u>Gene Siskel's Flicks Picks</u> <<u>http://www.metromix.com/movies/1,1021,2060,00.html</u>>.

Stodgill, R. M. (1974). <u>Handbook of leadership.</u> New York: Free Press.

Tracey, J. B. and T. R. Hinkin (1998). Transformational leadership or effective managerial practices? <u>Group & organization management.</u> Thousand Oaks, CA: Sage. 23 (3) September, p. 220.

Turan, K. (1998). Soldiers of misfortune. <u>Los Angeles Times.</u> Friday, July 24. <<u>http://www.latimes.com/sbin/iawrapper?NS-search-set=/35bf5/aaaa001czbf5ee9&NS-doc-offset=0&NS-adv-search=1&</u>>.

Vroom, V. H. and Yetton, P. W. (1973). <u>Leadership and decision making</u>. Pittsburgh: University of Pittsburgh Press.

Whetton, D. A. and Cameron, K. S. (1995). <u>Developing management skills, 3rd Ed.</u> New York: Harper Collins.

Wilmington, M. (1998). Apocalypse then: Steven Spielberg's violent '*Saving Private Ryan*' depicts both the horror and humanity of World War II. <u>Chicago Tribune.</u> July 24. <<u>http://chicagotribune.com/leisure/movies/article/0,1051,ART-12665,00.html</u>>.

Epilogue

The D-Day landings were successful for the Allies, who continued their push across France and into Germany. The Germans resisted fiercely, especially in Holland where paratroop drops were unsuccessful (see the film "A Bridge Too Far"), and along the western border of Germany where they counterattacked in the winter of 1944 resulting in the Battle of the Bulge. Germany surrendered in 1945.

Teaching Note
THE SAFETY MEMO

Topics (* = Primary topic with teaching plan)
    *Decision Case
    *Leadership (delegation, empowerment, style)
    *Culture (assessment)
    *Organizational Culture, acceptance of
    *Communication (barriers, dysfunctional)
    *Positional Bargaining
    *Safety
    *Decision-making Process
    Ethics
    Interpersonal Conflict
    Large Corporation (non-banking) Context
    Synthesis Case

Case overview

    When Gordon Baldwin left his old job at Pacific Bell Telephone and joined The Cable Company, he was surprised at the lack of safety observations the field technicians exhibited. At Pacific Bell, he was given extensive training in safety practices and received regular updates and training to remind him of the safety precautions. At The Cable Company, the extent of Gordon's training was a two-week "drive along," where he was to receive on the job training. He noticed many unsafe practices when the technicians were dealing with overhead cable lines and installation. When he expressed his concern to his supervisor, he was asked to join the safety committee. In a short time, Gordon was asked to spend 40 percent of his time on safety issues and he was told that his performance evaluation would be tied to succeeding in reducing the out-of-control workman's comp claims filed at The Cable Company. Over time, Gordon became disheartened as he noticed that very few of the safety suggestions made by him or the committee seemed to be used consistently in the field.

    Gordon wrote a memo to his supervisor outlining what he perceived as lack of commitment from the company. Next thing Gordon knew he was being called to the office of Gil, the executive vice president of engineering. Gil had the reputation as the company hatchet man. When he asked his supervisor why he was being called in, he said, "You need to be careful what you write around here." Gordon spoke to several people to see what to expect at the meeting. None of it was good news. Gordon thought about what the memo had said and he knew all of it was true, so he wondered what could be the problem. When Gordon entered the Gil's office, Gil started out quietly but then very quickly worked up a head of steam. For two hours, Gil screamed at Gordon such things as "what the hell do you know about this company anyway? I've been in charge of safety long before you ever came here. What gives you the right to say the company doesn't care?" After the first fifteen minutes, Gordon gave up trying to say anything. After two hours of screaming and belittling Gordon, Gil looked at his watch, sat down in his chair, reached over to Gordon, shook his hand, and said, "I'm glad we had this little talk." Gordon left wondering why Gil hadn't fired him on the spot and why he was waiting to fire him at a later time.

This teaching plan was prepared by Gordon Baldwin and Teri C. Tompkins, University of Redlands. The case and teaching note were prepared as basis for class discussion rather than to illustrate either effective or ineffective handling of administrative situations. Suggestions for improvement of this note should be sent to Teri.Tompkins@pepperdine.edu. Credit will be given in the next revision.

Industry

Telecommunications, cable industry. Very fast paced, entrepreneurial, nonunion organization. One of the largest cable company services, covering nationwide. Organization and peoples' names are disguised.

Teaching objectives

1. To develop skill in identifying and analyzing problems.
2. To develop skill in designing solutions and plans for implementation.
3. This case can also be used to understand and apply concepts of leadership (delegation and empowerment, style), culture (assessment), communication (barriers, methods), and positional bargaining in the context of safety issues.

Other related cases in Volume 1

Handling Problems at Japan Auto (interpersonal conflict). Heart Attack (ethics). Julie's Call: Empowerment at Taco Bell (empowerment). La Cabaret (ethics). Moon over E.R. (safety). No, Sir, Sergeant! (interpersonal conflict). Problems at Wukmier Home Electronics Warehouse (interpersonal conflict). Questions Matter (interpersonal conflict, dysfunctional communications). Shaking the Bird Cage (decision making process). Temporary Employees: Car Show Turned Ugly (ethics, positional bargaining).

Other related cases in Volume 2

A Selfish Request in Japan (assessment of culture, ethics, positional bargaining). Angry Branch Manager (decision making process, interpersonal conflict). Changing Quotas (decision making process). Cost and Schedule Team at AVIONICS (empowerment). Incident on the USS *Whitney* (interpersonal conflict). Insubordination or Unclear Loyalties? (decision making process). Preferential Treatment? (interpersonal conflict). Reputation in Jeopardy (interpersonal conflict). The Volunteer (assessment of culture, ethics, safety). Violence at the United States Postal Service (interpersonal conflict, safety).

Intended courses and levels

This case is a comprehensive case that covers a variety of topics. It can be used in management, organizational behavior, and human resources management courses. It has been classroom tested with undergraduate students, and mid-career executive students with good results. In addition to the individual topics, it can be used as an examination case, or as a semester long case.

Analysis

All related analysis and references are embedded in the answers to the questions.

Research methodology

This case was written from the perspective of Gordon Baldwin and review of certain company memos. This case is a true incident. Names and organizations have been disguised.

Teaching plan

This comprehensive case has a variety of topics to explore. It can make an interesting ethics and social responsibility case by asking students *"Does Gil put employees and the public in danger by his intimidation tactics to the part-time safety manager?"* The case could be used for a comprehensive exam either take-home or in class. What issues will students notice? Or you can name a list of eight topics and ask them to address four or five of them. The table below provides a basic framework for a discussion of any topic.

Topic: Decision Making Process on any Topic
60-minute teaching plan

Pre-assignment: Read case (15 minutes)

	Timing	Activity	Organization	Student Outcomes
I	0-5 minutes (5)	Summarize the case facts.	Ask or appoint a "volunteer".	Orientation and refresher on case.
II	5 - 15 minutes (10)	Ask: *What are the critical issues and problems in this case?*	Full class discussion. List ideas on left side of board.	Students might note: KEY SYMPTOM: Company's safety record, danger to employees, govt. standards, danger of lawsuits, workers' comp costs. POTENTIAL ISSUES/PROBLEMS: Company culture and senior leadership appear to be uncommitted to safety. Entrepreneurial company too busy growing to focus on details and procedures. Gil's Leadership style. Gordon's lack of cultural assessment. Gordon's lack of authority to act on delegated responsibility. Gordon's naivete, assuming The Cable Company is the same as Pacific Bell.
III	15 - 25 minutes (10)	Ask: *Which theories and models might apply to this case?*	Full class discussion. Write theory next to each critical issue. For example: "Gil's leadership style (theories of delegation and empowerment)."	Leadership (delegation, empowerment, style). See Questions 1, 2, 3, 8, 9. Culture (assessment). See Questions 4, 5, 7. Communication (barriers, methods). See Questions 6, 7, 11. Positional bargaining. See Question 10.
IV	25 - 30 minutes (5)	Ask: *From the perspective of Gordon and Gil's concern for safety, generate or brainstorm a list of potential solutions. Do not evaluate your list.*	In pairs or triads (based on seating proximity), create a quick list to report out. (This method saves board space.) Alternative: Full class discussion.	Students will jot down a variety of solutions based on their understanding of the key problems. In addition to what Gordon and Gil can do, some ideas may emerge about what The Cable Company management can do about safety.
V	30 - 35 minutes (5)	*Circle the three solutions that you suspect may be most appropriate and be ready to report to the class.*	Same as IV.	Same as IV.
VI	35-40 minutes (5)	*Quickly list your best alternatives on the board.*	Ask pairs/triads to quickly report one of their alternatives.	Some possible answers: Gordon: • take time to get to know his audience • careful assessment of The Cable

	Timing	Activity	Organization	Student Outcomes
			Continue around the room until all ideas have been expressed.	Company's environment • present his concerns and knowledge more effectively • taking time up front would have allowed him to get a basis of support • solicit feedback on the message content and style • seek out allies who might allow him to channel his concerns to people with more influence Gil: • remain open-minded and seek ways to collaborate • don't personalized the issue • focused on the facts • utilize Gordon's significant experience, and seek alternatives together • use an industry standard (such as OSHA), as a means for discussing the issues.
VII	40 - 55 minutes (15)	Discuss the alternatives. *What are the benefits and costs of each of these alternatives?*	Time is short, so it might help if the instructor selects four or five of the most viable (or one that isn't mentioned).	Possible benefits: • Reduces accidents • Socially responsible • Decreases costs (due to litigation and workman's comp costs) • Increase number of ideas • Increases worker commitment Possible costs • Increased short-term costs • Safety training takes busy technicians out of the field • Possible loss of face to prior safety leaders • There will be many ideas.
VIII	55-60 minutes (5)	Wrap-up. You might ask, "What is the _first_ step(s) that needs to be taken to reduce the workman's comp rate? Hand out or read epilogue.	Full class discussion.	Many of the solutions need to be implemented. Asking for first step helps student's prioritize their concerns, and to begin thinking of implementation issues.

25-minute teaching plan on decision making process on any topic.
Pre-assignment: Read case before class (15 minutes)
Activities. Do activities II (7 minutes), VI (5 minutes), VII (10 minutes), and VIII (3 minutes) in the 60 minute plan.

Discussion questions and answers

How was delegation used properly or improperly to enlist Gordon's assistance with the safety program?

<u>Analysis skills</u> (breaking a concept into its parts and explaining their interrelationships, distinguishing relevant from extraneous material)

Answer

As noted in <u>Management Leadership in Action</u>, (Mosley, Pietri, & Megginson, 1996, p. 260) "Delegation is the process by which managers distribute and entrust activities and related authority to other people in the organization. Authority is the right to do something , or tell someone else to do it, in order to reach organizational objectives. Responsibility is the obligation created when an employee accepts the manager's delegation of authority. Delegation occurs when the following actions take place:

- The manager assigns objectives or duties to lower level employee.
- The manager grants the authority needed to accomplish the objectives or duties.
- The employee accepts the delegation, whether implicitly or explicitly, thereby creating an obligation or responsibility.
- The manager holds the employee accountable for results."

In this case incident, only three of the four delegation actions took place. Items one, three, and four were initiated. However, item two was overlooked when Gordon was asked to create and oversee the risk control function. Gordon was told that he would be accountable on his performance review for positively impacting the safety of other employees. Although Gordon accepted the delegation and was advised of the responsibility to achieve certain measurable results, his manager failed to grant him any authority to accomplish safety objectives.

Did Gordon feel empowered? Explain.

<u>Evaluation skills</u> (using a set of criteria to arrive at a reasoned judgment of the value of something)

Answer

Apparently, when the manager delegated these loss-control responsibilities, Gordon presumed that he was empowered to do what seemed necessary. He understood that he was expected to identify opportunities for improvement, suggest alternatives, make recommendations, and so on. Over a period of several months, Gordon submitted numerous reports on safety or regulatory compliance issues. Various managers positively acknowledged Gordon's analysis and his suggestions for improvement but little remedial action was taken. At least part of this problem was due to the lack of clout and stature that burdened the safety coordinator's position.

Gordon's response to this situation was to push a little harder against the inertia of those from whom he was seeking supportive action. He did this mostly through memos. Gordon became increasingly frustrated as time progressed, and his written reports and requests for help became more strongly worded. He still felt empowered to conduct risk control activities, and knew that he was being held accountable for improving safety results. However, he had no real control and only marginal influence over the processes that generated those results.

Why would knowledge of delegation and empowerment principles be useful to Gordon?

<u>Synthesis skills</u> (putting parts together to form a new whole; solving a problem requiring creativity or originality)

Answer:

Early recognition of the hole in the delegation model would have prevented Gordon from assuming empowered ownership of the development of a loss-control program. This fact would have undoubtedly prevented the problem by restraining the tone of the memo that caused Gil such extreme agitation. However, since Gordon did not identify this critical gap, he went on to experience with Gil what Robbins (1993, p. 685) reported when he stated that, "Certain managerial personalities can be a handicap to implementing an empowerment program. For example, managers with a high power need are reluctant to give up control they have worked hard to earn."

In retrospect, Gordon should have carefully reviewed the structure of the function he was asked to perform when he was first enjoined to coordinate safety activities. He might have recognized the faulty delegation model. Had he discussed that situation with his manager at the outset, it would have been possible for the manager to restructure and truly empower the safety role. If redefining the role was not possible, Gordon could have chosen to decline the safety duties altogether, thereby averting the confrontation with Gil.

Question 4

Compare and contrast differences between cultural elements of Pacific Bell and The Cable Company.
Analysis skills (breaking a concept into its parts and explaining their interrelationships, distinguishing relevant from extraneous material)

Answer

Gordon had recently worked for a highly structured organization (Pacific Bell) in which unsafe actions or hazardous conditions brought immediate attention and appropriate responses from the management team. Gordon expected the same responsiveness from his new company and became quite concerned when it did not manifest. He did not take the time to learn the similarities and the differences between these two companies' values and priorities.

Pacific Bell was a company with a long history. It's policies and procedures were well established. The Cable Company was an entrepreneurial company with a history of moving quickly to capture market share. Its policies and procedures were developed "on the fly" in order to be responsive to emerging opportunities. Pacific Bell focused on managing expenses. The Cable Company focused on generating revenue. Pacific Bell employees were likely evaluated on their ability to follow procedures, thus helping to manage costs. The Cable Company employees were likely evaluated with how quickly they could install equipment and how many customers they serviced, thus helping to generate revenue. It is also likely that Pacific Bell executives accepted established communication channels and procedures for making decisions. In contrast, The Cable Company executives were likely more like mavericks, making decisions as the need arose and without detailed consultation with top management.

Sternberg (1997, p. 9) stated that the skills and approaches that allow someone to be successful in a previous company, may not work in the present organization. "Each company is different—with its own set of working conditions, its own organizational culture, its own competitive context, and so on. The result is that someone who succeeds in one environment may not succeed particularly well in another." Gordon expected that The Cable Company would value the culture of controlling costs and did not understand that it valued generating revenue and responding quickly to changing market conditions.

Question 5

What might the outcome have been if Gordon had taken the time to become familiar with the cultural differences between the new company and his former employer?
Hypothetical question (poses a change in the facts or issues)

Answer

If Gordon had taken the time to become familiar with the cultural differences, he might have noticed that there were variations between the cultures of Pac Bell and his new employer. He might have taken more time up front to assess those differences and build relationships with the managers who would be reviewing and acting on his safety reports and recommendations. Performing in this manner would have helped Gordon gain critical understanding of the new culture and how he could best apply his skills and past experiences in the new surroundings.

Question 6

What are the major barriers to effective communication noted in the case?

Application skills (using information in a new context to solve a problem, answer a question, or perform a task)

Answer

Management Leadership in Action (Mosely, et al., 1996) listed a number of interpersonal barriers to effective communication. Two barriers played a large part in the critical incident confrontation. These were, differing perceptions and the status of the communicator.

Differing Perceptions

Gordon's perception of the condition of safety and loss-control programs and practices at his new company prompted the examples given in his memo and colored his descriptions of the type and amount of training that had been overlooked. Based on his prior experiences, Gordon assumed the point of view that his observations reflected either right or wrong, safe or unsafe behaviors. There was no middle ground for Gordon, and he communicated this in forceful and unyielding terms. However, his perceptions were in high contrast to Gil's assessment of the situation.

Status of the Communicator

Gordon probably did not have much credibility is Gil's eyes. Not taking the time to discover this, Gordon postured his report as a factual representation of the status of the safety program. Gil did not agree with that status assessment. After all, Gordon was a new, hourly wage employee offering safety research, observations, and recommendations to a tenured group of more senior managers. In attempting to communicate safety concerns, Gordon may have appeared to be challenging the status quo of a very profitable enterprise, as well as Gil's position and authority. Without a high credibility rating in Gil's eyes, Gordon's "attempts to motivate, persuade, and direct work efforts (were) greatly handicapped from the start (Mosely et al., 1996, p. 334." Therefore, Gordon's leadership of the safety awareness effort was faulty.

Question 7

Suppose that Gordon had taken the time to meet the key players, ask their opinions, and make a careful assessment of the new business environment. How would this have changed the ways that Gil and Gordon communicated?

Hypothetical question (pose a change in the facts or issues)

Answer

If Gordon had taken the time to get to know his audience, meet the key players, ask their opinions, and make a careful assessment of his new employer's business environment, Gordon's credibility would have risen in spite of being new to the company. He could then have presented his concerns and knowledge about safety much more effectively. This approach would also have reduced the potential for Gil to become angry. Taking this time up front would have allowed him to form a base of support for his positions. His failure to do this was unfortunate, and helped lead to Gil's misinterpreting the contents and implications of the safety memo.

Other strategic approaches that Gordon could have taken were to solicit feedback on the message content and style, in order to massage it into a form that might be more easily accepted in this company. Additionally, he might have sought out allies who shared his concerns but held more respectable positions within the organization. He could then channel his written concerns about the safety program through more highly placed and respected employees. However, Gordon failed to explore these options. As a result, he appeared to be challenging Gil and the prevailing company status quo.

Question 8
How would you characterize Gil's leadership style and how effective was it?
<u>Exploratory question</u> (probes facts and basic knowledge), and <u>evaluation skills</u> (using a set of criteria to arrive at a reasoned judgment of the value of something)

Answer

Gil's leadership style was like the planet-smashing tactics of a famous science-fiction villain. In <u>Leadership vs. Autocracy: They Just Don't Get It!</u> (Harari, 1996, p. 43) the author asks, "What exactly is wrong with the Darth Vader School of Management?" Harari feels that a lot is wrong with it and says that autocratic approaches might have made ". . . sense in a bygone era, where employees weren't expected to think. . ." However, other managers had asked Gordon to think, research, and recommend options to the organization. They understood Harari's point that, "In today's knowledge-based nanosecond economy, adherence to obsolete principles is deadly. Sustainable competitive vigor is dependent on the leader's capacity to harness and fan intellectual capital—a.k.a. people's minds" (Harari, 1996, p. 43). Gil did not accept Gordon's information. Gil did not attempt to identify any valid points or potential focus issues in the report. He instead behaved like a cruel drill sergeant verbally hazing a new recruit. This leadership style forced Gordon to reconsider if this company was the best place to invest and fan his intellectual capital.

Question 9
Why didn't Gil acknowledge the validity of any of the concerns that Gordon had listed in his memo?
<u>Cause-and-effect question</u> (asks for causal relationship between ideas, actions, or events)

Answer

According to Muczyk and Steel (1998, p. 4), "organizational members are unlikely to embrace decisions and goals if their naked self-interest is it at odds with those decisions and goals." By extrapolating this point, it was easy to see that Gil was not going to embrace the safety coordinator's findings and recommendations because to do so would be an admission:

- that significant safety problems existed in organization
- that Gil had not been effective in preventing them
- that they were apparent—even to a new employee
- that company management had been remiss in not spotting and correcting safety deficiencies

According to Larsen and King (1996, p. 50) in their article, "The Systematic Distortion of Information: an Ongoing Challenge to Management," "...researchers working in the area of perception documented the natural tendency for individuals to accept information favorable to their self-image and beliefs, and to reject or misinterpret negative or critical information." Gil rejected and misunderstood the memo from Gordon for several reasons:

It was not consistent with Gil's opinions and perceptions and did not support Gil's beliefs that he had personally contributed substantially to the company's health and safety programs.

It was written by someone who, until recently, was employed in a different industry. Gil assumed that someone so new could not possibly know how safety practices needed to be applied in this company.

It was written by a wage-earning employee in a low-status job within the organization. In addition, Gil felt that the memo was presenting numerous inaccurate conclusions regarding the company's safety program.

Question 10
How did Gil's choice to adopt a positional bargaining standpoint predispose the outcome of his conversation with Gordon?
Cause-and-effect question (asks for causal relationship between ideas, actions, or events)
Answer

In <u>Management Leadership in Action</u>, the authors presented some typical sources of conflict in an organization. In this case, conflict probably arose from Gil's communication style, as well as his personal style. As previously noted, Gil was predisposed to reject input that he deemed too critical. As the aggressor in this incident, Gil placed himself in a "positional bargaining" environment where he was determined that he would win and Gordon would lose. Gil's win strategy was to behave as though he had been personally insulted and then react to this fallacious assumption. In reacting, he imposed his view in a very powerful way. While in this process, he denied the accuracy and validity of Gordon's report, and spent a significant amount of time venting his anger on the subordinate.

Question 11
What might be a more appropriate approach for Gil when communicating with Gordon?
Synthesis skills (putting parts together to form a new whole; solving a problem requiring creativity or originality)

Answer

A more appropriate approach would have been to remain open-minded and seek ways to collaborate from the perspective that Gordon and Gil had valuable though not necessarily congruent points of view. Collaboration was preferable because it was in the best interests of the stakeholders to identify opportunities to save money and reduce accidents and injuries. Ideally, the incident could have been avoided by a "principled negotiation" with these components: "(1) Separating the people form the problem. (2) Focusing on interests, not positions. (3) Generating a variety of possibilities (4) Insisting that the results be based on some objective standards" (Mosley et al., 1996, pp. 435-439).

Regarding the first point, Gil should not have personalized the issue by claiming that Gordon insulted him. As soon as Gil assumed insult, his anger and feelings of indignation assumed control, invective flowed, and all logic was set aside together with the best interests of the stakeholders.

Regarding the second point, it would have been simpler to have a discussion that focused on the facts. In this case, facts would have included results of workplace safety observations, accident statistics, reports from the insurance providers and a review of the Cal/OSHA regulations impacting this company's work operations. The discussions between Gil and Gordon would have centered on correct interpretations of this information and perhaps on a going forward strategy for bringing the company into compliance.

Regarding the third point, Gil and Gordon both had significant experiential backgrounds in the telecommunications business. Had there been a discussion based on identifying options for the company, it would have benefited everyone. In addition, such a discussion might have been developmental for Gordon in as much as he would have been involved with a problem solving/brainstorming exercise with someone on the senior leadership team. No doubt Gordon would have benefited from this experience.

Regarding the fourth point, it would have been simple to arrive at some industry-standard measures that Gordon and Gil could have referenced as part of their discussion. These standards might have included the company's insurance "X-mod", the company's OSHA recordable accident rate, and the costs per subscriber for work-related accidents.

References
Harari, O. (1996). Leadership vs. autocracy: They just don't get it!. <u>Management Review, 85</u>: 42-45. (WilsonSelect No. BBP196066383)

Larsen, E. & King, J. (1996, Winter). The systemic distortion of information: an ongoing Challenge to Management. Organizational Dynamics, 24: 49-64. (Wilson Select No. BBP196024039)

Mosley, C., Pietri, P., & Megginson, L. (1996). Management leadership in action. New York: Harper Collins College.

Muczyk, J. & Steel, R. (1998). Leadership style and the turnaround executive. Business Horizons, 41. (WilsonSelect No. BBP198037299)

Ramsey, R.D. (August 1996). Conflict resolution skills for supervisors. Supervision, 9-11. (WilsonSelect No. BBP196067611)

Robbins, (1993). Organizational behavior: concepts, controversies, and applications, 6th Edition. Englewood Cliffs, NJ. Prentice Hall

Solomon, R. (July 1998). The moral psychology of business: Care and compassion in the corporation. Business Ethics Quarterly, 8. (WilsonSelect No. BSSI98028654)

Sternberg, R. (1997). Managerial intelligence: why IQ isn't enough. Journal of Management, 23. (WilsonSelect No. BBP197082006)

Epilogue

What became of the traumatized safety coordinator? He recovered from the shock of the verbal assault and came to understand it better. He also re-evaluated his writing style and began to try and see how many ways that his reports could be reasonably misinterpreted. With these fresh perspectives, he attempted to find ways of communicating more clearly. He went on to work in the loss-prevention field, eventually serving as corporate safety manager for that same company. He was never actually grateful for the chewing-out he received, but he did realize that after that event not much else in business could make him more uncomfortable. That knowledge was sort of freeing.

What happened to Gil? He and Gordon formed a cordial relationship, working together to support a variety of loss-control initiatives. Gil stayed with the firm for another 5 years, then retired and took a job building cable television systems in Europe.

What happened to the others?

Lawrence: He remained in the industry as a senior leader.

Joan: She continued to work in the industry as a senior leader.

Bob: Bob was poorly matched to this leadership position. Just about two years later, he was asked to leave the company. His current whereabouts are unknown.

Terry: Terry continued to work in the industry as a senior engineer. He remained a vocal supporter of workplace safety.

Ron: Continued to manage technical operations for a large telecommunications firm in California. He remained a strong supporter of safety on the job.

What happened to the company?

It continued to grow and prosper. It developed a respectable safety program and realized increasingly better safety performance for the next several years. Overall profitability rose significantly as well. It was acquired by a larger firm in 1999.

Teaching Note
THE VOLUNTEER

Topics (* = Primary topic with teaching plan)
*Whistle blowing
*Ethics
*Authority, acceptance of
*Environmental context, closed systems
*Decision case
Interviewing
Municipal organization
Volunteer management

Case overview

Linda served as the new volunteer coordinator at a small but well-visited museum. Linda had not had a job outside of the home for a while and she looked forward to the challenges she would receive from her work. Soon after starting her job, she discovered that the museum had ignored memo after memo from the city requesting that the museum fingerprint all volunteers, especially those who work with children.

Linda went to her supervisor, Mr. Tanaka, and he told her not to worry about the memos because the most the city ever did was send another memo. He would accept responsibility for being an compliance. Linda was worried about not following through with the request. She soon discovered that Mr. Tanaka was trying to protect a friend of his from being kicked out of the volunteer program. The problem was that the man was a convicted child molester and had spent several years in jail.

Not wanting to confront Mr. Tanaka, and knowing his reputation for revenge, Linda decided to tell him that the city had called and were now enforcing the screening process. He told her to ignore the request, but she decided to proceed with the screening anyway. When the day of the fingerprinting came, the convicted child molester lied and said that he had already been fingerprinted and he refused to be printed.

Linda decided to go to the office manager, who was Mr. Tanaka's equal, to see if she could help. After the office manager spoke to Mr. Tanaka, he raged at Linda and very soon after began making public remarks about the poor quality of her work. The felon volunteer, however, was released.

Shortly after his release, a female volunteer came to Linda telling her that she had been dating the felon volunteer and when she pressed him about why he was released he told her why. She decided to end the relationship and he began stalking her. Linda now realized that the museum could face a possible lawsuit from negligence. Linda decided to put in safety precautions to keep the felon out of the museum's volunteer program. She also encouraged Mr. Tanaka to speak to the museum director and Linda saw him go to her office and speak to her for an hour. The next day she found out that the director knew nothing about the problem.

In case B, the director is advised by city attorneys to fire Mr. Tanaka. She argues in his favor and he is allowed to stay, but with no supervision over the volunteers.

Industry

Municipal museum. Primarily run by volunteers with a few professional staff.

Prepared by Teri C. Tompkins, University of Redlands, and Louise A. Palermo. The case and teaching note were prepared as basis for class discussion rather than to illustrate either effective or ineffective handling of administrative situations. Suggestions for improvement should be sent to Teri.Tompkins@pepperdine.edu. Credit will be given in the next revision.

Teaching objectives:
1. To discuss when insubordination of authority is acceptable.
2. To examine the consequences of whistle blowing.
3. To identify unethical behavior.
4. To evaluate procedures and timing to end unethical behavior.
5. To illustrate how closed systems can become dysfunctional.
6. To recognize that weak leadership can lead to poor organizational decisions or procedures.

Other related cases in Volume 1

A New Magazine in Nigeria (acceptance of authority). Costume Bank (nonprofit organizations). Donor Services Department in Guatemala (nonprofit organizations). Heart Attack (ethics). La Cabaret (ethics). No, Sir, Sergeant! (acceptance of authority). Pearl Jam's Dispute with Ticketmaster (environmental context). Questions Matter (acceptance of authority). Temporary Employees: Car Show Turned Ugly (ethics).

Other related cases in Volume 2

A Selfish Request in Japan (ethics). Costume Bank (nonprofit organizations). Incident on the USS Whitney (acceptance of authority). Insubordination or Unclear Loyalties? (acceptance of authority, nonprofit organizations). Reputation in Jeopardy (acceptance of authority). The Safety Memo (ethics). When Worlds Collide (environmental context).

Intended courses and levels

The case would work well in any management, organizational behavior, or human resources course dealing with the topics of dysfunctional closed environments, authority, weak leadership, ethical behavior and whistle blowing. It is appropriate for undergraduate, graduate, or executive students.

Analysis

All related analysis and references are embedded in the answers to the questions.

Research methodology

Research on this case was based on written records, interviews, and personal observation of the casewriter. This case is a true incident. The names and organization have been disguised.

Teaching plan

This classroom-tested case will generate a lot of discussion and interest. The situation of a convicted child molester working with children creates lots of student involvement. The case works well with small group discussion of the assigned questions and then debriefing.

Some students question why Linda didn't act more quickly. They may find it difficult to recognize how difficult it is for most individuals to resist authority. Provocative discussions can center around why people don't fight against tyrants during such times as the cultural revolution in China, Hitler's regime, or brutality in the former Yugoslavia, the middle east, Central America, Congo, or during the civil rights movement in America. When a person sees someone in charge (political leaders, military leaders, or the police) performing questionable acts, the person often questions his or herself rather than the authority. You might want to introduce the Milgram experiments (see, for example, Robbins, 1998, p. A 20-21; Ivancevich & Matteson, 1999, p. 382-383) during this case. (In the Milgram experiment, more than 60 percent of the participants administered an electric shock to a "learner" because the man in the white coat told them to do so.)

After the discussion on authority, you can talk about when it is appropriate to question authority. You may also want to use a related case from the Volume I casebook, No, Sir, Sergeant! The case will probably generate more disagreement among students about when it is acceptable to question authority than <u>The Volunteer</u> because the person in <u>No, Sir, Sergeant!</u> was questioning authority while in the military.

It can be used as a decision case by following the standard decision case format (Erskine, Leenders, Mauffette-Leenders, 1998, p. 128). Allow at least 60 minutes. Assign the case and pre-analysis by individuals or groups:

a) Defining the issue.
b) Analyzing the case data with focus on causes and effects as well as constraints and opportunities.
c) Generating alternatives.
d) Selecting decision criteria.
e) Analyzing and evaluating alternatives.
f) Selecting the preferred alternative.
g) Developing an action and implementation plan.

Topic: Ethics/Whistle Blowing
60- minute teaching plan

Pre-assignment: none

	Timing	Activity	Organization	Student Outcomes
I	0-1 minute (1)	1-minute introduction of class activity.	After introduction, form students into small groups of 4-5 students	Prepare students to discuss case.
II	1–15 minutes (14)	Students read case.	Individual	Familiarity with case facts.
III	15-25 minutes (10)	Q1. Answer the question: *Quickly outline the timing of events.*	Small group discussion	Students become familiar with the timing in the case. This question sets up a later question on evaluation of timing and effectiveness. See answer to Q1.
IV	25-35 minutes (10)	Answer the question: *What were the ethical problems Linda and the museum faced?*	Small group discussion	(1) How to remove the felon after her supervisor insisted he stay; (2) How to preserve the good name of the museum; (3) When to tell all the superiors about the situation; (4) Whom to tell; (5) How to protect the female volunteer; (6) What were the back-up plans if the director failed to act appropriately; (7) When and whom should inform the city.
V	35-45 minutes (10)	Q3. *Did Linda act in an insubordinate way toward her manager? Explain why or why not. What factors caused the need to go against Tanaka's orders?*	Small group discussion	Most students say she did not act insubordinately; however, from Tanaka's point of view, she did. Potential factors: (1) Closed system isolated from main headquarters created the environment; (2) Weak leadership above Mr. Tanaka; (3) Linda's personal ethics, high standards; (4) Safety and liability responsibility; (5) She was new to the system, so able to "see" problems more

	Timing	Activity	Organization	Student Outcomes
		Was the situation urgent?		easily; (6) Was there a question of urgency? Most students argue there was.
VI	45-50 minutes (5)	Answer the question: *Evaluate Linda's action in terms of timing and effectiveness.*	Small group discussion	Most students feel that Linda was very effective and that her timing was good. A few students will wonder why she didn't move more quickly. See <u>Teaching Plan</u> for additional ideas about how to handle this concern.
VII	50-55 minutes (5)	Answer the question: *What lessons do you draw from this case?*	This question can be answered quickly by instructor facilitation. Use quick "popcorn" style brief answers. Students remain seated in small groups to save time.	Here are some potential answers. (1) Documentation was effective. (2) Get legal counsel. (3) Strong leadership was needed. (4) Question authority if legal or liability issues are at stake. (5) Fresh eyes, new ideas help keep an organization from getting stagnant.
VIII	55-60 minutes (5)	Read or hand out part B and C and epilogue.	Still seated in small groups, but facing the instructor.	Conclusion: It is difficult for whistle blowers to stay in a job after the whistle is blown. Fortunately, in this case, the experience paid off for Linda and she landed an even better job. Students will draw their own conclusions about the museum's future.

<u>25-minute teaching plan for ethics</u>
Pre-assignment: Student's should read the case before coming to class (15 minutes reading time).
Activities IV, V, VI in 60-minute plan above

Discussion questions and answers

<u>Question 1</u>
What were the main events in this case and in what order did they occur?
<u>Comprehension skills</u> (understanding the meaning of remembered material, usually demonstrated by restating or citing examples.

<u>Answer</u>
1. Linda was hired after 15 years away from the job force.
2. Linda learns from past memos in the files that volunteers are required to be fingerprinted.
3. Linda signs up for training from the city and then tells Mr. Tanaka.
4. To Linda's surprise, Mr. Tanaka tells her to ignore the memos from the city because it is too time consuming.
5. Linda decides to quietly take the training anyway and then to show Mr. Tanaka that fingerprinting is not too difficult.
6. Shortly after the fingerprint training, the person in charge of recruiting and training volunteers, Erica, tells Linda that a convicted child molester wants to return to the program and that Mr. Tanaka has enabled the volunteer's participation for several years.
7. Linda decides to fingerprint Erica's group, but the felon refuses, saying his prints are already on file.
8. Linda goes to Mr. Tanaka and assertively tells him the risks the museum faces.
9. Mr. Tanaka tells Linda to stay out it; it is his responsibility.
10. Linda and Erica confide in Mrs. Phillips, the office manager and a peer of Mr. Tanaka.
11. Mr. Philips gets Tanaka to release the volunteer.

12. Mr. Tanaka begins to berate Linda and Erica in front of the other staff.
13. A female volunteer comes to Linda on the advice of her attorney to find out why a convicted child molester was allowed to volunteer at the museum. The woman had been dating the male volunteer until she found out about his conviction. He was now stalking her.
14. Linda decides the museum must take action to protect the female volunteer and goes to Mr. Tanaka telling him he must talk to Dr. Monroe about the incident.
15. Mr. Tanaka goes into Dr. Monroe's office and talks for an hour.
16. The next day, Linda brings in a picture of the felon to Dr. Monroe and finds the museum director doesn't know anything about the incidents.
17. Dr. Monroe consults the city attorneys and is advised to fire Mr. Tanaka.
18. Instead, Dr. Monroe removes Tanaka from direct supervision of the volunteer program.
19. Erica quits her job due to problems with Mr. Tanaka.
20. Linda finds a new job at a large, prestigious museum.

Question 2

What are the key issues in the case?
Analysis skills (breaking a concept into its parts and explaining their interrelationships, distinguishing relevant from extraneous material)

Answer

- When is it okay to go against authority?
- What can happen in a closed system?
- When is it okay to blow the whistle?
- What considerations must be taken into account if you decide to blow the whistle?
- What are the safety and security issues?
- Is there a "true and present danger"?
- Why do we have to follow policies?
- Is there danger of retaliation from Mr. Tanaka?

Question 3

Did Linda act in an insubordinate way toward her manager? Explain why or why not. What factors caused the need to go against Tanaka's orders? Is this situation urgent?
Evaluation skills (using a set of criteria to arrive at a reasoned judgment of the value of something) and cause-and-effect question (asks for causal relationship between ideas, actions, or events)

Answer

The first question students might ask when evaluating this question is whether or not Linda indeed acted with insubordination. From the perspective of most students, Linda acted appropriately and expertly. Mr. Tanaka was the one who was insubordinate (to the rules of the city). The instructor can point out however, that from Mr. Tanaka's perspective, it is likely that he perceived Linda acting insubordinately. This question is helpful for encouraging students to think about when it is appropriate to go against their supervisor's wishes. The Milgram experiment can be used (60 percent of the subjects followed direct orders and didn't question authority, even though potentially deadly to the "victim.")

Several factors in this case study forced Linda to act in an insubordinate way toward her manager and become, in a fashion, a "whistle blower" to the series of events. It was the corporate culture determined by Dr. Monroe, the director, which allowed the director's subordinates to act independently and without thought to the whole organization. Her hands-off approach covertly sent a message to Mr. Tanaka that he could act with impunity in any matter. This is graphically illustrated by his allowing the felon to enter a volunteer program even after Dr. Monroe determined he was not to be allowed to participate.

Under Dr. Monroe's management, the museum had developed into a closed system that worked to keep out any outside influences, even from the parent organization, the city. The environment was simple/stable. By never changing the programs, educational offerings, or volunteer organization, Dr. Monroe's managers could glide along in their jobs without increasing effort. This also kept them out of the city's focus whereby they might be required to take on other actions besides the ones they complacently filled.

Linda could not turn to Mrs. Grant, the president of FRIENDS—the volunteer program, to help solve her dilemma; Mrs. Grant had little business experience, was very submissive to Mr. Tanaka, and did not have the strong personality Linda felt was necessary to see the problem to a positive conclusion.

Some students might feel that Mr. Tanaka used his power in an unethical, authoritarian way and that Linda might feel weak and powerless. She felt responsible for the people and organizations listed above and this likely took precedence over abiding to Tanaka's authority. She consciously acted in an insubordinate way because of ethical implications. Although she was under a tremendous amount of stress during the several months that this incident played out, she felt strongly that she had no other choice of action.

Students might also mention the following:
- Linda's personal ethics, high standards.
- Safety and liability responsibility.
- She was new to the system, so able to "see" problems more easily.
- Was there a question of urgency? Most students argue there was.

Question 4
What were the ethical problems Linda and the museum faced?
Evaluation skills (using a set of criteria to arrive at a reasoned judgment of the value of something)

Answer
The museum experienced a series of ethical problems. Dr. Monroe established a "head-in-the-sand" attitude about any problems. In this manner she enabled Mr. Tanaka to work autonomously and with impunity. Mr. Tanaka appeared to be unethical in his decision making and in his managerial practice. Linda faced an ethical problem when she realized Mr. Tanaka would not release the felon from the volunteer program. In pushing the point, she stood to lose her job. She felt a female volunteer's safety and reputation were at risk. She also felt a responsibility to the museum to keep it protected.

Mr. Tanaka's unethical conduct caused a conflict of interest that should have become evident to Dr. Monroe if she had been paying greater attention to the daily work at the museum. The conflict became compounded when Mr. Tanaka made the decision to put the entire museum, children, and the female volunteer at risk when he developed a personal relationship with the felon that outweighed his responsibility to the organization.

Question 5
Evaluate Linda's action in terms of timing and effectiveness.
Evaluation skills (using a set of criteria to arrive at a reasoned judgment of the value of something)

Answer
Most students will argue that Linda was very effective and most will feel her timing was appropriate given the multiple stakeholder concerns she was trying to balance (the museum's continued existence if the news broke, her reputation and job security, the safety concerns of children, the security concerns of volunteers and staff, the right of a felon to exist after completing his punishment). Some students will argue that she did not act soon enough and could have moved more aggressively.

Linda moved slowly and carefully, a gamble that paid off for her in the long run. However, she was lucky that no incidents occurred during her tenure. When confronted with the problems facing Linda, she could have made a chart of the problems clearly identifying the objectives she wished to achieve and the decisions she needed to make. Some of the decisions she faced were:

- How to remove the felon after her supervisor insisted he stay.
- How to preserve the good name of the museum.
- Whom to tell.
- When to tell all the superiors about the situation.
- How to protect the female volunteer.
- What were the back-up plans if the director failed to act appropriately.
- When and whom should inform the city.

Some students will argue that Linda felt that her most important responsibilities, in order, were 1) to the children, 2) the female volunteer, 3) the museum's mission, and 4) the museum's management. In terms of protecting the children and the female volunteer, Linda was very effective. In terms of the long-term health of the museum's ability to react to change, Linda had little impact. This is not a reflection on Linda's ability, but she had no authority to act in these terms and it would have taken much more time for the culture to change at the museum.

Question 6

What lessons do you draw from this case?
<u>Synthesis skills</u> (putting parts together to form a new whole; solving a problem requiring creativity or originality)

Answer

1. Documentation was effective. It is important to document conversations, decisions, and actions, especially if liability is at stake.
2. Get legal counsel. This was a difficult case, and asking for legal counsel can help sort out some considerations not normally considered by non-legal personnel.
3. Strong leadership was needed. Weak leadership can lead to closed systems and dysfunctional behavior.
4. Question authority if legal or liability issues are at stake.
5. Fresh eyes, new ideas help keep an organization from getting stagnant. This is why many companies change auditors every three or four years, or change security guards at key locations.

References

Erskine, J.A., Leenders, M. R., Mauffette-Leenders, LA. (1998) <u>Teaching with cases.</u> Richard Ivey School of Business, The University of Western Ontario: Ivey.

Ivancevich, J.M. and M. T. Matteson (1999). <u>Organizational behavior and management, 5th edition.</u> Boston: Irwin McGraw-Hill.

Robbins, S. P. (1988). <u>Organizational behavior: concepts, controversies, applications, 8th edition.</u> Englewood Cliffs, NJ: Prentice Hall.

Epilogue

Three months later, Linda sent her resume to a large, very prestigious museum and was offered the position. The problem-solving abilities that she gained from resolving the incident were what got her the new position. Upon learning that his nemesis was leaving, Mr. Tanaka politicked to place the woman with whom he was having an affair into Linda's position. Linda had foreseen this and had long before recommended a woman who very closely matched Linda in work philosophy. Although Mr. Tanaka was allowed to be part of the interview team, he was not invited to be part of the decision.

The Volunteer

Mr. Tanaka is still at the museum. He continues to have no authority over the volunteer program because Dr. Monroe took it away from him. Mrs. Grant resigned as president because she no longer wished to work with Mr. Tanaka. The museum has not changed in any way and is feeling the competition of the new museum across the way. The female volunteer went to court and got a 10-year restraining order against the felon.

Teaching Note
THEN THERE WAS ONE

Topics (* = Primary topic with teaching plan)
 *Hackman-Oldham model
 *Job satisfaction
 Motivation
 Alderfer's ERG theory
 Leadership
 Small business context

Case overview

  Sarah worked in a three-person human resources department at a money management firm that had 115 employees. Sarah, who had worked for the company for almost three years, was a human resources assistant. She had been hired fresh out of college. She reported to Mary, human resources director. Mary had been with the company two years, although she had twenty years experience in human resources. Sarah's coworker, Ann, had been with the company eight years. Tom, the owner of the company, allowed a great deal of autonomy among his managers. However, when he got fed up with an employee, he usually ended their employment with the company.

  Sarah was not very satisfied with her job. Part of the problem was conflict between departments. Mary, who made many mistakes, was often in conflict with either the director of compliance or the controller. One of these "mistakes" occurred when the director of compliance and Mary met to discuss the severance details of a layoff. Mary drafted the severance agreement and presented it to the employee with important details incorrectly written. Mary and the director of compliance were also in conflict about who was responsible for various work.

  The human resources manager, Ann, was also a problem because she was known as the office gossip. She would sometimes share confidential information with employees. Because of these problems, Sarah grew weary of being associated with a department with such a bad reputation. The department had been under scrutiny for about three months and no new projects were coming into the department. She wanted new challenges and the opportunity to grow. Consequently, she decided that after she returned from her honeymoon, she would seek new employment where she could better develop her human resources management skills.

  Two weeks after her honeymoon, the owner of the company, Tom, invited Sarah out to lunch. She wondered if she was going to be fired. Instead, he told her that he was going to layoff Ann and Mary. She would remain in charge of some of the HR functions. The rest would be distributed among the managers or outsourced. Sarah had mixed emotions. She was sad for her two coworkers, she felt guilty that she knew about the layoff before them. She felt excited about new job opportunities and that she could continue to work for the company without having to worry about being associated with a bad department. She wondered if she could do the job.

  Over time, Sarah discovered that she knew a lot more about human resources than she thought. Her self-confidence grew. Her co-workers were very encouraging. She found that she had to let go of control of many aspects of the traditional HR role in order to do the job that was formerly done by three people. For example, hiring and salary negotiations went to line managers. Sarah was able to work autonomously. She eventually adjusted to finding information on her own and developed an external mentor. She felt that she was a better employee after the layoff.

This teaching note was prepared by Susan Pippert and Teri C. Tompkins, University of Redlands. The case and teaching note were prepared as basis for class discussion rather than to illustrate either effective or ineffective handling of administrative situations. Suggestions for improvement of this note should be sent to Teri.Tompkins@pepperdine.edu. Credit will be given in the next revision.

Industry

     Financial services industry. Small company of 115 employees.

Teaching objectives
1. To drill students on the Hackman-Oldham model of job enrichment.
2. To apply motivation theories to the case.
3. To evaluate the leaders' responsibility for what happened in the case.

Other related cases in Volume 1

     A Team Divided or a Team United? (job satisfaction). Split Operations at Sky and Arrow Airlines (job satisfaction).

Other related cases in Volume 2

     Saving Private Ryan and Classic Leadership Models (leadership).

Intended courses and levels

     This course works best for undergraduate students to drill them on motivation concepts and to help them apply these theories to a case. The questions on leadership are appropriate for graduate students as well. The topics fit best under the individual level in organizational behavior courses and under the leading function in management courses.

Analysis

     Analysis is embedded in the discussion questions and answers section.

Research methodology

     This case is based on the recollections of Sarah in the case. The company and people are disguised.

Teaching plan

     The table below provides a considerable drill on the Hackman-Oldham model. Alternatively, you can assign the case as a pre-reading assignment, and then discuss two or three topics described in the discussion and answer section: 1) Hackman-Oldham model of job enrichment/ job satisfaction, 2) Alderfer's ERG theory of motivation, and 3) evaluation of the leadership qualities of Mary and Tom.

     Graduate students can use this case to evaluate the responsibility of leaders for managing job enrichment and other motivational issues. The case could be used as a quick 40 minute assignment. Read the case (15 minutes). Then answer questions 8 and 9 (15-20 minutes). End with a discussion of the challenges and advantages of monitoring motivational issues in their own work place (10-15 minutes).

Topic: Hackman-Oldham Job Enrichment Model

60-minute teaching plan

Pre-assignment: none

	Timing	Activity	Organization	Student Outcomes
I	0-15 minutes (15)	Read case.	Individually	Familiarity with case facts.
II	15 - 20 minutes (15)	Instructor reviews the Hackman-Oldham model for job enrichment.	Mini-lecture	Review from textbook, or See answer to question 1, or See summary of questions 1 – 4 for list of characteristics.
III	20-30 minutes (10)	*Q2. Use the Hackman-Oldham model to look at*	Full class discussion or small groups	See summary of questions 1 – 4 for list of characteristics.

	Timing	Activity	Organization	Student Outcomes
		Sarah's job characteristics before the layoff.		
IV	30 - 35 minutes (5)	*Q3. Use the Hackman-Oldham model to look at Sarah's job characteristics after the layoff.*	Full class discussion or small groups	See summary of questions 1 – 4 for list of characteristics.
V	35-40 minutes (5)	*Q4. Is the Hackman-Oldham a good model to use when looking at job satisfaction? Why?*	Full class discussion or small groups	Yes, it is a good model for job satisfaction. See answer to question 4.
VI	40 - 50 minutes (10)	Mini-assessment—Focused listing. See Angelo & Cross (1993). Stick to the 10-minute time limit.	Step-by-step procedure. Write Hackman-Olmham at top of sheet of paper as a heading. Make a list of important words and phrases that are related to and subsumed by the heading. Look over the list quickly, adding any important items you may have left out. (Angelo & Cross, 1993, p. 129)	Focused listing is a tool for quickly determining what learners recall as the most important points related to a particular topic. It can help faculty assess how well students can describe or define a central point in the lesson, and it can begin to illuminate the web of concepts students connect with that point. Practicing this technique can help students learn to focus attention and improve recall (Angelo & Cross, 1993, p. 126).
VII	50 - 60 minutes (10)	Students hand in focus list. Instructor quickly reads through, clarifying any common points that seem to missing for a number of students	Large group. Alternatively, you may read the list after class and clarify the beginning of the following class.	To give immediate feedback to students about the concept.

<u>25-minute teaching plan on Hackman-Oldham Model</u>
Pre-assignment: Read case before class (15 minutes). Read about the Hackman-Oldham model in your text before class (15 minutes).
Activities. Do activities III, IV, and V in the 60-minute plan.

Discussion questions and answers
<u>Question 1</u>
Review the Hackman-Oldham model for job enrichment.
<u>Knowledge skills</u> (remember previously learned material such as definitions, principles, formulas).

<u>Answer</u>
Hackman and Oldman developed a comprehensive model for job enrichment. It is a type of job design that combines horizontal job enlargement and vertical job enrichment to increase employee

motivation and satisfaction. It focuses on two areas, core job characteristics and critical psychological states. There are five core characteristics, which are skill variety, task identity, task significance, autonomy and feedback. There are three critical psychological states, which are experienced meaningfulness, experienced responsibility, and knowledge of results. This model shows that the job characteristics and psychological states are interrelated. The job characteristics determine what psychological state one has which ultimately leads to certain outcomes. Attached is a copy of this model. The four possible outcomes are high internal work motivation, high quality work performance, high satisfaction with work, and low absenteeism and turnover. Lastly, there are moderating factors that contribute to the job characteristics and the critical psychological states ultimately leading to these four outcomes. These three moderating factors are knowledge and skill, growth-need strength, and context satisfaction.

Question 2

Use the Hackman-Oldham model to look at Sarah's job characteristics <u>before</u> the layoff.
<u>Application skills</u> (using information in a new context to solve a problem, answer a question, or perform a task).

Answer

Let's look at Sarah's job characteristics before the layoff and compare them to those in the model. Of the five job characteristics, the following three were missing: skill variety, task significance, and autonomy. Skill variety is defined as the variety of different activities and the use of different personal skills involved in performing the job. Task significance is the impact the job has on the lives of others, such as coworkers or others in the surrounding environment. Lastly, autonomy is the freedom, independence, and discretion involved in performing the job.

In looking at the case, Sarah was frustrated in her job because no one respected her department. Because of that, it was very difficult to get the approval from the president, Tom, to initiate new projects because he wanted to limit the human resources function. Some of the projects stopped were upward performance appraisals and job evaluations. Though he never stated why he did not like these projects, we might surmise that it was primarily due to human resources' bad reputation. Perhaps he was concerned that anything from HR department would not be well received and he had doubts as to the validity of the projects. Since there were not any new projects, Sarah was left to do the administrative tasks which became routine and lacked the variety new projects would offer. She did have contact with others in the office, but not at a level that was challenging her to use new personal skills. Furthermore, she felt that these routine tasks had little significance. This is not to say that the tasks were not important, but they were not difficult, nor did they take a great deal of intelligence to complete. This illustrates the lack of skill variety and task significance in her job.

In the past, Sarah had been involved in meaningful projects such as upward appraisal and job classifications. When these projects ended, she was left with routine tasks and felt that her autonomy had been taken away. She was given some freedom, probably more than others at her level, and she likely learned many new skills in the two years she had been there, yet she never really had the freedom to use them. An example of this was employee relations. People told her their problems and she discussed her recommendations with Mary. Once she discussed it with her, Mary would take over the project. She would contact the person and implement the solution. Sarah indicated in the case that she wished that she could have participated in that process.

In addition to lacking some of the core job characteristics, she was also missing two of the psychological states, which were experienced meaningfulness of work and knowledge of results. Experienced meaningfulness refers to the degree that a worker views their job as being useful and valuable to the company and surrounding environment. Part of the job of HR is to answer a benefit question or let employees know how much vacation they had. This could be experienced as helping them, but for Sarah, it was likely not enough. She appeared to want to do more meaningful work, such as solving an employee conflict or helping someone with their career path, but these tasks were done by Mary and Ann.

The other psychological factor that was missing was the knowledge of results. This is the awareness of how effective one's work is. Mary might have given Sarah feedback regarding projects she did for her, but Sarah seemed to hunger for a sense of what others felt about her work. Usually no news is good news, but she may have felt better knowing that others thought highly of her work. Because she did not get feedback from others, she wondered if those outside the department considered her a waste of money, like Ann and Mary, or a saving grace to the department. It was only after the layoff that she learned that people thought very highly of her and what an affect that had on her motivation and job satisfaction, though this will be discussed in another question.

Because some of the core job characteristics and critical psychological states were missing, she did not achieve any of the desired outcomes. Another part of this model is the moderating factors that further determine whether the core job characteristics will trigger the critical psychological states. These factors are knowledge and skill, growth-need strength (which is the need for personal growth), and context satisfactions (satisfaction with pay, job security, coworkers, and so on). She had the knowledge and skill, though she did not feel she had the growth potential. The department was small so there was not much room for growth and she was no longer learning new skills. She may have also missed some of the context satisfactions such as job security and satisfaction with coworkers. Knowing that the human resources department had been under scrutiny for three months, she may have surmised that it was a matter of time before they eliminated the department or Mary. She stated that she was looking for a new job because of the reputation of the department due to Mary's mistakes and Ann's lack of confidentiality.

Using the Hackman-Oldham model, it is clear that Sarah did not have the elements necessary for complete job enrichment before the layoff.

Question 3

Use the Hackman-Oldham model to look at Sarah's job characteristics _after_ the layoff.
<u>Application skills</u> (using information in a new context to solve a problem, answer a question, or perform a task).

Answer

Looking at the Hackman-Oldman model before the layoff, Sarah was lacking three of the five core job characteristics: skill variety, task significance, and autonomy. The changes in her circumstances fulfilled these areas, especially skill variety. She may have had too much variety because she delegated some of her responsibilities to the managers.

Task significance changed as well. She used to participate in the big projects when the department had them. Now she was suddenly determining what projects needed to be done and was solely responsible for them. For example, a significant project was to redesign the human resources department. The last area she was lacking was autonomy. This was quickly rectified after Ann and Mary left. It was obvious that after they left that she was left pretty much alone to do her work. At first, she was concerned about this but as her confidence increased, she learned how capable she really was. In the past, she could always go to Mary if she had a question, but without her she was left to use the resources she had to find the answer. This appeared to be one of the most valuable things she gained from this experience. One doesn't have to know everything, so long as they know where to go to find the answer.

Having fulfilled the five core job characteristics, the critical psychological states fell into place. She suddenly had meaningfulness in her job and was slowly getting knowledge of results. Other workers praised her work, which was important for her self-esteem.

Lastly, the outcomes in the model were achieved because she had high internal work motivation, high quality work performance, high satisfaction and we might assume low absenteeism. She appeared to be rejuvenated with the changes in her job after the layoff. She worked long hours because she liked her job and may have felt that she was making an important contribution to the company. She was motivated and satisfied with her work and appeared to strive to do her best.

Question 4

Is the Hackman-Oldham a good model to look at job satisfaction? Why?
<u>Evaluation skills</u> (using a set of criteria to arrive at a reasoned judgment of the value of something).

Answer

The Hackman-Oldman model is a good indicator of job satisfaction. Using Sarah's case as an example, it is evident that when she was lacking in the job characteristics and psychological states she was very unsatisfied in her job. When she had fulfilled these areas her level of satisfaction dramatically increased. It is likely that one of the key factors to her satisfaction was the increase in self-confidence at work. Hearing the positive feedback from her peers and managers was very encouraging.

The chart below summarizes our discussion of the Hackman-Oldham model in this case.

Summary of Questions 1 – 4

Hackman-Oldham Model of Job Enrichment	Before layoff	After layoff
Core Characteristics		
• Skill variety	Missing	Present
• Task identity	Present	Present
• Task significance	Missing	Present
• Autonomy	Missing	Present
• Feedback	Present	Present
Psychological States		
• Experienced meaningfulness	Missing	Present
• Experienced responsibility	Present	Present
• Knowledge of results	Missing	Present
Outcomes		
• High internal work motivation	Missing	Present
• High quality work performance	Missing	Present
• High satisfaction with work	Missing	Present
• Low absenteeism and turnover	Unknown	Present
Motivating Factors		
• knowledge and skill	Present	Partially missing
• growth-need strength (which is the need for personal growth)	Missing	Present
• context satisfactions (satisfaction with pay, job security, coworkers, and so on).	Partially missing	Present
Conclusion: Hackman-Oldham model is a good indicator of job satisfaction.		

Question 5

Review Alderfer's ERG Theory.
<u>Knowledge skills</u> (remember previously learned material such as definitions, principles, formulas).

Answer

Alderfer's ERG theory suggests that behavior is driven by the desire to fulfill three essential needs: existence, relatedness, and growth. This theory was developed to further explain Maslow's need hierarchy. Maslow's need hierarchy lacked research support, so Alderfer reformulated the theory and reduced the need hierarchy from five levels to three. Research has supported his findings and determined that these three needs are a reliable and constructive measure of motivation.

Alderfer developed a survey that asks questions in each of the three areas. The survey determines how people rate in each of three categories. The existence needs consist of things needed to survive, such as pay and fringe benefits. The relatedness needs includes respect from supervisors and coworkers, belonging (love), and status (esteem). The last area is growth needs which is about continually being challenged and using a variety of skills.

Question 6

Use Alderfer's ERG theory to evaluate Sarah's motivation before the layoff.

<u>Application skills</u> (using information in a new context to solve a problem, answer a question, or perform a task).

Answer

Many of the ERG needs were not being met in Sarah's job. While the <u>existence</u> needs were being met, for the most part, the latter two needs were not being met. Regarding the existence needs, Sarah was likely paid fairly and had acceptable benefits, such as insurance and vacation. This is based on the fact that she did not complain about those issues in the case. The <u>relatedness</u> needs were not being met in the area of respect from her peers. She might have been liked as a person, but she did not know how they felt about her work. Even if Sarah knew that she worked hard and did a good job, she was fearful that being associated with the human resources department would hurt her career at the company. Because the department did not have a good reputation, she did not feel fulfilled in the status part of the relatedness needs. Finally, her <u>growth</u> needs were not being met as evidenced by her feelings of stagnation in her job.

Question 7

Use Alderfer's ERG theory to evaluate Sarah's motivation after the layoff.

<u>Application skills</u> (using information in a new context to solve a problem, answer a question, or perform a task).

Answer

Before the layoff Sarah's existence needs were met but she was lacking in the relatedness and growth needs. After the layoff those needs were fulfilled. She felt she had earned the respect of her superiors and peers. Soon after the layoff, people told her that they had always thought highly of her, despite the poor reputation of the department. She felt that she had a job that was important. She went from being at the bottom of a department of three to being the whole department. Finally, the growth needs were met because she had much to learn and was being challenged everyday, which was important to Sarah.

Question 8

Evaluate Tom's responsibilities for the performance of Mary and the HR function.

<u>Evaluation skills</u> (using a set of criteria to arrive at a reasoned judgment of the value of something).

Answer

Tom was much to blame for what had happened. Tom's tendency to ignore personnel problems hindered Mary's ability to perform her job. Mary was frustrated with the conflicts with the director of compliance and may have realized that her continual mistakes might eventually get her fired. Tom's reluctance to be a leader was a problem. The case tells us that even if he knew there was a problem with a manager, he didn't address the manager with his concerns. In fact, it appeared that he waited until the problem had gotten out of hand and then he would terminate the person. This was the case with Mary. Tom let the problem go for too long so that he had no other choice but to terminate Mary and Ann. If he had been more proactive he might have saved human resources' reputation by working with Mary, and if that was not successful, then he could have replaced them with more qualified people.

The first action he should have taken was to tell Mary his concerns. If he felt that she was constantly making mistakes on projects, then he should have told her that this was unacceptable. He could have looked for the source of her mistakes to see if there was a pattern. If there was a pattern, such as she was unclear on the goals of the project or unfamiliar with the business, then he could have worked with her to solve this. It is likely that part of human resources' bad reputation came because he did not address these issues before they became public knowledge.

The downside to this would be that it would have taken more time and, like most owners, Tom probably had a busy schedule. It is helpful to have employees who get the job done correctly the first time and who need very little support. Deciding how much effort you want to take to help an employee improve are functions of your personal values, the difficulty and expense of replacing the employee, and how well the employee responds to feedback. Apparently Tom found it easier to let an employee sink or swim. If they sunk, he would terminate and look for another candidate who was capable of handling the job without guidance from him.

Question 9
Evaluate Mary's responsibilities for the performance of the HR function.
Evaluation skills (using a set of criteria to arrive at a reasoned judgment of the value of something).

Answer
Mary should have dealt with Ann's lack of confidentiality. The human resources function commonly receives confidential information and it is vital that the department have a reputation for integrity. Each employee must feel safe to come to the department with its concerns and feel confident that his or her case will be handled professionally. Mary should have been very clear that confidential information was not to be leaked to anyone. Consistent feedback and consequences whenever a violation occurred would have educated Ann about confidences. Then, if she continued to fail to maintain confidences, a case for termination would have been documented. If Mary had handled the confidentiality problem, the reputation of human resources would have been better, which would have given Sarah greater job satisfaction and might have helped Mary keep her job.

Question 10
Evaluate Sarah's responsibility in relation to Mary.
Evaluation skills (using a set of criteria to arrive at a reasoned judgment of the value of something).

Answer
Sarah was not honest with Mary. She could have let her know her feeling of stagnation in her job. If she had talked to her about her desire for more autonomy, skill variety, and task significance, Mary might have helped her in these areas. Sarah appeared to have become impatient with the internal problems in their department and wanted out instead of trying to find ways to make the situation work. If she had expressed more of an interest in dealing with employee relations and other areas Mary was involved in, she might have been more motivated and satisfied. Furthermore, she might have felt that there was more of a growth opportunity for her in that department.

However, Mary was a passive person and did not sense Sarah's dissatisfaction with her job. Could she have really been able to target what Sarah needed to feel fulfilled? If she had followed the steps in the path-goal theory, she might have realized what she needed to be happy, though she may have not been able to address all of her needs. Furthermore, Sarah did not want to confide in Mary about how bored and fed up she was with the department. It is likely that Mary did not know how bad her reputation and the reputation of the department was. Was it Sarah's place to discuss this with her? Did Sarah have the clarity about the situation that she later gathered toward the end of the case?

References
Angelo, T.A. & Cross, K. P. (1993). Classroom Assessment Techniques: A handbook for college teachers, 2nd ed. San Francisco: Jossey-Bass.

Epilogue
Two years after the layoff, Mary was working on long-term temporary assignments. She also did special projects for people such as writing employee handbooks, doing AQMD plans, policy and procedure manuals, and so on. Although she seemed happy, she would have preferred to have a regular full-time job or a temporary assignment near her home. In her current job, she was driving from Orange County to West Los Angeles four days a week. Since this was temporary, she was not getting benefits. There appeared not to be many top-level human resources positions available to her.

Ann was doing very well. She took off a year to complete her master's degree in psychology and was working towards her 3,000 hours of experience in the field. This experience is usually unpaid. Since it would take quite a while to earn these hours, she found a job at a nonprofit firm in the human resources department.

Teaching Note
UNPROFESSIONAL CONDUCT

Topics (* = Primary Topic with teaching plan)
>   *Job fit
>   *Career choice
>   *Personal goals
>   Perception
>   Johari window
>   Recruitment and training
>   Leadership
>   Interracial differences and conflict
>   Large corporation (non-banking) context

Case overview

Andre Hamilton, a young African-American male, had grown up realizing that not many young men like him would ever make it to college. After eight years in the military, where he learned how to conduct himself professionally and to respect other people, he went to college and got his bachelor's degree in management. Graduating from college gave him the feeling that he was going to make it and accomplish his dream of becoming successful in a good career with a good company.

After attending a job fair, he narrowed his choice to two companies that seemed like good companies to work for. He first interviewed with G.M.A.C., a mortgage company. Before his interview with the second company, The Office Supply Store, Andre was offered and accepted a position with G.M.A.C. The job was that of a loan officer paid on straight commission. On his first day at work at G.M.A.C., Andre was impressed with the professional attitude of the employees and the welcome he received from everyone. He enjoyed the feeling of being one of the other professionals. On his second day at work, Andre attended an interview with The Office Supply Store. After listening to the opportunities of training to become a manager, combined with office location and a steady salary, Andre decided to quit G.M.A.C., and begin work with The Office Supply Store. The district manager of The Office Supply Store sent him a letter telling him to report to Mrs. Richards, "one of their best training managers."

On his first day at The Office Supply Store, Andre entered Mrs. Richard's office and introduced himself. "What are you doing here? You're supposed to be at orientation," she said rudely. Andre flushed and showed her the letter telling him to report to her store. Mrs. Richards cursed, "Those a—holes don't know what their doing. Go wait in the next room while I straighten this mess out."

As Andre waited, he became very angry thinking about how he had been treated and how unprofessional Mrs. Richards was. He thought about punching her in the face, but knew it wouldn't accomplish anything except to land him in jail. He decided to try and make the best of it. After several weeks of similar behavior from Mrs. Richards, he wondered what he should do. Had he carefully chosen his career or did he base it simply on working for a good company?

Industry

A large retail chain store selling office supplies, computers, and office furniture. Nonunion.

Teaching objectives

1.   To examine career choice options.
2.   To illustrate how a person's perceptions and goals are important to job fit.

176

This teaching note was prepared by Andre Hamilton and Teri C. Tompkins. The case and teaching note were prepared as a basis for class discussion rather than to illustrate either effective or ineffective handling of administrative situations. Suggestions for improvement should be sent to Teri.Tompkins@pepperdine.edu. Credit will be given in the next revision.

Other related cases in Volume 1

Costume Bank (career choice). Heart Attack (interracial differences and conflict). La Cabaret (interracial differences and conflict). Problems at Wukmier Home Electronics Warehouse (interracial differences and conflict). The Day They Announced the Buyout (perception). Unmovable Team (career choice). Your Uncle Wants You! (recruitment).

Other related cases in Volume 2

Angry Branch Manager (interracial differences and conflict, perception). Cafe Latte (perception). Negotiating Work Hours (perception). Preferential Treatment (interracial differences and conflict). The Volunteer (career choice). Violence at the United States Postal Service (interracial differences and conflict).

Intended courses and levels

This case is useful for undergraduate students examining career choice, which might fit well in the early part of a management course or the later part of organizational behavior courses. It can be used to examine job fit or perception for undergraduate and graduate students. Finally, recruitment and training policies can be evaluated for management and human resources management courses.

Analysis

All related analysis and references are embedded in the answers to the questions.

Research methodology

This case is based on the personal experience and perceptions of the author. The case is a true incident. The Office Supply Store is a disguised name. G.M.A.C is undisguised. All names, except the author, have been changed.

Teaching plan

This case tends to stir up some judgment for people as they evaluate Mrs. Richards and Andre's interaction and Andre's perception of the interaction. There are numerous directions you can take the case. The teaching plan below is a good one for undergraduate students. Alternatively, if you are comfortable with strong student emotion, then using the case to evaluate diversity issues and perception issues can be very good. These topics will stir up the most energy and difference of opinion in the class. See some of the questions and answers for ways to begin discussion.

Finally, you might consider using this case to evaluate recruitment and training policies of stores. What mistakes were made that got this trainee off to such a bad start?

Topic: Career Choice and Personal Goals
60-minute teaching plan

Pre-assignment: None

	Timing	**Activity**	**Organization**	**Student Outcomes**
I	0-15 minutes (15)	Read case.	Individually	Familiarity with the case facts.
II	15-20 minutes (5)	Mini lecture. Factors to consider when evaluating a career.	Entire class	See answer to question 1. 1. Self assessment 2. Explore opportunities 3. Make decisions and set goals 4. Action planning 5. Follow-up
III	20-30 minutes (10)	*Q2. Evaluate Andre's process of finding a job.*	Form small groups of 4 to 5 students.	1. Not a thorough self-assessment. 2. Good at exploring opportunities 3. Set goal for management training

	Timing	Activity	Organization	Student Outcomes
				(but why?). 4. Took action by going to career fair.
IV	30-32 minutes (2)	Professor summarizes answer.		See final paragraph to answer Q2. Weakness is self-assessment. Perhaps due to internal dilemma to "make-it," based on moving beyond his upbringing or to a match to his personal skills and values.
V	32-45 minutes (13)	Have students develop a personal vision for themselves (adapted from Senge, et al., pp. 201-206). *Imagine achieving the results in your life that you deeply desire. Why would they look like? What would they feel like? What words would you use to describe them?*	Individually answer the questions. Record on paper, but it will not be collected (assure them privacy).	Areas students might examine: • Self-image • Tangibles • Home • Health • Relationships • Work • Personal pursuits • Community • Other • Life Purpose
VI	45-59 minutes (14)	Pick a partner in the class to talk about your vision. Have partner B listen as partner A answers this question about several elements from his/her vision, *"If I could have it now, would I take it?"* Partner B and A switch roles after time is up. Monitor the time and let students know they have 5 minutes for each partner (which you can allow to go 1 or 2 minutes longer). Tell them when to switch.	Have students turn their chairs (if possible) to face each other. Partner B listens or asks "If you could have it now, would you take it?" Or partner A can read his/her answer to each area (e.g., self-image, tangibles) and ask him/herself the question. B's job is to listen, not to comment or offer advice.	This helps students determine if there are conditions to the item. It can also help them clarify their process and become more precise.
VII	59-60 minutes (1)	Debrief and read short epilogue.	Full Class	Andre is still searching for his career. Sometimes it takes time. Understanding yourself and your goals can help you avoid *some* frustration, but not all!

<u>25-minute teaching plan for Career Development</u>
Pre-assignment: Student's should read the case before coming to class (15 minutes reading time).
Do activities II, III (15 minutes), IV, and VII from 60-minute plan above.

Discussion questions and answers

Question 1

What kinds of factors should one consider when evaluating his or her career choice?

Knowledge skills (remember previously learned material such as definitions, principles, and formulas)

Answer

The following factors are important to consider when evaluating career choices:

1. Do a self-assessment (values, interests, skills, abilities, and preferred activities. What makes you happy in work? How closely is self-image tied to your occupation? What rewards are important to you?) Daft, 1994, p. 789.
2. Explore opportunities. What opportunities are around you? What is the job market like? What is the economy like? Is training and development made available?
3. Make decisions and set goals. What are your short-term and long-term goals? What work do you need to do to accomplish that work?
4. Action planning. Set deadline dates; identify resources needed, and barriers. How will you get the resources or get around the barriers?
5. Follow-up. Periodic evaluation. "How am I doing? Am I growing?"

Question 2

Evaluate Andre's process of finding a job.

Evaluation skills (using a set of criteria to arrive at a reasoned judgment of the value of something).

Answer

It is not apparent in the case whether Andre conducted a self-assessment. It appeared that Andre was most concerned about the quality of the company and opportunities for advancement, rather than assessing his particular skills and interests. Andre appears to value the environment that he works in the most. It would be helpful if he would also assess his particular values, interests, skills, and abilities. In this way, he can discover his own "internal" needs to match with the organization that meets those needs.

Andre appeared to be good at exploring opportunities. He and his buddies in the military discussed the types of organizations that they thought were good. It is not apparent whether he explored the economic conditions, but we know that in the late 1990s the economy was in excellent condition and unemployment was low.

Andre had a goal of going into management training (although we are not sure why he chose that field), and he was able to reassess his organizational choice based on his goal. He decided to use the career fair as a method to act on his goal. It appears that he is skillful at setting goals and acting on them. It also appears that he evaluated his choices and was able to reassess.

In summary, Andre's weakness appears to be in self-assessment. It may be that he has an internal dilemma. On the one hand, he wants to "make it," which he defines as moving beyond his upbringing. On the other hand, he may not have the personal interests, or skill sets, to succeed in the type of business he has targeted. Andre appears to value people and professionalism. Perhaps his job search should include more assessment of himself and the company culture. In this way, he can match his interest and skills with the company's mission and culture.

Question 3

How do perception and judgment influence Andre's behavior in this case?

Application skills (using information in a new context to solve a problem, answer a question, or perform a task).

179

Answer

Perception and judgement refers to how people see others and interact with them. Wagner and Hollenbeck (1995, p. 139) explain that "perceptual processing can be either controlled or automatic and moves through four stages: attention, organization, interpretation, and judgement.

According to Wagner and Hollenbeck in the attention stage, "we select a small subset of the information that is available to our five senses for processing. The degree to which any stimulus attracts our attention is a complex function of characteristics of the object and of ourselves (p 141). When a person is touched or moved by something, they react to it. Andre used his basic senses to process the verbal and nonverbal information he received from Mrs. Richards at The Office Supply Store. Mrs. Richards's behavior attracted his attention because her actions were not what he expected in a professional environment.

In the organization stage, a person takes a small perceptual sample of another person to form a view of that individual. Wagner and Hollenbeck (p. 144) state, "information is simplified and they convert complex behavior sequences into scripts and represent people by prototypes. When Andre placed Mrs. Richards into a group (people with chips on their shoulder against young black men), he displayed a classic example of stereotyping in his organizational process.

In the interpretation stage, Wagner and Hollenbeck (p. 150) explain that they use the condensed information from the organization stage and selectively pick and choose the information that helps us to understand why people act the way they do. Andre stereotyped Mrs. Richards into a single category; he was able to explain to himself why she was acting the way she did (by seeing her as a bigot).

In the final stage, judgement, Wagner and Hollenbeck state "we use the information processed in the prior stages to come up with an object, person, or event. This evaluation, once made, affects our decisions, behavior and subsequent perceptions" (p. 154). In looking at this stage, it became clear the anger he felt was a result of how he processed the information regarding Mrs. Richards and why he had developed hard feelings toward her.

Question 4

Why didn't Andre confront Mrs. Richards about her behavior?
Diagnostic question (probes motives or causes).

Answer

An individual's culture is derived from people, places, and institutions that have made inputs into their life. The differences in cultures impact perceptions of people by providing a window from which they judge each other. In his cultural upbringing he was taught not to react outwardly toward behavior such as the type Mrs. Richards displayed because it could fuel the fire to her anger. He wanted to stop Mrs. Richards and ask her to refrain from using bad language, but he didn't because he was afraid of the consequences he might have faced if she got angry (loss of job).

Question 5

Using the Johari window as a frame, examine Andre and Mrs. Richard's viewpoints
Application skills (using information in a new context to solve a problem, answer a question, or perform a task).

Answer

The Johari window can be helpful in understanding this case study, because it allows us to see ourselves from the viewpoint of others. In The Organizational Behavior Reader (sixth edition), Jay Hall explains the four regions of the Johari window. According to Hall, "the Johari window is essentially an information processing model; interpersonal style and individual effectiveness are assessed in terms of information processing tendencies and the performance consequences thought to be associated with such practices (p. 231)". This is how well they interact with people and how our input plays a role in influencing individuals' opinions of us. The Johari window is a window divided into four parts, each part representing an area of personal space. One half of the window represents how you see yourself and the other half of the window represents how others see you.

Figure 1

	Known by other	Unknown by other
Known by you	Arena	Facade
Unknown by you	Blind spot	Unknown

In looking at the upper left region, sometimes called the "Arena", the information in this cell is known by self and known by others. The larger the arena becomes, the more rewarding, effective, and productive are a person's relationship. The more you know about yourself and the more others know about you, the better the chances are that the relationship will be positive. In the case study, Mrs. Richards and Andre had not reached this point in their relationship. Neither she nor Andre knew enough about each other to allow this process to work.

In region II, information is known by others, but unknown to you. This area is also known as the "Blind spot". Mrs. Richards could have seen something about Andre that he didn't know about himself. Her perception of his behavior could have played a role in how she saw him as a person. In region III the information is known by self, but unknown by others; it is also known as the "Facade" and has a natural protection of an individual's self. In applying this to the case, Andre knew Mrs. Richards had hurt his feelings, but he was not going to let her know about it. There are many ways this could apply to the case study. Another possibility is that Mrs. Richards could have been angry with someone else or a project was overdue and she just decided to divert attention from herself to buy some time. Finally, in region IV the information is unknown by self and unknown by others; this is also called the "Unknown". This means there may be many things about a person that surface at different times in different situations. Had he been in the same situation with another person, would the results be the same?

According to Jay Hall, "we should just focus on those pieces of information which have a bearing on the quality and productivity of the relationship. This should be considered as a appropriate target for the information processing practices prescribed by the model" (p. 233). In reviewing this model, it will help him to be aware of how people see him and how he sees others.

Question 6
How would you improve The Office Supply Store's recruitment and orientation practices?
Action question (calls for a conclusion or action).
Answer
This question addresses what courses of action might be taken to prevent this type of situation in the future. Start by having the recruitment manager send duplicate letters (sent to new employees) to the general managers of each store. This way they could know who to look for and give them an opportunity to correct any inaccurate information before new employees physically get to the wrong locations. This would also save time and money, because the company would not have to interrupt daily schedules to focus on oversights.

The Office Supply Store could have invested in leadership training. This may ensure the time and money spent advertising, interviewing, and training new employees would not be wasted due to managers who may not carry out the company's philosophy of caring for employees and providing a comfortable work environment.

The Office Supply Store should develop a training program that will allow new manager trainees an opportunity to train at another store if they do not feel things are working out in the store they were initially assigned to. This would allow for greater success among new management trainees because it could potentially reduce personality conflicts. It would give a stronger account of the new manager trainees credibility and integrity, by ensuring misunderstandings were clearly consistent with that new employee. Finally, this type of process on behalf of The Office Supply Store would create a win-win situation for manager trainees and general managers who have been assigned to train them. Additionally, the store should make the human resources department available so that a concerned employee can go to the department for help and advice.

Some of the downsides of implementing the suggested changes are: increased workloads on recruitment officers, added cost in training all employees, and overloading of task training of some general managers. One of the concerns of implementing the suggested changes is that sending manager trainees to other stores could result in an over tasking of training for other general managers and place trainees at a disadvantage because they may not receive the individual attention they need during the training process. Additionally, the amount of money it would cost the company to provide leadership training for all of its employees could affect the bottom line (profits).

Question 7
What could Mrs. Richards have done better when Andre came into her store?
Diagnostic question (probes motives or causes).
Answer
Upon his initial arrival to the store Mrs. Richards could have introduced him to his coworkers and showed him around the store. This would have given him a feeling of being wanted and would have reduced the awkwardness that he was feeling coming into a new environment. She could have then taken this opportunity to explain to him that he needed to attend the orientation. This approach would not have given him the impression that he was part of the problem that she was experiencing. This method of communication would have benefited both her and Andre in establishing a foundation for a good working relationship.

Mrs. Richards could have spoken with her boss, the district manager, and expressed her concerns in regards to her workload. Perhaps her current workload would prevent her from effectively handling a new manager trainee or giving this manager trainee the attention he deserved. This would have allowed her to operate the store's daily functions with her trained personnel to ensure they offered the same high quality and standards expected of them by their customers. Mrs. Richards also could have requested that he start working at the store at a later time. This would have allowed her to give him the attention required for his training.

Mrs. Richards could have provided a more comfortable working environment by presenting herself in a professional manner. By behaving in an unprofessional manner she may destroy the good efforts made by The Office Supply Store and its recruiting team. It is therefore possible that Mrs. Richards could benefit from employee relations and multicultural training to make her aware of how her behavior could affect new employees and The Office Supply Store Corporation.

Question 8
What could Andre have done to improve his situation?
Action question (calls for a conclusion or action).
Answer
In looking at himself in this situation, Andre could have applied Johari's window region IV to Mrs. Richards and himself. Region IV is known as the "unknown". When he walked into The Office Supply Store, Andre did not know anyone and no one in that store knew him. But because of the negative response he received from Mrs. Richards, both from her body language and her verbal response to the letter, he drew the conclusion that he knew her and his knowledge of her was that she did not like him. But in reality, he really did not know her. If he could have refrained from taking her response toward him personally, since she did not know him, perhaps they would have had time to develop a positive relationship.

He could have called the store before he arrived that morning, to establish himself with the general manager (Mrs. Richards) before he showed up at the store. He could have sought out more information about himself from friends, which could have allowed him to communicate with Mrs. Richards in a different way, such as explaining to her that he was not comfortable with how she was responding toward him. He could have been aware of the expectation he had built up regarding how great it was going to be to work for The Office Supply Store; this could have resulted in a smoother transition from G.M.A.C. to The Office Supply Store.

In looking at the downsides in this situation, if he had called the store, Andre may have risked being viewed as an over-aggressive pest by the district manager. Also, if he would have told Mrs. Richards he was not comfortable with her form of communication, this could have resulted in her concluding that he was sensitive. Thus they might not have been able to communicate openly and frankly.

References

Daft, R. (1994). Management, 3rd ed. Fort Worth, TX: Dryden.

Hall, J. (1995). Communication revisited. In J.A. Hall, J.S Osland, and I.M. Rubin (Eds.) The Organizational Behavior Reader, 6th ed. Upper Saddle River, NJ: Prentice Hall.

Senge, P., Roberts, C., Ross, R. B., Smith, B.J. and Kleiner, A. (1994). The fifth discipline Fieldbook: Strategies and tools for building a learning organization. NY: Doubleday.

Wagner, J., & Hollenbeck, J. (1995). Management of organizational behavior. Upper Saddle River, NJ: Prentice-Hall.

Epilogue

Even though Andre appreciated the treatment he experienced at G.M.A.C., he didn't go back to this job because he knew that the work at G.M.A.C. was not really something he was interested in. Andre received his master's degree in human resources development from Claremont Graduate University. He did not find a job in this field. He is currently employed as a teacher.

VIOLENCE AT THE UNITED STATES POSTAL SERVICE

Part A: The Killing of James Whooper by Bruce Clark
Part B: Organizational Climate at the Postal Service

Topics (* = Primary Topic with teaching plan)
  Workplace Violence
  Prediction of violent behavior
  Levels of workplace violence
  Transient criminality
  Management of workplace violence
  Stress
  Interpersonal conflict
  Interracial differences and conflict
  Government context
  Labor/management context

Case overview

This unusual case describes an incident of workplace violence at the United States Postal Service office in City of Industry, California. Part A presents the story of the killing of James Whooper by Bruce Clark and possible explanations. Part B considers the backdrop of violence at the Postal Service—a history of authoritarian management practices and confrontational labor-management relations, and implementation of massive downsizing, restructuring, and technological change since the 1980s.

The literature on workplace violence posits that violent incidents result from the interaction of the person who is the perpetrator and the environment. Two of the questions posed by this case are whether the shooting could have been prevented, and whether the general organizational climate at the Postal Service, which is said to be conducive to workplace violence, played a role in a workplace homicide at a model postal facility.

Industry

United States Postal Service processing plant. Governmental. Large-size company. Union employees.

Teaching objectives
  1. To familiarize students with the data on workplace violence.
  2. To explore case facts and related readings to determine if workplace violence can be prevented.
  3. To evaluate whether it is possible to predict violent behavior.
  4. To learn about the theory of transient criminality.

Other related cases in Volume 1

Heart Attack (interracial differences and conflict). La Cabaret (interracial differences and conflict). Moon over E.R. (workplace violence). No, Sir, Sergeant! (interpersonal conflict). Problems at Wukmier Home Electronics Warehouse (interpersonal conflict, interracial differences and conflict). Questions Matter (interpersonal conflict).

This teaching note was prepared by Dianne Layden, University of Redlands. The case and teaching note were prepared as basis for class discussion rather than to illustrate either effective or ineffective handling of administrative situations. Suggestions for improvement should be sent to Teri.Tompkins@pepperdine.edu. Credit will be given in the next revision.

Other related cases in Volume 2

Angry Branch Manager (interracial differences and conflict). Cafe Latte (interpersonal conflict). Incident on the USS *Whitney* (interpersonal conflict). Preferential Treatment? (interpersonal conflict, interracial differences and conflict). Reputation in Jeopardy (interpersonal conflict). The Safety Memo (interpersonal conflict). Unprofessional Conduct (interracial differences and conflict).

Intended courses and levels

This case is primarily intended for graduate students in human resources management, although it can be useful as an overview of workplace violence for undergraduate students. The topics include workplace violence, levels of workplace violence, theory of transient criminality, and prevention of workplace violence.

Analysis

See the supplemental material at the end of this teaching note.

Research methodology

Major references include: *USA vs. Clark*, Case #95-CR-652, US District Court, Central District of California (Western Division), filed July 28, 1995, and terminated May 6, 1996; interviews with Thomas Dugan, Postal Inspection Service, Pasadena California, and Miguel Rodriguez, Business Agent/Vice-President, California Area Local, American Postal Workers Union, Montclair, California; and materials furnished by the Santa Ana Postal District, City of Industry, California, and US Postal Service, Washington, DC

Teaching plan

The teaching plan below responds to Part A. The discussion and answer section has appropriate questions for Part B of the case. There are supplemental handouts at the end of the teaching note to guide professors in teaching this topic since not much information is usually available in textbooks yet.

Topic: Workplace Violence
60-minute teaching plan

Preassignment: Instructor may want to make copies of the supplemental handout at the end of this note.

	Timing	Activity	Organization	Student Outcomes
I	0-1 minute (1)	1-minute introduction of class activity.	After introduction, form students into small groups of 4-5 students	Students are prepared to discuss case.
II	1–15 minutes (14)	Students read case.	Individual	Students become familiar with case facts.
III	15-25 minutes (10)	Mini-lecture: Overview of workplace violence Alternative 1: Students describe experiences with workplace violence	Mini-lecture while students remain in their groups Alternative 1: Professor facilitates discussion or students discuss in	Students become familiar with the employer's obligation to provide a safe workplace, prevalence on nonlethal workplace violence, rise in workplace homicides, and utility of prevention programs.

	Timing	Activity	Organization	Student Outcomes
			their groups.	
I V	25-35 minutes (10)	Answer this question: *Speculate as to the possible causes of the rise in workplace homicides since the 1980s.*	Small group discussion	Students recognize influence of such factors as a violent culture, widespread gun use, economic climate of downsizing and job insecurity, and role of workplace as social world in workers' lives.
V	35-55 minutes (20)	As a group, discuss these questions: *Could the killing of James Whooper by Bruce Clark have been prevented? What are the implications for management of the difficulty in preventing workplace violence?*	Small group discussion	Students recognize that removal of Clark from the workplace after his assault on Whooper might have saved Whooper's life. Employers should anticipate violence and watch for warning signs.
V I	55-60 minutes (5)	Summarize and share epilogue.	Students remain seated in small groups	Workplace violence is a social problem. Employees may respond with lethal violence to fear of job loss and perceived injustice on the job. Prevention programs by employers may deter violence.

25-Minute Teaching Plan for Workplace Violence

Pre-assignment: Students read the case before coming to class (Activity II: 15 minutes).

Activities I, III, V, VI in 60-minute plan above (Activity IV: 10 minutes)

Activity V: Assign each group *one* question to answer, not two (10 minutes)

Discussion questions and answers

Part A: The Killing of James Whooper by Bruce Clark

Question 1

Could the killing of James Whooper by Bruce Clark have been prevented? Explain why or why not. Be sure to address the issues of changes in management, warning signs of potential violence, and security at the City of Industry postal facility. Were Postal Service workplace violence policies effective in this case?

Action question (calls for a conclusion or action) and cause-and-effect question (asks for causal relationship between ideas, actions, or events).

Answer

Changes in management are known to have an impact on employees. One study of workplace violence found that at the organizational level, changes in management were significantly related to both witnessed and experienced aggression at the workplace. The Clark case presents an example of the impact of a change in supervision on a single employee. Whooper was a new supervisor at the facility, and his managerial style, although clearly not abusive, apparently upset Clark. Clark's statement that he was singled out by his supervisor, although not amplified in the record, indicates that he perceived that he was being treated unjustly. As a long-term employee, he may have feared the loss of his job. Furthermore, it appears that his workplace and social world were synonymous. The arrival of Whooper apparently threatened Clark's world at the Postal Service, and Clark murdered Whooper in an effort to remove him from the workplace and restore order in his workplace-social world.

In hindsight, the only clear warning sign was Clark's physical assault on Whooper about 45 minutes before he shot him; that is, when Clark escalated to level 3 in Baron's model (see supplemental handout A). Afterwards, Whooper sent Clark back to work after Clark said that he was okay, that he did not have a gun, and that he was able to go back to work. Instead, Clark should have been removed from the workplace. He could have been placed on leave with pay until an investigation determined whether there existed any provocation by Whooper or extenuating circumstances that affected Clark's behavior. Whether or not disciplinary action was warranted and the nature of such action could then have been decided. Thomas Dugan, who led the investigation of the killing for the Postal Inspection Service, agreed that Clark should have been removed from the site after the assault, or detained at the site but not sent back to work.

Security measures vary at different postal facilities, and the question arises as to whether metal detectors should have been installed at the entrances to this facility. According to Dugan, postal security people and metal detectors, which are present in some locations, were not provided at the city of Industry facility because violence was not anticipated there. He stated that the decision whether to provide increased security requires a balancing of the interests of employee security and employee privacy. Student opinions will vary regarding the desirability of metal detectors at the workplace.

Postal Service workplace violence policies were not effective in this case. Before Clark's assault, there was no evidence of behavior by either party prohibited by the "zero tolerance" policy. Neither was there evidence that the six strategies of selection, security, policy, climate, employee support, and separation played a role in inhibiting violent action by Clark. Although Whooper received four hours of workplace violence training, he allowed Clark to return to work after he struck Whooper. The "no firearms" policy was not adopted until a month after Whooper was killed, but Clark obviously was undeterred by federal law and policy prohibiting the possession of firearms in a postal facility.

Question 2

Review the composition of the threat assessment team at the City of Industry postal facility. Why is the team composed of members from different functional areas of management? The threat assessment process sometimes requires management to consult with mental health professionals. What are the implications of such collaborations? Finally, what risks are present in the administration of threat reporting and assessment procedures?

Synthesis skills (putting parts together to form a new whole; solving a problem requiring creativity or originality) and evaluation skills (using a set of criteria to arrive at a reasoned judgment of the value of something).

Answer

Threat assessment is a delicate process that requires a balancing of the interests of employer and employee. When an employee is alleged to have made a threat, information and expert opinions must be gathered confidentially from a variety of sources and evaluated in terms of all that is known about the employee and the environment. The appropriate managerial action must also be determined. Alternatives include no action, voluntary or mandatory counseling, a disability leave of absence, an offer of the opportunity to resign, dismissal, obtaining a temporary or permanent restraining order, notifying law enforcement agencies or filing civil or criminal charges, notifying persons who are the targets of threats so that they may protect themselves, and providing additional security at the workplace. An interdisciplinary team is a necessity so that information about an employee may be considered from the viewpoints of the legal, human resources, security, and mental health professions, on the assumption that the most accurate assessment of potential dangerousness will result from a collaborative effort. An error could result in loss of life; at the same time, an employee's right of privacy and expectation of just cause and due process in discipline must be respected throughout the investigation and subsequent management actions.

Mental health professionals currently work with employers through employee assistance programs, which offer counseling services to assist employees in resolving personal and work-related problems. Direct contact with members of management may be limited, however, given the emphasis on confidentiality. The literature on workplace violence favors direct involvement of a mental health professional in threat assessment; that is, use of a psychologist to conduct the interviews with the employee who is the subject of the investigation, the person who reported the threat, and persons who are knowledgeable about the employee's state of mind. To be productive, collaborations between mental health professionals and management will require both parties to adapt to this new working relationship. Mental health professionals must develop expertise in workplace violence prevention, and management must be receptive to information about the psychological state of an employee throughout the assessment process.

Several risks are inherent in threat reporting and assessment procedures. Experts on workplace violence propose the use of telephone hotlines for reporting threats and triggering investigations of any employees who inspire fear. Such programs may generate other forms of conflict. Postal workers, for example, are said to have filed reports against each other alleging threats at the slightest hint of trouble rather than attempting to resolve the problem, which has created an atmosphere of paranoia. Moreover, false allegations may be made. New legal issues are likely to arise if investigations are conducted without cause, or employees are defamed or adversely affected in their employment opportunities by allegations of having made threats. Also, employees may be afraid to file reports because of fear of retaliation. Threat reporting procedures should seek to protect employees by prohibiting the filing of knowingly false allegations, retaliation for reporting threats and violent incidents, and misuse of information obtained in investigations of potential violence. Another concern is that for threat reporting procedures to be taken seriously, employees who file reports must be informed of their status, but without revealing confidential information about the subjects of investigation. Finally, there is a need for careful handling of managerial actions that follow an investigation, so as to avoid triggering a violent incident.

Question 3

Mental health professionals routinely advise that the dangerousness of individuals is extremely difficult to predict. What are the implications for management of the difficulty in predicting workplace violence?

Application skills (using information in a new context to solve a problem, answer a question, or perform a task).

Answer

The danger of individuals is extremely difficult for mental health professionals to predict, and general models for predicting violence apparently do not apply to workplace homicides; furthermore, given the size of the labor force and the small number of workplace homicides annually, the base rate is said to be too low to permit accurate prediction. The implications for management are that emphasis must be placed on violence prevention programs rather than on identification of potentially violent employees through the use of profiles of perpetrators. Fox and Levin have observed that many more employees will fit the profile than will seek revenge at work, and the attempt to identify problem workers may create a self-fulfilling prophesy whereby combative employees become enraged when singled out in a negative way.[4]

Violence prevention programs should include provision of security measures to limit exposure of employees, promotion of an organizational climate free of stress and abuse, maintenance of sound human resources management and labor relations practices (particularly in the areas of selection), performance appraisal, discipline, and lay-offs; ongoing management development, organization-wide training on the potential for workplace violence (particularly warning signs), adoption and communication of policies that declare violence of any sort to be contrary to business purposes, provision of threat reporting and assessment procedures (followed by intervention through counseling when appropriate), formation of a broad-based, crisis-management team to respond to warning signs and violent incidents, and post-incident implementation of trauma response procedures.

Mawson's theory of transient criminality asserts that a law-abiding and controlled individual is capable of criminal behavior under conditions of extreme stress and in the absence of social supports (see supplemental handout A). Thus, many employees might be moved by their circumstances to commit a violent act at the workplace. This prospect should encourage management to provide stress reduction programs and counseling on stress through employee assistance programs. Management also should be sensitive to changes in the work environment that might disrupt an employee's workplace-social world, such as introduction of a new supervisor, work rules, or work methods, or removal of close friends through downsizing, dismissal, or other management action.

Part B: Organizational Climate at the Postal Service

Question 4
Do you think the general organizational climate at the Postal Service played a role in the workplace homicide at the city of Industry facility? Explain why or why not.
Cause-and-effect question (asks for causal relationship between ideas, actions, or events).
Answer
Bruce Clark has not disclosed his motive for killing James Whooper. Thus, we cannot know whether the general organizational climate played a role in the homicide at the city of Industry facility. The managerial disciplines of human resources management and organizational behavior, however, are built on the presumption that organizational climate is a factor in productivity and job satisfaction. Furthermore, researchers have postulated a linkage between workplace violence and employee perceptions of organizational justice. Folger and Baron's theory linked injustice to frustration, resentment, the desire for vengeance, and ensuing violence. In summary, individuals perceive that they have been treated unfairly under certain conditions. When other circumstances also prevail (e.g., when individuals have certain personal characteristics that predispose them to attribute malevolence to others, when they believe that the treatment they have received violates widely accepted norms of fairness or 'fair play,' and when they readily can imagine much better outcomes for themselves that are consistent with such principles), these feelings may translate into strong resentment and a powerful desire for revenge.[6]

Question 5

In the 1990s, according to the US Department of Labor, workplace homicide became the second leading cause of death at the workplace after traffic accidents, up from third place; moreover, researchers have found that the incidence of employees killing their supervisors has doubled since the 1980s. Speculate as to possible causes of the rise in homicide at the workplace.

Evaluation skills (using a set of criteria to arrive at a reasoned judgment of the value of something).

Answer

Social causes of workplace violence include the existence of a violent culture in the United States. Notably, the majority of homicides result from various forms of conflict, not the commission of felonies.[7] A 1998 study by the U.S. Centers for Disease Control and Prevention found the United States has by far the highest rate of gun deaths among the world's 36 richest nations.[8] In 1998, Polsby and Kates reported that 40 to 50 percent of American households had one or more guns, and that there are nearly as many guns as there are people: "If an American is overcome with rage, or with any other urgent reason for wishing to arm himself, chances are he will be able to outfit himself with a gun forthwith."[9] As a means of dispute resolution, the gun is viewed as the "great equalizer." A changing economy, characterized by massive downsizing since the 1980s, is another factor, as rising unemployment is associated with increases in violence, crime, and disease; a 1995 survey by *The New York Times* concluded that the downsizing has resulted in the most acute job insecurity since the Great Depression.[10] Additional factors cited by Fox and Levin are an increased rate of divorce, greater residential mobility, and a general lack of neighborliness; thus, for many Americans, work is the only source of stability and companionship.

Footnotes

[1]Robert A. Baron and Joel H. Neuman, "Workplace Violence and Workplace Aggression: Evidence on Their Relative Frequency and Potential Causes," *Aggressive Behavior*, 22, No. 3 (1996), pp. 161–173. Increased use of part-time workers, changes in management, pay cuts or pay freezes, and increased workforce diversity were significantly related to both witnessed and experienced aggression. Other changes, particularly budget cuts, reengineering, and job sharing, were significantly related to witnessed aggression. A linkage was found between downsizing and workplace violence, but the correlation was not as strong as correlations to other types of organizational change.

[2]Stuart Silverstein, "The War on Workplace Violence," *Los Angeles Times*," March 18, 1994, pp. A1, A20.

[3]See, for example, Randy K. Otto, "On the Ability of Mental Health Professionals to `Predict Dangerousness': A Commentary on Interpretations of the 'Dangerousness Literature,'" *Law and Psychology Review*, 18 (Spring, 1994), pp. 43–68. Regarding the difficulty of predicting workplace homicide, see Frank E. Kuzmits, "When Employees Kill Other Employees: The Case of Joseph T. Wesbecker," and John Monahan, "Editorial: Violence in the Workplace," *Journal of Occupational Medicine*, 32, No. 10 (October, 1990), pp. 1014–1021.

[4]See, generally, James Alan Fox and Jack Levin, "Firing Back: The Growing Threat of Workplace Homicide," *The Annals of The American Academy of Political and Social Science*, 536 (November, 1994), pp. 16–30.

[5]See, generally, Dianne R. Layden, "Violence, the Emotionally Enraged Employee, and the Workplace: Managerial Considerations," *States of Rage: Emotional Eruption, Violence, and Social Change*, Renee R. Curry and Terry L. Allison, eds. (New York: New York University Press, 1996), pp. 46–49; see, generally, pp. 35–61.

[6]Robert Folger and Robert A. Baron, "Violence and Hostility at Work: A Model of Reactions to Perceived Injustice," *Violence on the Job: Identifying Risks and Developing Solutions*, Gary R. VandenBos and Elizabeth Q. Bulatao, eds. (Washington, DC: American Psychological Association, 1996), p. 61; see, generally, pp. 51–85.

[7]See, for example, US Department of Justice, Federal Bureau of Investigation, *Uniform Crime Reports for the United States, 1995* (Washington, DC: US Government Printing Office, 1996). In 1995, of a total of 20,043 murder victims, 3,649 (18 percent) were killed as the result of felonies or attempted felonies, 10,592 (53 percent) were killed as a result of various forms of conflict, and 5,802 (29 percent) were killed under unknown circumstances.

[8]"US Leads in Gun Deaths Among Wealthiest Nations," *Los Angeles Times*, April 17, 1998, p. A18.

[9]See, generally, Daniel B. Polsby and Don B. Kates, Jr., "American Homicide Exceptionalism," *University of Colorado Law Review*, 69, No. 4 (1998), p. 970.

[10]Richard L. Vernaci, "Crime, Disease Linked to Economy," *Riverside Press-Enterprise*, October 16, 1992, pp. A1, A10. Merva and Fowles found a 1 percent rise in unemployment resulted in 17,654 deaths annually from heart disease, 1,386 deaths from stroke, 730 homicides, 31,305 violent crimes, and 111,775 property crimes. See also The New York Times, *The Downsizing of America* (New York, NY: Times Books/Random House), 1996. Based on an analysis of US Department of Labor data, *The New York Times* estimated that 43.5 million jobs were eliminated between 1979 and 1995. Despite the loss, the number of jobs grew from 90 million to 117 million over the 17-year period.

Supplemental Handout A: Violence in the Workplace

Overview of Workplace Violence

Violence at the workplace is highly prevalent in American society. One well known study estimated that one in four full-time workers was harassed, threatened, or attacked during the one-year survey period in 1992–1993.[1] Other key findings were that a high percentage of incidents go unreported. The health and productivity of victims and other workers are negatively affected by violence and harassment; and job stress is strongly correlated with violence and harassment on the job. On a more positive note, workers who believed their organizations had effective security programs, grievance mechanisms, and harassment policies also reported lower rates of workplace violence.

The U.S. Department of Labor has published complete national data on workplace homicides since 1992. In the 1990s, although still a rare occurrence, homicide became the second leading cause of death at the workplace after transportation accidents, up from third place. The vast majority of homicides occur in the course of robberies or other crimes, or involve police officers and security guards who are killed in the line of duty. In 1995, 1,024 homicides occurred, as shown below.[2]

	Number		*Percent*	
TOTAL	1,024		100%	
Work associates	113		11%	
Co-worker, former co-worker	88		9%	
Customer, client	25		2%	
Personal acquaintance	44		4%	
Husband, ex-husband		14		1%
Boyfriend, ex-boyfriend	11		1%	
Wife, ex-wife; girlfriend, ex-girlfriend	4		–	
Other relative		10		1%
Other acquaintance	5		–	
Robberies and other crimes	727		71%	
Police killed in the line of duty	81		8%	
Security guard killed in the line of duty	59		6%	

In 1995, homicides by co-workers or former co-workers rose to 9 percent of the total (88 deaths) from 5 percent in 1994, 6 percent in 1993, and 4 percent in 1992 (45, 59, and 49 deaths, respectively).

Workplace homicide data for 1992 through 1997 are presented in Figures 1 and 2. In summary, about 80–85 percent of the homicides occurred during the course of robberies or other crimes, about 10 percent resulted from business disputes, and about 5 percent resulted from personal disputes. In their study of murders of employers by employees from 1976 through 1992, Fox and Levin found the incidence had doubled since the 1980s. Currently, nearly two cases occur each month in the United States. At the same time, workplace homicides are rare. One observer has noted that in 1993, for example, that 59 employees were killed by current or former co-workers in a total labor force of 120.8 million workers. Thus, the chance that a homicidal incident would occur was only one in 2.1 million. The National Weather Service puts the odds of getting struck by lightning at one in 600,000.[4]

Workplace homicides may be likened to airplane crashes; they occur infrequently, but they terrify people when they do. In a 1996 survey of its members by the Society of Human Resources Management, 45 percent of the respondents said employees at their organizations were concerned that violence could occur at work.[5]

Fear of job loss, perceived or actual, is widely cited as a cause of workplace violence. Fox and Levin, for example, concluded that vengeful workers are typically middle-aged, white males who face job loss, see little opportunity for finding another job, and blame others for their plight. They tend to be loners for whom work provides the only meaningful part of their lives. Some vengeful employees come to feel invulnerable to job loss because of long-term employment. A related characteristic common to workplace violence perpetrators is the perception of an injustice at work.

In his book of cases of workplace violence, Baron found that warning signs of violence existed, but they often went undetected. These included attendance problems, extensive counseling of the employee required of the supervisor, decreased productivity, inconsistent work patterns, poor working relationships, concentration problems, safety problems, poor health and hygiene, unusual or changed behavior, fascination with guns or other weapons, evidence of possible drug or alcohol abuse, evidence of serious stress in the employee's personal life, continual excuses or blaming, and unshakable depression.[6] Baron outlined three levels in the forms that violence might take:

> Level one: Refuses to cooperate with immediate supervisor, spreads rumors and gossip to harm others, consistently argues with co-workers, belligerent toward customers/clients, constantly swears at others, makes unwanted sexual comments.

> Level two: Argues increasingly with customers, vendors, co-workers and management; refuses to obey company policies and procedures, sabotages equipment and steals property for revenge, verbalizes wishes to hurt co-workers and/or management, sends sexual or violent notes to co-workers and/or management, sees self as victimized by management (me against them).

> Level three: Frequent displays of intense anger resulting in recurrent suicidal threats, recurrent physical fights, destruction of property, utilization of weapons to harm others, commission of murder, rape, and/or arson.[7]

Baron's model for analyzing cases considers the employee, the environment, and the trigger for violence.[8] His review of the cases found that "emotionally enraged" employees have a history of one or more of the following: drug or alcohol abuse, serious stress or multiple life stressors, unshakable depression, pathological blaming, violent behavior and fascination with weapons, elevated frustration with the employer, poor interpersonal relationships, romance obsession, domestic disputes, or sexual harassment, impaired neurological functioning, behavioral disintegration and psychotic and/or paranoid behavior.

He listed the following organizational factors as predominant in employment related causes of violence: organizational personnel problems ignored, chronic labor-management conflict, preferential treatment because of title and responsibilities, employee perceptions of themselves as tools in the workplace, frequent and ineffective grievance procedures, lack of mutual respect in departments and among employees, ineffective horizontal and vertical communication, lack of consistency in senior management's actions, increased workloads with greater expectations, fewer resources and fewer rewards, work atmosphere that is repetitive, monotonous, and unfulfilling; overly aggressive, authoritarian management style; insufficient attention to physical environment and security measures; ineffective pre-employment screening and inconsistent application of organizational policies and procedures.

The triggering event, Baron averred, can be "literally anything"—a loud final argument between individuals, a courteous "no" to a disgruntled customer, or a lay-off notice.

Employers have legal obligations in the area of safety and health.[9] The Occupational Safety and Health Act of 1970 declares that an employer shall furnish a place of employment that is free from recognized hazards that cause, or are likely to cause, death or serious physical harm to employees. Under the common law tort theories of negligent hiring and negligent retention, an employer may be held liable for the violent acts of employees if the employer knew or should have known that the employee posed an unreasonable risk of harm because of violent propensities.

The Killing of James Whooper by Bruce Clark

Of relevance to the Clark case is Mawson's theory of "transient criminality," which attributes criminal behavior by well-controlled and law-abiding individuals more to situational factors than to enduring characteristics of the person committing the crime. The theory holds that "stressful events combined with the simultaneous absence or destruction of social bonds" can lead such individuals to commit criminal acts.[10] In summary, each individual has a "cognitive map" composed of familiar people, places, and objects, as well as abstract concepts of values, beliefs, and normative standards, including legal and moral rules (see appendix). When events occur that are perceived by an individual as incongruous with the cognitive map, he or she engages in behavior designed to maintain or restore congruity. Under conditions of stress and emotional arousal, and in the absence of close personal relationships, the failure to attain congruent sensory feedback is said to result in progressive disintegration of the cognitive map, among other adverse consequences, and an increased probability the individual will commit a criminal act that under normal circumstances would be inconsistent with his or her habits and lifestyle.

Regarding the importance of social supports, researchers have found "that individuals who have recently experienced a number of stressful life events, yet who have frequent and intimate contacts with relatives or other persons, are much less prone to become mentally or physically ill than those experiencing comparable amounts of stress, but with minimal supports. Thus, strong social bonds play a key role in 'protecting' individuals from the harmful effects of simultaneous environmental stress."[11]

The theory of transient criminality offers a psychological explanation for the shooting. Bruce Clark perceived the behavior of James Whooper as a supervisor as a threat to his own social world and perhaps his very employment. Clark's life revolved around the Postal Service and his cats, who were said to be his family. Whooper's presence jeopardized the social bonds with other workers that meant so much to Clark, and he lacked sufficient social supports outside of work to deal with the crisis he faced. In the wake of the disintegration of the cognitive map of his life, Clark sought to remove Whooper from the workplace in the most forceful way possible.

The Clark case has several implications for employers and employees. First, it exemplifies the difficulty of predicting and preventing workplace violence despite implementation of preventive programs. In recent years, the US Postal Service has instituted several measures designed to reduce this risk, such as pre-employment screening of applicants; training programs on workplace violence; promotion of sound human resources management practices and deterrence of abusive practices; procedures for reporting and assessing threats; and enhanced security measures. Second, the case reminds us of the need to train supervisors and employees in recognizing the warning signs of potential violence and taking appropriate action when such signs are displayed. Third, the case points out the sensitivities of supervisor-employee relations, particularly the impact of the arrival of a new supervisor on workfloor relations.

Footnotes

[1]*Fear and Violence in the Workplace* (Minneapolis, MN: Northwestern National Life Insurance Company, October 1993). The company has since changed its name to ReliaStar Life Insurance Company. See also *Violence in the Workplace*, Research Report #15 (Houston, TX: International Facility Management Association, 1994), a report prepared by the University of Southern California Center for Crisis Management in Los Angeles, California; *Violence in the Workplace: Risk Factors and Prevention Strategies*, NIOSH Current Intelligence Bulletin 57 (Washington, DC: US Department of Health and Human Services, Public Health Service, Centers for Disease Control and Prevention, National Institute for Occupational Safety and Health, June 1996); and Greg Warchol, "Workplace Violence, 1992–96," NCJ-168634, US Department of Justice, Office of Justice Programs, Bureau of Justice Statistics, July 1998. Data from the National Crime Victimization Survey for the period of 1992 through 1996 estimated that an average of 2,032,000 victimizations occurred annually at the workplace. The victimizations accounted for 18 percent of the annual total of 10,969,000 acts of violence. An estimated 11 percent of rapes, 7 percent of robberies, and 21 percent of assaults occurred while victims were working or on duty.

[2]*National Census of Fatal Occupational Injuries, 1995*, News Release, USDL-96-315 (Washington, DC: United States Department of Labor, Bureau of Labor Statistics, August 8, 1996), p. 6.

[3]See, generally, James Alan Fox and Jack Levin, "Firing Back: The Growing Threat of Workplace Homicide," *The Annals of The American Academy of Political and Social Science*, 536 (November 1994), pp. 16–30.

[4]See, generally, Erik Larson, "Trigger Happy – False Crisis: How Workplace Violence Became a Hot Issue," *The Wall Street Journal*, October 15, 1994, pp. A1, A10.

[5]See, generally, *1996 Workplace Violence Survey* (Alexandria, VA: Society for Human Resources Management, June 1996).

[6]S. Anthony Baron, *Violence in the Workplace: A Prevention and Management Guide for Businesses* (Ventura, CA: Pathfinder Publishing of California, 1993), pp. 50–52.

[7]*Ibid.*, p. 51.

[8]See, generally, S. Anthony Baron, "Organizational Factors in Workplace Violence: Developing Effective Programs to Reduce Workplace Violence," *Occupational medicien: State of the Art Reviews*, Robert Harrison, ed. (Philadelphia, PA: Hanley & Belfus, Inc., 1996), pp. 161–173.

[9]See "US Department of Labor Program Highlights, Fact Sheet No. OSHA 96-53." In 1996, OSHA issued voluntary guidelines for protecting workers against violence in the health care and social services industries. See also, for example, Stephen C. Yohay and Melissa L. Peppe, "Workplace Violence: Employer Responsibilities and Liabilities," *Occupational Hazards*, 58, No. 7 (July 1996), pp. 21–26.

[10]Anthony R. Mawson, *Transient Criminality: A Model of Stress-Induced Crime* (New York: Praeger Publishers, 1987), p. 20. The category of transient criminality "includes individuals for whom criminal deviance represents an occasional and usually not very serious aberration from an otherwise law-abiding existence." (pp. 6–7) A criminal act may be committed once, twice, or a few times in a lifetime. The act typically is a misdemeanor, but may be a felony such as murder. "The incidence in the

general population may be very high compared to crimes committed by persistent offenders . . ." (p. 10) See, generally, pp. 54–63.

[11]*Ibid.*, p. 19.

Additional References

Flannery, Raymond B. *Violence in the Workplace.* New York: The Crossroad Publishing Company, 1995.

Heskett, Sandra L. *Workplace Violence: Before, During, and After.* Boston, MA: Butterworth-Heinemann, 1996.

Kelleher, Michael D. *New Arenas for Violence: Homicide in the American Workplace.* Westport, CT: Praeger Publishers, 1996.

Kelleher, Michael D. *Profiling the Lethal Employee: Case Studies of Violence in the Workplace.* Westport, CT: Praeger Publishers, 1997.

Labig, Charles E. *Preventing Violence in the Workplace.* New York: AMACOM, 1995.

Mantell, Michael, with Steve Albrecht. *Ticking Bombs: Defusing Violence in the Workplace.* Burr Ridge, IL: Richard D. Irwin, Inc., 1994.

Appendix*:* Mawson's Theory of Transient Criminality—The Cognitive Map

KEY ATTACHMENT FIGURES,
primary group/nuclear and
extended family, e.g., mother,
father, spouse, children;
concept of self

OTHER ATTACHMENT OBJECTS,
e.g., home, neighborhood; citizenship;
religious and other "sacred"
legal-moral beliefs

OTHER INTERNALIZED BELIEFS,
including laws, mores, customs, folkways;
theories about the external world

PERCEPTUAL/CULTURAL STANDARDS,
including culturally-specific standards for
recognizing and judging experiences

BASIC PERCEPTUAL-SENSORIAL EXPECTANCIES
i.e., expected quantities and types of sensory input,
e.g., visual, tactile, auditory, olfactory, gustatory

Schematic representation of an individual's cognitive map. Increasingly complex, abstract, and psychologically important types of internalized representations are assumed to be derived from combinations of "basic" sensorial experiences, as indicated by the wide base of the structure in relation to its apex.

Source: Anthony R. Mawson, *Transient Criminality: A Model of Stress-Induced Crime* (New York: Praeger Publishers, 1987), p. 88.

Figure 1: Circumstances of Workplace Homicides, 1992–1994

Type of Circumstance	1992 Number	%	1993 Number	%	1994 Number	%
TOTAL	1,004	100%	1,063	100%	1,071	100%
Business disputes	*87*	*9%*	*106*	*10%*	*100*	*9%*
Coworker, former coworker	45	4%	59	6%	49	5%
Customer, client	35	3%	43	4%	42	4%
Other	7	1%	*		*	
Personal disputes	*39*	*4%*	*45*	*4%*	*43*	*4%*
Relative of victim (primarily husband, ex-husband)	24	2%	21	2%	*	
Boyfriend, ex-boyfriend	7	1%	12	1%	11	1%
Other	8	1%	12	1%	*	
Robberies and miscellaneous crimes	*822*	*82%*	*793*	*75%*	*648*	*73%*
Police in the line of duty	*56*	*6%*	*67*	*6%*	*70*	*7%*
Security guard in the line of duty	*		*52*	*5%*	*76*	*7%*

Source: Census of Fatal Occupational Injuries, US Department of Labor, Bureau of Labor Statistics, Washington, DC. In 1993, the category Security Guard in the Line of Duty was added. The category Business Disputes was renamed Work Associates and the other subcategory was dropped. Also, the category Personal Disputes was renamed Personal Acquaintance, the Other subcategory was dropped, and separate data were provided for homicides by the victim's husband or ex-husband (15 or 1 percent) and other relative (6 or 1 percent); the subcategories not shown for 1994 are victim's husband or ex-husband (24 or 2 percent) and other relative or acquaintance (8 or 1 percent). The 1994 data do not add up to the 1,071 total because of data omission. The 1992, 1993, and 1994 data were revised to reflect 1,044, 1,074, and 1,080 homicides, respectively; the additional cases were not assigned to categories (Personal Communication, Janice A. Windau, Epidemiologist, Office of Safety, Health, and Working Conditions, Bureau of Labor Statistics).

Figure 2: Circumstances of Workplace Homicides, 1995–1997

Type of Circumstance	1995 Number	%	1996 Number	%	1997 Number	%
TOTAL	1,024	100%	927	100%	856	100%
Work associates	*113*	*11%*	*132*	*14%*	*81*	*9%*
Coworker, former coworker	88	9%	76	8%	56	7%
Customer, client	25	2%	56	6%	25	3%
Relative	*28*	*3%*	*28*	*3%*	*24*	*3%*
Husband, ex-husband		14	1%	17	2%	16	2%
Wife, ex-wife		4	--	--		3	--
Other relative		10	1%	9	1%	5	1%
Personal acquaintance	16	2%	26	3%	20	2%
Boyfriend, ex-boyfriend	11	1%	11	1%	11	1%
Other acquaintance	5	--	15	2%	9	1%
Robbery and other crimes	*727*	*71%*	*741*	*80%*	*731*	*85%*
Robbery	*		357	39%	338	39%
Police in the line of duty	*81*	*8%*	*		*	
Security guard in the line of duty	*59*	*6%*	*		*	

Source: Census of Fatal Occupational Injuries, US Department of Labor, Bureau of Labor Statistics, Washington, DC. See "Job-Related Homicides by Selected Characteristics, 1992–97" for 1996 and 1997 data. In 1995, the Relative and Personal Acquaintance categories comprised one category called Personal Acquaintance; the subcategory Wife, Ex-Wife also specified Girlfriend, Ex-Girlfriend. Also, the category Robbery and Other Crimes was called Robberies and Miscellaneous Crimes. In 1996, the Robbery subcategory was added. Also, the categories Police in the Line of Duty and Security Guard in the Line of Duty were deleted from the section on circumstances in reports of workplace homicides; these figures are listed in the Occupation section, under Protective Service Occupations. Most of these homicides are reported in the Robbery and Other Crimes category, with some reported in the Relative and Personal Acquaintance categories (Personal Communication, Janice A. Windau, Epidemiologist, Office of Safety, Health, and Working Conditions, Bureau of Labor Statistics).

Supplemental Handout B: Violence in the Workplace

1. Incidence

    In 1992, the Centers for Disease Control declared workplace homicide a serious national public health problem.

2. Types
    a. Robbery and commercial crime
    b. Law enforcement and security officers
    c. Domestic or spouse-related
    d. Employer-directed violence
    e. Terrorism and hate crimes

3. Cases

    Landmark case of Patrick Henry Sherrill, postal worker in Edmond, OK, who on August 20, 1986, fatally shot 14 people, wounded six others, and committed suicide at the U.S. Post Office, after being reprimanded by his supervisor and told that he would receive a poor performance report.

4. Social causes
    a. Disintegration of family life, high divorce rate.
    b. Violent culture: risk of being murdered in U.S. seven times greater than in most European countries; guns are present in 40 percent of American households; many people experienced with guns, including children, an estimated 20 percent of whom have carried guns to school at least once; the mass media have portrayed the use of guns as glamorous and acceptable.
    c. Economy: loss of belief in economic progress; a *New York Times* study found that 43.3 million jobs were eliminated in 1979–1995; a *Times* poll in late-1995 concluded that a result of the downsizing is the most acute job insecurity since the Great Depression of the 1930s.
    d. Career dissonance: loss by men of their anchor in job and profession, because of loss of long-valued, generalized expectation that loyalty, diligence, and hard work would be rewarded with job stability and security, and perceived challenge to authority and potency by women, who have gained ground in the struggle for equality at the workplace; violence against women and hate crimes against minorities also are rising.

5. Homicidal people

6. Managerial practices
    a. Negligent, unjust, and abusive practices
    b. Sound human resources management practices
        1) Careful selection and retention of managers, continuous development
        2) Open communications
        3) Absence of discrimination and favoritism
        4) Adequate compensation
        5) Training and promotional opportunities
        6) Employee participation in decision
        7) Feedback on performance
        8) Employee assistance programs
        9) Just cause and due process in discipline
        10) Impartial grievance procedures

11) Outplacement services

12) Exit interviews

13) Attitude surveys on managerial performance and satisfaction with HRM program

c. Procedural justice in HR decisions: procedures consistent across persons and over time, bias suppressed, decisions based on accurate information, opportunities to modify decisions, process represents concerns of all participants, decisions based on prevailing moral and ethical standards

7. Legal Issues

a) General duty clause, Section 5(a), Occupational Safety and Health Act, to provide a safe and healthy workplace free of recognized hazards

b) Negligent hiring: heightened duty of inquiry into applicant's background when jobs involve weapons, substantial public contact, and supervision of children; criminal records difficult to assess because past violent behavior may not be predictive, and use requires business necessity if applicant protected under Title VII, Civil Rights Act; psychological tests must be job-related and valid under Equal Employment Opportunity Commission guidelines, and may not be intrusive without compelling reason such as life-endangering occupation or high-stress position, and a questionable score should lead to a clinical interview, not outright rejection

c) Negligent retention: duty to take notice of threats and harassment within workplace, and to respond to employee complaints and warnings about potentially dangerous employees, same theory as applied to sexual harassment; Americans with Disabilities Act may require mental health counseling for employees with violent propensities related to mental impairment, and may preclude suspending or discharging employee suspected as posing a danger because of requirement of reasonable accommodation

d) Duty to warn victims of threats, covers independent psychiatrists and psychologists, employee assistance programs, mental health clinics

e) Post-discharge duty to protect employee safety by providing additional security, e.g., take keys and passcards or change locks and codes, consider transferring threatened employee or increasing security at work location

8. Costs

An estimated $250,000 per serious incident: medical and post-trauma stress treatment, lost wages to workers, training costs for replacement workers, lost productivity, property damage, property theft, increased physical and electronic security, enhanced training for supervisors and managers, diversion of attention of senior management to react to incident, respond to the crisis, and plan for the future, investigations using outside experts, diminished image in the minds of stakeholders and customers resulting in reduced sales potential and lower stock value, increased legal expenditures for lawsuits and legal defensibility measures

9. Comprehensive plans

a. Climate: reduction of stress

b. Employee relations: emphasis on selection, appraisal, discipline, layoffs

c. Security of facilities

d. Workplace violence policies

1) Statement that violence of any sort is contrary to business purpose

2) Reinforced communication through all possible means

3) Designated personnel to receive and act on threats

4) Hotlines

e. Policies on threats: reports, investigations, intervention through counseling

   f. Management training: psychology of job loss, warning signs of violence

   g. Crisis management team, use of specialists

   h. Post-incident trauma procedures

      1) Employees and families

      2) Medical personnel, police, communications media, clients

Teaching Note
WHEN WORLDS COLLIDE

Topics (* = Primary topic with teaching plan)
  *Environmental uncertainty & complexity
  *Mechanistic & organic structures
  *Stable & Changing environments
  Contingency theory
  Internal and external alignments
  Strategic alliance
  Differentiation & integration
  Rewards
  Organizational structure
  Restructuring

Case overview

Evergreen, a dominant player in the manufacture and delivery of preprinted paper forms to Fortune 1000 companies, had entered a new emerging market of electronic forms. In the initial thinking, it had rejected purchase of an electronic forms producer due to perceived product defects, retail market and simplicity of the offerings. They had, instead, decided to form a software product development division headed by a former senior sales manager and staffed with some outside talent. They had purchased a small electronic forms company to begin this division.

The company history was one of customer satisfaction and responsiveness. It was also sales-driven, with a strong manufacturing component. It beat the industry growth level in three out of four divisional categories, all except office products. Business forms comprised over one third of all business, and was at a 15 percent growth rate, compared to industry growth of minus 2.5 percent.

The recent entry into software required technical expertise, a different sales strategy, and changes in manufacturing. Those involved felt the company did not comprehend such changes. It was also in financial danger, with customers unsure of the delivery of the technology as promised.

Industry

A dominant player in the manufacturing and delivery of preprinted paper forms and a new player in electronic forms. Nonunion.

Teaching objectives

1. To examine contingency theory.
2. To analyze organizational fit among internal components of the firm, as well as between the firm and its external environment.
3. To illustrate elements of strategic alliances.
4. To illustrate how companies might meet newly emerging customer trends.

Other related cases in Volume 1

Fired! (rewards). Donor Services Department in Guatemala (organizational structure). Julie's Call: Empowerment at Taco Bell (contingency theory). Pearl Jam's Dispute with Ticketmaster (environmental context). Split Operations at Sky and Arrow Airlines (organizational structure). The Unmovable Team (rewards).

This teaching note was prepared by Russell Aebig, Ann Feyerherm (Pepperdine University), Rasool Azari (University of Redlands), and Teri C. Tompkins. The case and teaching note were prepared as basis for class discussion rather than to illustrate either effective or ineffective handling of administrative situations. Suggestions for improvement of this note should be sent to Teri.Tompkins@pepperdine.edu. Credit will be given in the next revision.

Other related cases in Volume 2

Insubordination or Unclear Loyalties? (organizational structure). Saving Private Ryan and Classic Leadership Models (contingency theory). The Volunteer (environmental context).

Intended courses and levels

This case is intended for undergraduate, graduate and executive students in organizational theory, general management, or a portion of strategy courses dealing with strategic positioning and alliances. The case can be positioned midway to late in the term.

Analysis

Analysis can be found in the introduction to the teaching plan and in the answers to the questions.

Research methodology

This case was written based on first hand observation and company annual reports. The company and the people are disguised.

Teaching plan

The first part of the discussion centers around a diagnosis of the issues, about 25 minutes would be appropriate. A contingency theory is appropriate background to use for this case. You could also include what Evergreen did well, what they could build from. The second part of the discussion would be the students' suggestions of what to do at this juncture, taking about 20 minutes for the students to justify their suggestions. At the end of the teaching note is the epilogue, which can be used in the final summation of key points by the instructor.

Diagnosis: The first set of questions deals with the alignment (or misalignment) of systems and design within the organization structure. The second deals with the external environment; what is influencing this organization from its outside resources and constraints?

Internal alignment

The major concepts to be covered would be differentiation and integration, (Lawrence & Lorsch, 1986), examining the sales force, including their rewards and their skills, skills of manufacturing personnel, and the culture and how it might influence what happened with a new division. Also, current technology consists of large batch and mass production (from Woodward's definitions). This may not be the case with the new software development.

External alignment

One could use the grid of stability and complexity to analyze the uncertainty of the environment with printed forms versus electronic forms. Originally published by Robert Duncan in 1972, "Characteristics of Organizational Environments and Perceived Environmental Uncertainties" in Administrative Science Quarterly, it is used in several major textbooks (e.g. Daft, Organization Theory & Design).

After conducting an examination of the internal and external alignment, you could look at what they did well, and then spend some time trying to "fix" those elements that are misaligned and discuss new strategies that might be available for the company.

Topic: Contingency Theory on Internal & External Alignments; Mechanistic/Organic Structure
60-minute teaching plan

Pre-assignment: Read case (15 minutes)

	Timing	Activity	Organization	Student Outcomes
I	0-5 minutes (5)	Summarize the case facts	Ask or appoint a "volunteer"	Orientation and refresher on case

	Timing	Activity	Organization	Student Outcomes
II	5 - 15 minutes (10)	Ask: *Diagnose the alignment (or misalignment) of systems and design within the organizational structure?*	Full class discussion.	Students should note: • Differentiation & integration (Question 1) • Sales force reward (doing, not selling system), technical level, and contacts (Question 2) • Manufacturing personnel's skill level (lower than required for software development) (Question 3) • Culture ("yes" culture combined with perceived malleability of software added potential delays and dissatisfied customers. (Question 4)
III	15-25 minutes (10)	Ask: *Diagnose the external alignment of the company.*	Full class discussion. Use the stability and complexity grid (see question 5 & 6) on board or overhead.	Current business: (Stable and Simple). Response to low uncertainty = mechanistic structure. (Question 5) Future business: (more unstable, more complex). Requires more organic, lower formalization. (Question 6)
IV	25 - 30 minutes (5)	Ask *What did they do well?*	Full class discussion.	Anticipated future market growth. Positioned themselves ahead of the competition. Culture of saying yes is useful for developing new solutions. R&D department already established (Question 7).
V	30-50 minutes (20)	*What suggestions do you have for Evergreen at this juncture?*	Full class discussion. Encourage students to justify their suggestions.	Realignment of elements: 1. Re-educate and incentives for sales people. 2. Task force to deal with manufacturing aspect of software. 3. Acquire new skill levels (hire or retrain). New strategies (Question 9). 1. Strategic alliance with original electronic forms company they chose not to buy to get technical know-how. 2. Subcontract software development and concentrate few salespeople on intensive customer contact/problem solving, acting as "brokers."
VI	50 - 60 minutes (10)	Hand out or read epilogue found in this teaching note. Ask for reactions.	Individual or full class reading, followed by full class discussion.	Student reactions will vary. Point out or ask for places where there was agreement and disagreement between student suggestions and Evergreen's response.

25-minute teaching plan on environmental complexity/ external alignment
Pre-assignment: Read case before class (15 minutes)
Activities. Do activities I, III, and VI in the 60-minute plan.

25-minute teaching plan on internal structures/ internal alignment
Pre-assignment: Read case before class (15 minutes)
Activities. Do activities I, II, and VI in the 60-minute plan.

Discussion questions and answers

Question 1

Explain how organizational design structure (e.g., differentiation/integration) can be matched or mismatched with its environment (e.g., stable/changing). Reference: Hellreigel, Jackson, Slocum (1999). Management, 8th edition. Cincinnati, OH: South-West, pp. 363-364.

Comprehension skills (understanding the meaning of remembered material, usually by restating or citing examples)

Answer

Paul Lawrence and Jay Lorsch (1967) found that organizations perform better if they match their organizational design to the challenges posed by an organization's external environment (e.g., stable versus changing). Differentiation is the measure of the differences among departments with respect to structure, tasks, and goals. Integration is the measure of coordination among departments with respect to structure, tasks, and goals.

The salespeople are characterized by having a short time horizon, social interpersonal orientation, and high formality of structure. The manufacturing people also have a short time horizon, an interpersonal orientation that is task-oriented, and a high formality of structure. The new group of electronic forms developers are more like the current small group of R&D, a long time horizon, primarily task-oriented (developing new products), and a low formality of structure. There is currently little need for integration, yet with a new entry there is going to be a higher need for integration.

Question 2

Diagnose the sales force's alignment (or misalignment) within the organizational structure.

Analysis skills (breaking a concept into its parts and explaining their interrelationships, distinguishing relevant from extraneous material)

Answer

Sales force: Their rewards systems must be examined. The rewards are often for doing a job instead of on selling the system. They are not given incentives for the current needs of electronic forms selling. They are used to selling through long-term relationships with their customers. The technical level of these people was appropriate for selling business forms, labels, direct mail, and office products. The requirements were limited to getting camera-ready copy of the form or label and scheduling the production of the product. The sales force was not equipped to sell advanced software technology. Their general contacts were purchasing agents and sometimes line managers of their client organizations. They were unable to talk to the MIS departments of the customers they were dealing with. Without this relationship, they were unable to break into this market on a large-scale basis.

Question 3

Diagnose the manufacturing personnel's alignment (or misalignment) within the organizational structure.

Analysis skills (breaking a concept into its parts and explaining their interrelationships, distinguishing relevant from extraneous material)

Answer

Manufacturing Personnel: Currently, the manufacturing personnel had lower skill levels, which was fine for operating a printer or printing press. Development of software required much higher, and different types of skills and training. Developers of software are generally considered professional employees, with expectations of autonomy, salary, and respect that accompany professionals.

Question 4

Diagnose the culture alignment (or misalignment) within the organizational structure.

Analysis skills (breaking a concept into its parts and explaining their interrelationships, distinguishing relevant from extraneous material)

Answer

The culture, "Find a way to say yes", was easier to fulfill when they dealt with printed forms. There was a subtle trap in this belief system when it came to software, especially in a start-up of developing electronic forms. Since there was often not a predefined target, a commitment to "say yes" would mean endless delays. The perceived malleability of software—implying it could be changed easily—also added to this potential for delays and dissatisfied customers.

Question 5

Diagnose the current business's alignment (or misalignment) with the external environment.
Analysis skills (breaking a concept into its parts and explaining their interrelationships, distinguishing relevant from extraneous material)

Answer

The current business of printed forms could be characterized as stable (on the stable to unstable dimension) and simple (on the dimension of simple to complex). Therefore, there is very low uncertainty. As a response to this low uncertainty, it is likely that the organization will have a mechanistic structure with a formal, centralized operation. This is true at Evergreen, a business printing company. It has a number of formal rules, centralized decision making at the plant (for job-based decisions), or at headquarters for central processing and other business decisions.

It also should have relatively few departments, also true here with a sales department, manufacturing, a small R&D group and administrative support. There are no integrating roles. There are two groups: manufacturing and sales. They cooperate only through the manufacturing manager. There is also little imitation by competitors and they are currently operations-oriented. Finding the next job is the orientation of the sales force. Producing the current job is the orientation of the manufacturing people.

Question 6

Diagnose the future business's alignment (or misalignment) with the external environment.
Analysis skills (breaking a concept into its parts and explaining their interrelationships, distinguishing relevant from extraneous material)

Answer

The future business is not so certain. On the dimension of stability, it is more unstable; on the dimension of complexity, it is more complex. This leads to a higher degree of uncertainty. There are a large number of external elements that are dissimilar. They are unpredictable as the technology changes very quickly. Being able to keep pace with the changes is a significant challenge for any company in the industry. Using Daft's Organization Theory and Design text, there are two significant structural implications for Evergreen. The first is the imitation of similar organizations. Evergreen will need to look beyond its own walls in order to successfully compete.

The other structural design is that a company needs to be more organic. This means lower formalization. Software development is largely problem solving, and those problems are often undefined. The developers are usually creative by nature and require little formalization to thrive. With a more organic structure, employees contribute to the common tasks of the department; tasks are adjusted and redefined through employee teamwork; and communication is horizontal rather than vertical. There is less hierarchy of control and fewer rules. Knowledge and control of the tasks are located anywhere in the organization. Because of the variety of technology that must be monitored and implemented, it is difficult to centralize the information.

Question 7

What did Evergreen do well?
Evaluation skills (using a set of criteria to arrive at a reasoned judgment of the value of something)

Answer

This might be a more "appreciative perspective" and include the following. They did anticipate future market growth into the electronic forms. They seemed to move to position themselves well in front of major competition. The culture is one that could be geared to serving customers in their transition to electronic forms. They have a "find a way to say yes" mantra, which could be useful in developing what is proving to be new solutions, provided it didn't fall into the endless cycle of always changing the product. There is already an R&D department that might be useful in this effort.

Question 8

What suggestions do you have for Evergreen's internal alignment at this juncture?
Synthesis skills (putting parts together to form a new whole; solving a problem requiring creativity or originality)

Answer

In terms of realignment of elements, there are a couple of options:

1) Play off the current culture by getting people together across the divisions to solve problems. The case seems to indicate the software division is isolating itself. Expand into a small task force that deals with the manufacturing aspect of this software.

2) Hire new people or find likely candidates to retrain. The skill levels are very different than the company currently possesses.

Question 9

What suggestions do you have for new strategies at this juncture?
Synthesis skills (putting parts together to form a new whole; solving a problem requiring creativity or originality)

Answer

In terms of new strategies, there are a couple of possible scenarios. Encourage student brainstorming of "what next"—form a few of the choice scenarios. Here are a couple suggestions:

1) Go back to the original electronic forms company they chose not to buy and see if any of their retail applications might be modified to fit the needs and form a type of alliance or licensing agreement with them. They have the technical know-how (which is lacking in Evergreen).

2) Subcontract the software development and concentrate a few salespeople on intensive customer contact and problem solving. The electronic forms salespeople would act as "brokers," finding the problems and then subcontracting out for solutions.

References

Duncan, R. (1972). Characteristics of organizational environments and perceived environmental uncertainties. Administrative Science Quarterly, 17 (3), start p. 313.

Hellreigel, Jackson, Slocum (1999). Management, 8th edition. Cincinnati, OH: South-West, pp. 363-364.

Lawrence, P. R., and Lorsch, J. W. (1986). Organization and Environment : Managing Differentiation and Integration . Boston: Harvard Business School Press.

Epilogue

Alliance and Consolidation

The purchase of the electronic forms company satisfied the customers that Evergreen was able to provide a transition strategy from their current paper forms into electronic forms. This immediately led to a contract with revenues five times greater than the price paid for the company. Other contracts soon followed for similar reasons. From a financial perspective the acquisition was deemed a great success.

Due to the inability to sell custom electronic form software through the sales force (and subsequent lack of revenues), and the estimates for the production of custom electronic forms product being significantly longer than expected, a decision was made to ally with a current electronic forms vendor.

The company that was under evaluation several years earlier had undergone a transformation. The defects were removed from the product, and it had been enhanced to the point where it was being marketed directly to enterprises as a corporate electronic form solution.

An alliance was formed between Evergreen and the vendor in which Evergreen would provide all the customer marketing through its sales force, and all of the customization through its electronic forms division. For its part, Evergreen would receive the software product at discounted prices and be able to sell in volume to its customer base.

This also led to further alliances between Evergreen, the electronic forms vendor, and third parties such as credit card companies that would provide access to their information and merge it into electronic forms.

Ultimately, the electronic form division was consolidated into the central operations. The division was downsized during this consolidation as the new business model, and support of an external software package, required fewer people.

Part III

CRITICAL INCIDENT CASE ASSIGNMENT HINTS

If you are like me, you may be concerned about how to help your student's think more critically about management theories. You may also be searching for a way to improve student's ability to write, even if you feel that your skills are not that of a professional writer. The critical incident case and analysis will help your students think and write more critically about their own experience. It will also help them learn to apply management concepts to their experience.

According to the North American Case Research Association (NACRA), cases are real-life descriptions of actual organizations. Even so, some students have difficulty believing that a case is real and may discount its value to their learning. A self-written case helps students identify strongly with the facts in the case and increases their understanding of the conceptual material because it directly applies to their own experience. The learning is anchored in an emotional event, so the concepts connected to the analysis of that event are retained over longer periods of time[1].

The critical incident case also increases student's ability to write and think critically. Professors are being held accountable across every discipline to help improve student's writing skills; yet, designing effective writing assignments that relate strongly to our discipline is not always easy. The critical incident case exercise is divided into distinctive steps, which helps students improve their ability to

- describe vividly, yet objectively
- think critically and conceptually
- explore a topic using different levels and types of questions
- and to improve clarity and specificity.

The professor doesn't need to be an English teacher to help student's improve their writing. Davis (1993, p. 205 - 207) writes that the hard work of writing, the use of peer review, and the emphasis on revision helps students improve their writing skills. As management professors, we can concentrate on the theory of the student's case and analysis, while providing students the opportunity to develop their ideas, compose drafts, get feedback from others, revise drafts, edit and present finished work, which supports improving their writing skills.

I have been using some version of student-written cases for eight years. I've also been teaching case method in my Managing Change class about the same length of time. However, it's only been recently that I have taught a case study for a graduate course called Groups and Leaders *and* assigned the critical incident case as an assignment. I was surprised when I notice the writing of the critical incident cases improved significantly over previous ones from the same course, and student's analysis of the cases improved after they wrote their own analysis. It appeared to me that there is an interaction effect when students learn from cases written by others and write their own case and analysis.

There is significant detail in Cases in Organizational Behavior and Management to guide you and your students in writing a case and then analyzing it. But I imagine that you would also like some tips in helping students' do this assignment. I hope you find the following ideas useful.

Helpful hints for the instructor
Class size and planning logistics

What's the ideal class size? Classroom size varies by institution. Here are some suggestions for planning logistics depending on your class size. In ½ semester courses, e.g., seven-weeks, small classes of 12 students is ideal. This is because turn-around time has to be one week. I've had up to 24, and the one-week turn-around time was challenging.

---

[1] Erlbaum. Spear, N.E., & Riccio, D.C. (1994). Memory: Phenomena and Principles. Boston, MA: Allyn & Bacon.

If you have medium-size classes of around 24, then give yourself two weeks to grade before you promise to turn it back to them. I tell the students on the very first day of class that I will need two weeks to grade each part, otherwise they wait anxiously for the feedback.

If I had large class sizes (I've had 70 students in basic OB courses as an adjunct), I would modify the assignment by having groups of students write and analyze a single case. Groups of 3 to 4 would be ideal. If you use the group writing method, I strongly suggest they do a peer group review to determine how they will distribute their grade. Here's how I explain it to students (source: A. Cohen, S. Fink, H. Gadon, and R. Willets Instructor's Manual for Effective Behavior in Organizations):

Peer Evaluation if choose Group Paper: To ensure balance of participation, your group will use peer evaluation. As a group, you will determine the percentage of the group grade each member receives. No group member can receive less than 80% (unless they did not contribute to the project) or more than 120%. For example in the table below the group agrees that Joe and Alice did the same amount of work but Sally did more than Joe and Alice. Joe and Alice give away 2% points to Sally in recognition of her contributions to the project:

	The group assigns a **peer grade** of		I assign a **project grade** of		**Actual Grade** in instructor's grade book
Joe	98%	X	85%	=	83.3%
Alice	98%	X	85%	=	83.3%
Sally	104%	X	85%	=	88.4%

I've found that I get excellent participation from students because they are aware from the beginning that they are being judged by their peers, not by just me. Encourage students to discuss their evaluation criteria frequently. If a student does not participate, then the group removes that person completely from the list (this means that they cannot use his/her points to boost their own grade. It's as if he/she was never in the group).

Scheduling

How long does the entire assignment take? I have frequently had students do this assignment in a seven-week, ½ semester course. Of course, it works well during longer terms, such as quarter or semester. Here is my seven-week schedule.

Table 1: Suggested schedule for due dates and grading time

	Student	**Professor**
Week 1	Turn in notes to get you started. Professor evaluates concept and give feedback before students go home.	This can be written in class or outside of class. I like to give them comments on the first night, so they can begin writing their narrative right away. With a small class, you can go around the room and have each student describe their critical incident (give them 5 to 10 minutes to write it down first). The advantage is they get to hear the others describe their ideas and your response.
Week 2		Professor returns grades and comments from Step 1: Notes to get you started. Allow 5 to 10 minutes to grade each Notes to Get You Started. Alternatively, you can not grade this assignment and just give them feedback on the first night of class.
Week 3	Turn in narrative.	Ask students not to put their work in special binders. A paper clip or staple works best for faster grading.
Week 4		You return graded narrative. Allow about 30 to 60 minutes to grade each case narrative.
Week 5	Turn in analysis.	
Week 6		You return graded analysis. Allow about 45 minutes to 1½ hours to grade each case analysis.
Week 7	Turn in final edited.	

	version of narrative and analysis.	
Grades due!		You grade final versions. Allow about 15 to 30 minutes to grade the final edited version.

Grading Hints

Teach students how to separate fact from opinion. This is one of the hardest things for them to do. Fact is like a reporter, being careful of adjectives. If he/she wants to express an opinion, then recognize it as opinion by attributing it to the person holding the opinion (usually in quotes). Hold opinions until the analysis.

Teach students to write better. Teach students that writing is a skill that needs to be developed. I tell them that the narrative and analysis use very different writing styles. The narrative is like presenting a written history or report. You must learn to present the report factually, but with flair, so that the report gets read. The analysis usually follows the report or is written as an executive summary. It is also like a research paper. The idea is to back your opinion up with facts (from the case) and theory (from experts, including yourself). In business, we need both kinds of writing.

What are some good criteria for grading the narrative? I find it hardest to grade the narrative because it is about someone's experience, and how do you judge that? There are some key items that I look for however, and I've put them in a grading template on the next page. Following that are some sample narrative grade sheets that I have used.

What are some good criteria for grading the analysis? One way to guide your thinking for grading is to use Bloom's taxonomy and evaluate the level of their cognitive ability. Some cases lend themselves more naturally to analysis, and not to synthesis and evaluation. I'd use my judgement and give a higher grade if they've done a very good job at the analysis level. The table below assumes good answers to these types of questions.

Table 2: Suggestions for grading by using Bloom's taxonomy

Bloom's taxonomy level (The chart assumes good answers to these type of questions. Grade lowers if poorly written answer to question type. Grade higher if excellent answer to question type).	Undergraduate	Graduate
All Knowledge and Comprehension	D to C	F to D
Knowledge, Comprehension and Application	C+ to B	C- to C+
Comprehension, Application, Analysis	B to B+	C+ to B-
Application, 2 Analysis	B+ to A-	B- to B+
Analysis, Synthesis, Evaluation	A- to A	B+ to A

Use the question type labels to evaluate their work, but there is a caution. Many students do not correctly label their questions. You must re-label the question types using the chart above. I think it is only fair to tell the students ahead of time that you want them to move beyond knowledge, comprehension, and exploratory-type questions. Many students want to use a knowledge question first to demonstrate that they know the theory. Tell them you already know the theory, and that all they have to do is reference it and you'll figure it out. I try to teach my students to briefly (1 to 2 sentences) describe the concept, and then build on the concept to apply, analyze, create and evaluate.

What are some good grading criteria for the Final edited version of Narrative and Analysis (Step 4)?

Have student mark one copy of their final paper. If you have the students "track their changes" or mark their copies on their final paper so that you can see where they made changes from the first graded

213

narrative and analysis, then grading can be very easy. This is a real advantage at the end of a term. Make sure they compare the New document to the Old document, and not vice versa, otherwise you'll get a lot of strikeouts and red ink! I always have my students submit their previously graded work as well (in a large self-addressed stamped envelope), so I can look at my "margin notes" in my first grading.

If they substantially changed their document, have them submit a clean copy of the document. (It's too hard to read the "track-changes" document when there are significant changes.) They should hand-mark the sections that stayed the same!

The chart below might guide you in how to evaluate the final version.

Table 3: Suggestions for grading Final Edited Version

Did the student ignore suggestions made in margins and grading template?	Lower grade one full grade (e.g., if they got an 84 on narrative (step 2) and 82 on analysis (step 3), then they would get a 73 on their final version (step 4).
Did the student respond to some of the suggestions, mostly copy edit, but not substantive requests?	Lower grade ½ grade (e.g., if they got an 84 on narrative (step 2) and 82 on analysis (step 3), then they would get a 78 on their final version (step 4).
Did the student respond to all suggestions, but you didn't have many substantive suggestions on their first two papers?	Give them the average between the two grades (e.g., if they got an 95 on narrative (step 2) and 89 on analysis (step 3), then they would get a 92 on their final version (step 4).
Did the student significantly improve his/her paper either because they responded well to your suggestions for substantive change or because they added their own ideas?	I give significantly higher grades on the final version, if it was poorly done in the first place, and then brought up to standard, e.g., from 75 (step 2) and 65 (step 3) to 88 (step 4). If it was brought up to excellence, then I give them 95-100 on the final version.

<u>Grading Template for Narrative</u>[2]

<u>Length and Straightforwardness</u>

❑ Selection of Facts is ___ poor ___adequate ___ very good ____ excellent. [Need to know which facts to keep and which ones to let go.]

    ❑ Some of the facts are extraneous (see marked case). ____ Develop better (see marked case).

    ❑ Appropriate Length (6-13 pages). ___too short___ too long ____just right!

    ❑ The case doesn't lend itself to analysis very well. ___There is not much to work with.

    ❑ Missing Information. Facts I'd like to know:

<u>The Story</u>

❑ The "hook" is ___poor ___adequate ___very good ___excellent (really got me!). [Should help me know what the case is about and make me want to read on.]

    ❑ Doesn't reflect the nature of the case.

    ❑ Lifeless/boring. [Suspense or wondering what happened makes it interesting.]

    ❑ Other:

❑ The body is ___ poor ___adequate ___very good ___excellent (compelling!). [Needs to be like a good story so that I can't stop reading it.]

    ❑ Not very interesting.

    ❑ Needs reorganizing or rewriting to bring in more __focus ___spark ___ drama/suspense ___flow

    ❑ Needs editing to bring in more __focus ___spark ___ drama/suspense ___flow

    ❑ Needs better description of: ___ see below ___ see notes on the narrative

    ❑ Other:

❑ The conclusion is ____poor ____adequate ___ very good ____ excellent. [The conclusion in a decision case leaves us wondering what to do. In an analysis case, it leaves us wondering WHY it happened.]

    ❑ Told too much, put the ending in the epilogue.

    ❑ Left me confused.

    ❑ Other:

<u>Case Organization</u>

❑ Organization/style is ____poor ___adequate ___ very good ___ excellent. [Style depends on the case facts.] I've checked the style(s) I think might fit.

    ❑ Better if time-sequenced.

    ❑ Tell it like a story. ___ Blend key players background into the story.

    ❑ Provide an overview/context first.

    ❑ Tell the critical incident story (circle appropriate one) first middle last in the story.

<u>Tone and Tense</u>

❑ Objectivity is ___ poor ___ adequate ___ very good ___ excellent. [Point of view should be neutral observer or reporter.] ___ There was some writing that left me feeling that you had "blind spots" to your character.

    ❑ Describe more, tell less.

    ❑ Tell both sides of the story. More from the perspective of….

    ❑ Did you leave out any information? Seems biased toward:

❑ Past tense. Write in past tense ___the company information ____the people need to be in past tense

❑ Third Person. Write in third person.

❑ Grammar is __poor __adequate __very good __excellent.

❑ Editing. __minor editing (didn't effect grade) __ more than minor editing needed __major editing needed

❑ Sentence/paragraph structure is ____ poor ___adequate ___very good ____ excellent

<u>Potential topics or questions for analysis:</u> See back of page for more.

---

[2] Adapted from Naumes, W. and Naumes, M. J. (1999). <u>The Art and Craft of Case Writing</u>. Thousand Oaks, CA: Sage, pp. 91 –102.

Grading Samples of Critical Incident Narrative

Diane
11/11/1997

The subject in this case is important to groups and leadership (and organizational behavior in general). You have chosen an incident that obviously had an impact for you. You write well and have the beginnings of a good case for analysis. To sufficiently analyze the case however, I feel that the case needs further development and information.

I urge you to provide the reader (me and some of your classmates) with more details about the groupware process. I think it is very interesting to read about the theory of group ware and the actual outcomes your group experienced. Primary organizational behavior theory as I see it: Group-decision making

Include information that will help you evaluate the electronic meeting decision-making style: e.g., criteria for group effectiveness: 1) number of ideas 2) quality of ideas 3) social pressure 4) money costs 5) speed 6) task orientation 7)potential for interpersonal conflict 8) feelings of accomplishment 9) commitment to solution 10) develops groups cohesiveness. (Source: Murnighan, "Group decision making: What strategies should you use?", Management Review, Feb 1981, p. 61.)

Questions I have for additional information to analyze your case:

You implied that there was a lot of conflict among the support staff. Did it revolve entirely around Sally? Was it divided by where one was located or the type of administrators/faculty served? I'm thinking that a secondary analysis might include interpersonal conflict or communications. (Reminder, your analysis requires you to examine at least two areas of organizational behavior).

You write, "needless to say the remaining weeks of the project were not as successful as the first. Walls had been built and sides had been taken…" What was the point of the project? Who was leading it? Could you write a section in the case about that person's hoped-for goals? Were they doing it as an experiment/research project? To solve interpersonal communication problems (as you imply with your comments) or to solve technical problems in the office work processes? Perhaps it is all of this… perhaps you had hoped for more interpersonal communication and were personally saddened that that wasn't accomplished. The organizational behavior theories that might apply would be goals and perceptions issues. Another interesting secondary or tertiary analysis.

The gender issue is interesting and it does the trick of demonstrating some of the problems with the groupware style of meeting. I think you have given us sufficient information in the case to guide the reader. In the epilogue, could you let us know if a man was selected to replace the dean?

Your final paragraph in the case is very interesting. Keep it, but divide into two sections. First, include what happened to the report in the case and develop it further as it demonstrates what happens to the material generated by groupware. In that section, address the gender issue just as you did in the case. In the epilogue, describe what eventually happened…"Eventually, the report and its contents faded…tensions over the sessions eventually cooled and were even laughed about later…"

In summary, for your final case, I suggest several sub-headings added to this case with information organized around them. 1. Introduction: The work of the people (as you have already done). 2. Problems and conflicts. Describe more fully the problems that were surfacing that led someone to believe that groupware was the solution to these problems. If there were more than one type of problems (e.g. I imagine there were work-process problems and interpersonal conflict problems) then describe them both. Use quotes to describe your personal feelings and frustrations to add color and interest. 3. Group ware project. Describe what group ware is. Who was leading the project and information about him/her. Describe the room (or rooms) in which the meeting took place. 4) Groupware fiasco. Keep this section. Add any details that you feel you might need to do your case analysis. 5) Outcome of groupware meetings.

Describe what happened to the report including the ignoring of the gender issue and **how you felt about it.** I think it must have felt terrible to know that your comments were not anonymous and that some people pointed fingers at you for standing up to a sexist comment. Describe (throughout the case) your feelings about what was happening to you. Use quotes when you are talking. 6) On a separate page, include an epilogue.

216

Grade on Step 1B: **B+ (87%)** (I felt that more information on the electronic meeting and the reasons for using it would have strengthened this case. That is, it would have been more fully developed and I would have fewer questions about what is the story behind the story). The writing and organization are good. I'm confident that you will have an excellent final case based on your understanding of organizational behavior theory that I saw demonstrated in class last week and your writing ability. If I can look at any drafts with you, please let me know. I look forward to working with you.

****

Jay
11/11/1997
At first reading of your case, I am not yet clear that it has the potential for an organizational behavioral (OB) analysis. However, after looking at the table of contents in several OB books, I think you could develop the case to look at several potential topics.

First possibility is the area of "work stress." If you were to give us some information about how the "impossible task" and the "constant rejections" affected you and your ability to work, you could examine work stress concepts more completely.

Another possibility might be in the area of "organizational culture" and/or "group norms." How do employees learn culture/norms…through rituals, stories, material symbols, language? If you could outline the ways that you were learning your organization's culture or the group norms, you might have a focus for your case.

Another angle might be in terms of "performance evaluation." What were you being evaluated on? How could your performance be measured, how did you know if you were doing well with all the rejections? How did the boss's interest in the final property impact your feelings of evaluation?

Regardless of the angle(s) that you decide to explore in your case, you will need to examine at least two organizational behavior concepts. I think your case has the making of a good case if you can add additional material to explain your feelings of approaching your boss one more time and the subsequent elation on both your parts.

I have some OB type cases in one of my textbooks that I'll bring to class for you to look at. It appears to me that you haven't been exposed to many cases before so you would benefit from getting a "feel" of how cases are written. You do an excellent job describing your feelings and imagining your boss's feelings…so I'm not concerned with your writing ability. The case, however, lacks the necessary structure and information for you to do an adequate job in the analysis section. Imagine that you are first presenting the facts (in an engaging format) to me (as if you were a medical student presenting the history and physical information—the case) and then you present your diagnosis to the attending physician (the analysis).

If you want to show me a draft copy of your case before the final one is due, I'd be happy to give you verbal feedback.

Grade: **C+/B- (79%).** You did good work describing the depth of feelings you felt during the critical incident. I felt that I jumped into the middle of the story and there were a number of background items missing that would have helped clarify your feelings and position (although you did include some important ones, too, e.g., the type of property desired and the apparent difficulty in getting this type of property). In your final case, include a little background on the company and on the owner (and/or boss). Tell us a little about yourself, how you got the job, and what your job title was…were you there only to look at property or was this an additional assignment on top of your other work? What experience had you had looking at property in the past? How did the other employees feel about the boss? Did he always reject everyone's ideas? What did it feel like to be young and eager to please the boss? Why did you persevere when others had quit searching? If you can weave this type of information into your story, then we can analyze this case from a number of interesting organizational behavior angles. Good luck.

Grading Template for Analysis

Name:_____

The type of question was identified and written correctly?   Yes   No

  _____Please look at the critical incident assignment and label each question by type.

  _____Some or all of your questions are not in the form as described in the critical incident assignment.

  _____Your questions are not complex enough, they can be answered with a simple yes or no or by a single-word answer. See especially: Q1 Q2 Q3 Q4 Q5 Q6 Q7 Q8 Q9

Appropriate references were cited?   Yes   No   Not needed.

  _____Please reference theory sections (e.g., knowledge type questions or definition sections).

  _____When referencing a primary source (e.g., Maslow) that was taken from another book (e.g., your textbook) follow this example: Maslow, year, p.# , as cited in textbook, year, p #)

Answers were edited, free from grammar, punctuation, and spelling errors?

  _____Minor errors (this did not affect your grade. Please edit carefully for next round)

  _____More than minor, but less than significant errors (this affected your grade somewhat)

  _____Significant errors (this affected your grade)

  _____Primarily editing problems

  _____Primarily clarity and sentence/paragraph structure problems

Content

  _____The most critical factors that influence the case were identified and discussed?

  _____Some or all of your answers were not thorough. See especially Q1, Q2, Q3, Q4, Q5, Q6, Q7, Q8, Q9

  _____Connect case facts more explicitly to the theory? (use words like: "For example", OR "because of" OR "due to."

Comments:

Continued on back page (if circled)

Suggestions for next round:

_____Some new case facts are in the analysis: be sure to include them in the narrative in the final case narrative.

_____You need a plan of action that considers the pros and cons of various options (including second-order consequences, that is, what might happen if you implement your idea).

_____You need a refection of how you might have done things differently if you knew then what you know now.

_____Add page numbers

Grade: _____% (Multiply the percentage by the total number of points possible to get your grade points)

How One Professor Does In-Depth Case Analysis

By Asbjorn Osland
George Fox University and former president of Western Casewriters Association

(Editor's note: Dr. Osland has laid out a case analysis plan that is useful for instructors who want to use case to a greater depth than I have suggested in the 25 and 60 minute teaching plans.)

The first step in teaching a case is to ask that students, outside of class, read it individually (1-2 hours) and then analyze it in groups (several additional hours) prior to the class. I give them the option of choosing which cases, assigned in the course, to write up. For the paper, I ask that students use the following section headings for their case analyses. The relative importance of each is indicated in parentheses with the total equal to 20 (though the number of points could certainly vary depending on the grading format of the professor). The case outline follows:

Analytical outline (4 points). An effective means used by students for writing up the case analysis is to work in small groups after having thoroughly read the case as individuals. Each student then jots down ideas on 3 by 5 Post-It pads, one idea per note, and places each on the wall, in columns, under one of the five categories (that is, situation analysis, problem analysis, theory application, solution and implementation analysis and anticipated consequences). They first complete writing down and posting their ideas and then begin discussing what idea should go in what category. This step can take several hours for a complicated case but once it's finished, the students have completed the analysis. Students are to attach this to their case printed out with columns. What the student describes in the situation (i.e., significant contextual factors and facts relating to the case) should lead into the problem that the student solves, which in turn is related to the solution & implementation, theory, and anticipated consequences. I prefer that all analytical outlines be done by groups; I find that they're generally superior to ones done by individuals. All that remains is the write-up (usually limited to five-seven pages plus exhibits) and the class discussion.

Situation analysis (3 points). Once students have thought through the case alone or talked it over with others and determined what the key problem(s) is (are), they are to list or discuss the information from the case that is relevant to their logical thought process and include this information in the situation analysis section. They are not to list problems they intend to solve here but may choose to list environmental or contextual problems that are important to their problem solving process but which are not the ones they identify to solve. For example, a culture of high power distance may be seen as an impediment to TQM, yet one cannot change basic culture. They are not to rehash all the details from the case; they are to assume that the instructor has read it. Limit to one page.

Problem analysis (3 points). Students are to begin this section with an explicit and direct statement of the problem(s) they've identified and chosen to solve. The problem must be further analyzed to clarify the variables or factors brought out in the case that influence it. Here students may also explain secondary problems they chose to avoid and why. This portion should be under a page.

Theory application (3 points). Students are to describe and apply relevant theories from the reading. They are to cite the theory and explain it, then describe how it's relevant to their case analysis. They should apply at least two theories for each case analysis. This section must be at least one page in length. I specify the length so that they don't answer too superficially.

Solution and implementation analysis (4 points). Here students are to present their solution to the case. They may also indicate which possible solutions they chose to avoid and why. They must recommend a course of action. They cannot conclude that more information be gathered or that a consultant be employed. In the implementation one must consider the feasibility, in terms of available resources, of the solution chosen.

Anticipated consequences (3 points). One must also attempt to anticipate the consequences of the solution chosen. Students are to write approximately one page. I've found that this is the section students tend to neglect.

Application (1 bonus point). Where possible, apply some aspects of the case to a situation they've experienced or observed. I include this because I hope they will better remember the case if they apply it.
Case write-ups usually consist of approximately 5-7 pages with additional exhibits.

One further note: I usually have students facilitate the case discussion. I ask which students wrote the case-up. I then select one to facilitate and another to serve as scribe for the white board. Both receive one bonus point as a token incentive. I find that when students facilitate, the discussion is livelier and more apt to foster a net-like communication pattern, rather than always bouncing back to the instructor. As much as one tries to empower the classroom, sometimes the best thing an instructor can do is to get out of the way. Then when the discussion is over, I may highlight some points that I felt were overlooked but I often find this is unnecessary.

HOMEWORK ASSIGNMENT QUESTIONS

Some instructors prefer to give assignment questions in preparation for class discussion. On the following pages you will find a list of all the questions from the teaching notes. You may wish to photocopy this list and circle the questions that you want students to answer. Alternatively, if you design your entire course before the term begins, you may wish to type these questions into your syllabus.

A SELFISH REQUEST IN JAPAN

1. According to Hofstede's four dimensions of culture, citing examples from the case, explain the Japanese management's reactions and concerns to Toby's request.
2. From a conceptual analysis of power and influence, examine NOGI's methodology in handling Toby's request. What types of power did each agent of NOGI possess?
3. Examining Maslow's needs hierarchy model, identify NOGI's failure to account for American attitudes towards needs in their school policies. Additionally, evaluate how the Japanese version of Maslow's model is infused into the contract that seems to disregard the law.
4. Understanding where the Japanese management system falls along Hofstede's four dimensions of culture, analyze its effectiveness in a corporation that employs American employees (i.e. NOGI). Specifically, citing examples from the case, examine and identify the cultural inaccuracy of NOGI's management policies within the context of Toby's critical incident.
5. Recommend a management strategy, at the local school level and at the corporate headquarters level, which incorporates Hofstede's four dimensions of culture to enhance employee satisfaction, minimize disruptions in the business process, and to promote a positive corporate culture.
6. Explain the importance of Toby's decision to recruit the help of the Tokyo South General Workers Union. Examine its role in the negotiation processes.
7. Evaluate the presence of Mr. Crawford and Mr. Allen from a power and influence perspective in the meeting between Toby and Mr. Miyake. How effective were they? Did one neutralize the other?
8. Explain NOGI's reasoning for drafting two employee contracts, one for Americans and one for Japanese.
9. If Ms. Nakamura had been aware of the illegality in the American employee contract, would their actions have been different?

ANGRY BRANCH MANAGER

1. Assuming that Henry's management style stayed consistent during his management tenure, why did his employees fail to disclose any wrongdoing during the first investigation performed by Michael Griffin, the Regional Manager?

2. What happened after the first investigation to change their behavior?

3. What part did the actions of human resources play in the differing responses of the employees?

4. How might cultural diversity account for the behavior of the branch employees?

5. What might have influenced Henry's statements about being a minority at Calwest?

6. How might have the different cultural perceptions created an unhealthy atmosphere within the branch?

7. What inferences might you make about a 56% turnover rate at Calwest?

8. Using the rational decision process, how would the group handle this situation?

CAFÉ LATTE, LLC

1. Define equity theory and its implications in family business. How does this theory explain Stuart's angry confrontations with Cynthia?

2. What are some perceptual problems that may explain the confrontation between Cynthia and Stuart? What were some other causes of Stuart's anger?

3. Suppose an anger management consultant visited Cafe Latte to help the partners deal with the issue of anger in the workplace, what might be his/her advise on anger management?

4. To what extent was the conflict due to a difference in communication style?

5. What are some of the unique challenges that family enterprises face?

CHANGING QUOTAS

1. Why did Susan seek to work with her old boss versus her current one? Why was her decision to do so successful?

2. If you were Susan, would you continue to work for Diebold? Why or why not?

3. How did Susan capitalize from creative problem solving?

4. Define Expectancy Theory. Could this define Susan's motivation to succeed before Diebold changed her quota? Why or why not?

5. If you were Susan's manager at Diebold, would you have opted to increase her quota in the middle of a sales negotiation? Why or why not?

COMPUTER SERVICES TEAM AT AVIONICS

1. Evaluate Williams' leadership of the team. What went wrong?

2. Under what conditions might the leaderless group idea have been more successful?

3. Why did the team do so poorly in responding to the mandate to become an integrated team?

4. If you were Barbara, the new manager, how would you handle the situation with the team (right after she got the new assignment)?

COST AND SCHEDULE TEAM AT AVIONICS

1. What were the factors that caused the team to be stressed during the first three months of the teams forming?

2. Why was the team able to succeed by the end of the case?

3. Was it a good idea for John to meet with the group without Dan? Why or why not?

4. Chart the team's development over the course of the nine months. Does Tuchman's model of forming, storming, norming, performing, and adjourning apply here? If so, what were the key transition points?

5. If you manage a team, given the answers to the first four questions, what lessons do you draw that would make you a better manager of teams? If you are a member of a team, what lessons do you conclude from this case that would make you a better member of a team?

GROUPWARE FIASCO

1. Summarize some of the factors that may have contributed to the conflict among the staff at the HSH division office.

2. What were some of the problems with Gordon's leadership style?

3. If you were the dean, what actions might you consider to reduce the conflict among the division office? Evaluate the pros and cons of your possible actions.

4. How successful was the groupware experiment in improving interpersonal relations? What were the key issues that lead you to this conclusion?

5. Suppose you were one of the secretaries in the pool, how might you try to effectively cope with the conflict and stress on the job?

INCIDENT ON THE *USS WHITNEY*

1. Is Lieutenant Commander Fuller primarily a transactional or transformational leader?

2. Would the situation be different if Lt. Cdr. Fuller were a transformational leader?

3. Using French and Raven's taxonomy of power, what were the bases of interpersonal power that Lt. Cdr. Fuller possessed over Ens. Beck?

4. What type of power, if any, did Ens. Beck possess?

5. How did implied norms account for the behavior noted in the narrative?

6. Was there any role conflict that can be identified in this case?

7. What roles did Lt. Wilson play in this case and how did they influence what happened?

INSUBORDINATION OR UNCLEAR LOYALTIES?

1. How do hierarchical, autocratic systems work against cross-program task forces?

2. What do new managers need to develop into competent managers?

3. To what extent is the problem with George personal and to what extent is it structural?

4. What should Ellen do?

5. What should George do?

LEADERSHIP OF TQM IN PANAMA

1. How would you describe and contrast the different implementation processes in each location?

2. Was the way the two leaders implemented TQM culturally and functionally appropriate?

NEGOTIATING WORK HOURS

Part 1
1. What are Susan's assumptions as she enters the negotiations?

2. What are the union's assumptions as they enter negotiations?

3. How do these assumptions influence their behaviors during negotiations?

4. What are the interests underlying the union's proposals (i.e., why is the union putting this proposal on the table)? What are the university's interests?

Part 2
1. Why did the negotiators fail to exchange any information?

2. What specific communication mistakes were made by the negotiators? Provide examples.

3. When are breaks effective in a negotiation? Comment on the use of breaks in this negotiation.

4. What needs to be done to get the negotiation back on track?

Part 3
1. Why did this interaction produce a better outcome? What were the turning points?

2. How did the initial assumptions of the negotiators impact the exchange of information in the first session? How did they affect the exchange of information in the second session?

3. Identify the elements of positive communication in this discussion.

4. Which questions were the most effective? Why?

PREFERENTIAL TREATMENT?

1. What factors, attitudes, beliefs, and circumstantial predicaments affected Dr. David's behavior towards Paul?"

2. What is discrimination?

3. Define equity. Was Paul treated fairly by Dr. David?

4. Define attraction. Using attraction as a factor, how did Dr. David's behavior towards the female student differentiate from his behavior towards Paul?

5. What other factors, if not discrimination, attraction, personality differences, and personal circumstances could have affected Dr. David's behavior towards Paul?

6. Define power/authority and explain its relevance when Paul did not confront Dr. David.

7. What would you do if you were Paul?

REPUTATION IN JEOPARDY

1. To what extent does the merger resolve the conflict?

2. What role did culture play in guiding performance and behavior before the merger? Were there any heroes in the organization before the merger? If so, who were Amber's heroes? What happened to Amber and her heroes' behavior and performance after the merger was announced? Why did the W.E. C.A.R.E. document no longer guide people's behavior after the merger announcement? What conclusions do you draw about the qualities of organizational culture after reading this case?

3. What are the essential management functions, and which ones were not demonstrated in this case?

RICHARD PRICHARD AND THE FEDERAL TRIAD PROGRAMS

1. The decision to be made in the case is whether or not Richard should come in to work on Saturday. Explore the two options available to Richard (Richard should go/Richard should not go). Tell whether the valence is positive, negative, or zero for each option and support your answer by listing the possible expectations resulting from each option.

2. What part do instrumentalities play in expectancy theory? Give some examples of possible instrumentalities leading to Richard's decision.

3. Based on expectancy theory, is it possible for Richard to put forth an effort while having low valence, instrumentality and expectancy? Use facts from the case to support or refute your answer.

4. Point out Richard's perception of his role in the organization as it relates to his goals and decision in the case.

5. Point out the importance of role theory and goals to explain why the coordinators possibly did not work as hard as Richard.

6. Suppose Richard made the decision of not going in to work, which may not have resulted in his role in the organization being changed by Dr. Duncan. Is there another way that he could have persuaded the coordinators to contribute more work to the program?

7. What possible sources of self-efficacy may have lead Richard to believe that he could accomplish the task that was asked of him?

8. What is the relationship between self-efficacy theory and the concepts of expectancy theory?

SAVING PRIVATE RYAN VIDEO CASE: CLASSIC LEADERSHIP MODELS

1. What traits does Captain Miller (Tom Hanks) display as a leader in the film <u>Saving Private Ryan</u>?

2. Does Captain Miller exhibit the behaviors of a successful leader suggested by the behavioral model of leadership?

3. Does Captain Miller change his leadership style in different situations consistent with the recommendations of the contingency model of leadership?

4. Is Captain Miller's behavior consistent with the decision making approach recommended by the Vroom-Yetton normative model of leadership?

5. Does Captain Miller provide the level of leader involvement that will result in the highest level of performance of his subordinates, according to path-goal theory?

6. Is Captain Miller a transformational leader?

THE SAFETY MEMO

1. How was delegation used properly or improperly to enlist Gordon's assistance with the safety program?

2. Did Gordon feel empowered? Explain.

3. Why would knowledge of delegation and empowerment principles be useful to Gordon?

4. Compare and contrast differences between cultural elements of Pacific Bell and The Cable Company.

5. What might the outcome have been if Gordon had taken the time to become familiar with the cultural differences between the new company and his former employer?

6. What are the major barriers to effective communication noted in the case?

7. Suppose that Gordon had taken the time to meet the key players, ask their opinions, and make a careful assessment of the new business environment. How would this have changed the ways that Gil and Gordon communicated?

8. How would you characterize Gil's leadership style and how effective was it?

9. Why didn't Gil acknowledge the validity of any of the concerns that Gordon had listed in his memo?

10. How did Gil's choice to adopt a positional bargaining standpoint predispose the outcome of his conversation with Gordon?

11. What might be a more appropriate approach for Gil when communicating with Gordon?

THE VOLUNTEER

1. What were the main events in this case and in what order did they occur?

2. What are the key issues in the case?

3. Did Linda act in an insubordinate way toward her manager? Explain why or why not. What factors caused the need to go against Tanaka's orders? Is this situation urgent?

4. What were the ethical problems Linda and the museum faced?

5. Evaluate Linda's action in terms of timing and effectiveness.

6. What lessons do you draw from this case?

THEN THERE WAS ONE

1. Review the Hackman-Oldham model for job enrichment.

2. Use the Hackman-Oldham model to look at Sarah's job characteristics <u>before</u> the layoff.

3. Use the Hackman-Oldham model to look at Sarah's job characteristics <u>after</u> the layoff.

4. Is the Hackman-Oldham a good model to look at job satisfaction? Why?

5. Review Alderfer's ERG Theory.

6. Use Alderfer's ERG theory to evaluate Sarah's motivation before the layoff.

7. Use Alderfer's ERG theory to evaluate Sarah's motivation after the layoff

8. Evaluate Tom's responsibilities for the performance of Mary and the HR function.

9. Evaluate Mary's responsibilities for the performance of the HR function.

10. Evaluate Sarah's responsibility in relation to Mary.

UNPROFESSIONAL CONDUCT

1. What kinds of factors should one consider when evaluating his or her career choice?

2. Evaluate Andre's process of finding a job.

3. How do perception and judgment influence Andre's behavior in this case?

4. Why didn't Andre confront Mrs. Richards about her behavior?

5. Using the Johari window as a frame, examine Andre and Mrs. Richard's viewpoints.

6. How would you improve The Office Supply Store's recruitment and orientation practices?

7. What could Mrs. Richards have done better when Andre came into her store?

8. What could Andre have done to improve his situation?

VIOLENCE AT THE UNITED STATES POSTAL SERVICE

1. Could the killing of James Whooper by Bruce Clark have been prevented? Explain why or why not. Be sure to address the issues of changes in management, warning signs of potential violence, and security at the City of Industry postal facility. Were Postal Service workplace violence policies effective in this case?

2. Review the composition of the threat assessment team at the city of Industry postal facility. Why is the team composed of members from different functional areas of management? The threat assessment process sometimes requires management to consult with mental health professionals. What are the implications of such collaborations? Finally, what risks are present in the administration of threat reporting and assessment procedures?

3. Mental health professionals routinely advise that the dangerousness of individuals is extremely difficult to predict. What are the implications for management of the difficulty in predicting workplace violence?

4. Do you think the general organizational climate at the Postal Service played a role in the workplace homicide at the city of Industry facility? Explain why or why not.

5. In the 1990s, according to the US Department of Labor, workplace homicide became the second leading cause of death at the workplace after traffic accidents, up from third place; moreover, researchers have found that the incidence of employees killing their supervisors has doubled since the 1980s. Speculate as to possible causes of the rise in homicide at the workplace.

WHEN WORLDS COLLIDE

1. Explain how organizational design structure (e.g., differentiation/integration) can be matched or mismatched with its environment (e.g., stable/changing).

2. Diagnose the sales force's alignment (or misalignment) within the organizational structure.

3. Diagnose the manufacturing personnel's alignment (or misalignment) within the organizational structure.

4. Diagnose the culture alignment (or misalignment) within the organizational structure.

5. Diagnose the current business's alignment (or misalignment) with the external environment.

6. Diagnose the future business's alignment (or misalignment) with the external environment.

7. What did Evergreen do well?

8. What suggestions do you have for Evergreen's internal alignment at this juncture?

9. What suggestions do you have for new strategies at this juncture?

INDEX OF TOPICS IN TEACHING NOTES